What About ProductManager?
(IBM's Solution for Engineering Change Control)

■ ■ ■

By David Curtis

What About ProductManager? (IBM's Solution for Engineering Change Control)

Other titles of interest available from Maximum Press:

* What About MAPICS/DB?, Blackshaw (#GB35–4289)

* IBM Client/Server Computing: A Business Perspective, Hoskins and Bolthouse (#G326–0466)

* Getting to Client/Server: IBM's Experience, Krantz

* IBM Personal Systems: A Business Perspective, Hoskins (#G325–0400)

* IBM RISC System/6000: A Business Perspective, Hoskins (#GA23–2674)

* IBM AS/400: A Business Perspective, Hoskins (#GA21–9990)

* IBM System/390: A Business Perspective, Hoskins (#G229–7220)

MaxFacts Special Reports available from Maximum Press:

* The PowerPC Revolution!, Hoskins

* Exploring the RISC System/6000 Model 41, Hoskins

What About ProductManager?

(IBM's Solution for Engineering Change Control)

■ ■ ■

By David Curtis

MAXIMUM PRESS
Florida

Photographs courtesy of International Business Machines Corporation and Sun Microsystems.

Recognizing the importance of preserving what has been written, it is a policy of Maximum Press to have books of enduring value published in the United States printed on acid-free paper, and we exert our best efforts to that end.

Library of Congress Cataloging-in-Publication Data

Curtis, David, 1946– What about ProductManager / David Curtis p. cm. Includes index. ISBN 0-9633214-4-7 : $34.97 1. ProductManager 2. Production management--Data processing. I. Title TS155.6.C87 1994
94–125 658.5′0285′5369–dc20 CIP

Printed in the United States of America
95 96 10 9 8 7 6 5 4 3 2 1

This book is dedicated to the ProductManager team. Over the years, this dedicated group has worked hard to bring ProductManager to the marketplace. Through their efforts and commitment, the ProductManager team continues to make it happen.

Contents

Foreword

These days, managing product information and controlling engineering changes is becoming ever more critical to a company's bottom line. After years of struggling with endless mounds of paper for part information, engineering change requests, bills of material, and all of the documentation associated with an end product, manufacturing companies now have the opportunity to place an umbrella of control over this information. The manufacturing industry's rapidly increasing exploitation of CAD/CAM/CAE applications, while it has increased productivity tremendously, has made the need to manage this data electronically much more critical to retain the control needed to capitalize on that productivity. An effective product data management (PDM) system can give these companies the ability to leverage the CAD/CAM/CAE data in many more of their business processes.

I can tell you up front that the road to managing the diverse types of product information is not a smooth one. The discussions, methods, and examples provided in *What About ProductManager?* provide an insight into what factors need to be considered when facing the product data management challenge.

IBM's ProductManager is a leading off-the-shelf solution that helps a company address its PDM needs. Its process management, change management, product definition, and document management functions provide an environment in which to manage product design, release, and change at the individual, department, project, company, or inter-enterprise level. It operates across a wide variety of environments. It's open--running either on a mainframe or any of a variety of UNIX and database environments. It's distributed: It provides client functions in a variety of environments from the desktop to the mainframe. It's flexible: As you optimize your operations, changing the way you do things, ProductManager can change too. No more "changing the process so the system can handle it." And it's scalable: You can use some of it, all of it, or you can stage your implementation and use more of ProductManager over time, as you continually optimize your processes.

What About ProductManager? provides good insight into ProductManager's capabilities. It talks about the variety of operating platform and database choices supported. It describes ProductManager's object-oriented implementation—a key technology that simplifies working with complex product information. Most importantly, however, it demonstrates ProductManager's flexibility and how tailoring your PDM environment to your way of doing business, today and tomorrow, is supported.

If you are looking for a PDM solution, reading *What About ProductManager?* is a good first step.

H. R. Pears
General Manager,
IBM Engineering Solutions,
Manufacturing Industry

Disclaimer

The purchase of computer software or hardware is an important and costly business decision. While the author and publisher of this book have made reasonable efforts to ensure the accuracy and timeliness of the information contained herein, the author and publisher assume no liability with respect to loss or damage caused or alleged to be caused by reliance on any information contained herein and disclaim any and all warranties, expressed or implied, as to the accuracy or reliability of said information.

This book is not intended to replace IBM product documentation or personnel in determining the specifications and capabilities of the products mentioned in this book. IBM product documentation should always be consulted, as the specifications and capabilities of computer hardware and software products are subject to frequent modification. The reader is solely responsible for the choice of computer hardware and software. All configurations and applications of computer hardware and software should be reviewed with proper IBM representatives prior to choosing or using any computer hardware and software. This book is not sponsored or endorsed by IBM, and the author and publisher are neither affiliated with IBM nor acting as IBM agents.

Acknowledgments

This book incorporates information attained through interviews and discussions with a broad group of people concerning the engineering field and the manufacturing industry. I appreciate the time everyone spent with me discussing the engineering profession and the challenges it faces.

A special thanks to Dennis McKaskey, April Stiles, and Herman Mitchell, who helped me understand what users are looking for in a product data management system and how they use it. Thanks to these IBM employees who spent time with me to discuss the specifics of ProductManager: Russ Carlson, Bob Abraham, Floyd Shackelford, Dan Sass, Don Curtis, Badari Panuganti, Joe Martinek, Jeff Stehlin, John Leneschmidt, Tom Rider, Vijay Vasandani, Ken Smith, and finally Jim Ryan, who worked with me to help produce this book, and Joel Lemke, who supported the project from the start. And, thanks to Bruce Jarvis, Ann Borgel, and Kevin Ray for their graphics support, to Marion Anderson for her editing, and to Judy Campbell and Carol Parker for their administrative support.

Last, but not least, many thanks to my wife, Lynda. She's not an engineer or a programmer, but her assistance and support were valuable to me.

Reader Comments

Any comments you would like to make are welcome. A reader feedback sheet is provided at the end of this book and can be copied and used to fax or mail in your comments. Alternatively, you can send it through IBM's electronic mail system to IBMMAIL(USBRCN7C).

Other Books in the Series

This book is the second in the *What About* series and joins *What About MAPICS/DB?*, which helps the reader understand, evaluate, and implement IBM's best-selling application program for manufacturers.

Subscribing to Revisions

You may subscribe to automatically receive future revisions of *What About ProductManager?* and any other book or MaxFacts Special Reports available through Maximum Press by calling (904)934–0819.

Trademarks

AIX™ is a trademark of International Business Machines Corporation.

AIXwindows™ is a trademark of International Business Machines Corporation.

AutoCAD™ is a trademark of AutoDESK.

BookManager READ/6000™ is a trademark of International Business Machines Corporation.

CADAM® is a registered trademark of CADAM Inc.

CATIA® is a registered trademark of Dassault Systèmes.

CATIA Data Management® is a registered trademark of Dassault Systèmes.

DataBase 2™ is a trademark of International Business Machines Corporation.

DataBase 2/6000™ is a trademark of International Business Machines Corporation.

DataBridge™ is a trademark of International TechneGroup Incorporated.

DataBuilder™ is a trademark of International TechneGroup Incorporated.

DB2/6000™ is a trademark of International Business Machines Corporation.

Distributed Application Environment™ is a trademark of International Business Machines Corporation.

Entry Communications System/6000™ is a trademark of International Business Machines Corporation.

Hewlett Packard® is a registered trademark of the Hewlett-Packard Co.

Hewlett Packard UX® is a registered trademark of the Hewlett-Packard Co.

IBM® is a registered trademark of International Business Machines Corporation.

IBM System/360™ is a trademark of International Business Machines Corporation.

IBM System/370™ is a trademark of International Business Machines Corporation.

IBM System/390™ is a trademark of International Business Machines Corporation.

INGRES™ is a trademark of INGRES Corporation.

Lotus 1-2-3™ is a trademark of Lotus Development Corporation.

MaxFacts™ is a trademark of Maximum Press.

MICRO CADAM™ is a trademark of MICROCADAM, Inc.

Microsoft Excel™ is a trademark of Microsoft Corporation.

Microsoft Word® is a registered trademark of Microsoft Corporation.

MOTIF™ is a trademark of Massachusetts Institute of Technology.

Oracle® is a registered trademark of the Oracle Corporation.

OS/2™ is a trademark of International Business Machines Corporation.

PC Storyboard™ is a trademark of International Business Machines Corporation.

Preview® is a registered trademark of Rosetta Technology.

Postscript® is a registered trademark of Adobe Systems Corporation.

ProductManager™ is a trademark of International Business Machines Corporation.

ProductManager/6000™ is a trademark of International Business Machines Corporation.

Pro/ENGINEER™ is a trademark of Parametric Technology Corporation.

Professional CADAM™ is a trademark of Dassault Systems of America.

QuickFit® is a registered trademark of Maximum Press.

RISC System/6000™ is a trademark of International Business Machines Corporation.

SPARCcenter 2000® is a registered trademark of Sun Microsystems, Inc.

SPARCcluster 1™ is a trademark of Sun Microsystems, Inc.

SPARCserver 10™ is a trademark of Sun Microsystems, Inc.

SPARCserver 1000™ is a trademark of Sun Microsystems, Inc.

SPARCstation 10™ is a trademark of Sun Microsystems, Inc.

Sun Microsystems® is a registered trademark of Sun Microsystems, Inc.

Sun Solaris® is a registered trademark of Sun Microsystems, Inc.

UNIX® is a registered trademark of UNIX Systems Laboratories, Inc.

X Window System™ is a trademark of Massachusetts Institute of Technology.

Introduction

What This Book Is

This book will help you better understand the engineering environment and give you a clear understanding of IBM's strategic ProductManager application program for engineering. Building on in-depth research, including many interviews with both the developers of ProductManager and actual users outside of IBM, this book takes a look at the capabilities of ProductManager and what it can do to help a business meet its product data management needs. The book will help you assess what ProductManager may add to your business and determine whether or not ProductManager is a good choice for your business; it will also provide information and examples that will help you successfully implement ProductManager in your business. ProductManager is a family of engineering management application programs developed by IBM that are designed to help you manage product information associated with the processes, releases, and ongoing changes involved in the development and manufacture of products. The software can be used at the workstation level, the department or team level, or the company level.

First, this book provides you with an overview of the engineering profession, including brief descriptions of the responsibilities of the various engineers involved in product development and manufacture. These are the engineers who will use ProductManager to manage product information. The book also gives an overview of some of the current trends in the engineering field and how businesses are dealing with these trends. In addition, we will look at some issues that will affect engineers today and in the future.

The book describes how ProductManager is put together, what each application program contributes to the product, and the functions within those applications. Afterward, you are introduced to QuickFit, a quantitative methodology that you can use to assess ProductManager based on the particular needs of your business.

Along with discussing how ProductManager can be used with other application programs, the book covers educational, technical support, and implementation issues that will help you decide if the product is the right engineering application program for your business.

Regardless of what program you choose to manage product data, *What About ProductManager?* will point out considerations that should go into the decision process when purchasing the necessary hardware and software. This book is intended for management and people involved with implementing a product data management solution for their business.

What This Book Is Not

What About ProductManager? does not attempt to cover all the operational aspects of the IBM RISC System/6000 product or any of the other hardware or operating systems on which ProductManager can reside. (Refer to *IBM RISC System/6000, A Business Perspective* [Hoskins] for details concerning the RISC System/6000 family.)

You are not provided detailed program descriptions or screen-by-screen instructions for running ProductManager, although the book does describe the documents available in the ProductManager library, which is composed of manuals that provide information on all aspects of using ProductManager. This book focuses instead on helping you understand the capabilities of ProductManager and evaluate whether or not it can meet your business needs.

You don't have to be a programmer or computer expert to use this book. Technical subjects are discussed as simply and concisely as possible while covering the information necessary to assess your need for ProductManager.

How to Use This Book

Chapter 1 provides an overview of the engineering world and looks at different engineering environments. It briefly describes basic engineering responsibilities and the current concepts and trends in engineering. The focus of the chapter is concurrent engineering and its derivatives, methods many industries are using to reduce product development time.

Chapter 2 explores ProductManager and its object-oriented implementation. Each application and the features it supports are discussed, along with practical uses for the application. There is also a brief overview of the platforms and operating systems on which ProductManager runs.

Chapter 3 assists you in determining whether ProductManager is right for your business. The chapter discusses product data management solutions and costs and how a product data management system can help a business. It also uses the QuickFit quantitative tool to help you assess whether ProductManager is the product data management solution for you.

Chapter 4 demonstrates by giving examples how small, medium, and large businesses can implement ProductManager. The chapter also discusses services and education to complement ProductManager.

Appendix A provides QuickFit worksheets you can use to assess whether or not ProductManager and its add-on programs can effectively meet your unique set of business needs.

Appendix B is a set of tasks to help guide you through preparing for and setting up ProductManager.

To help you understand the discussions presented in this book, key terms and phrases are highlighted in boldface when they are introduced and defined. These terms are also listed in the index at the back of the book. If while you are reading you forget the definition of a key term or phrase, the index will quickly guide you to the page or pages on which the term is defined or discussed.

A Word from the Series Editor

Computer systems continue to be ever more deeply woven into the fabric of business—all types of business. This is true because a properly implemented computer solution holds many real benefits for a business. Unfortunately, however, not every attempt to implement a computer solution within a business succeeds. The reasons for the failure are usually fairly clear with the benefit of hindsight.

Common reasons for failure include lack of real executive commitment, improper education, and selection of an application program that does not meet the needs of the business. A failed computer solution implementation can be a very frustrating and extremely costly event for all involved.

The purpose of the new What About series is to help reduce the risk associated with the implementation of a computer solution before the project begins. To this end, each book in the What About series will focus on one specific computer solution (in this case, IBM's ProductManager application program) and do three things. First, the book will introduce the intended environment and the specific computer solution in simple and understandable language to give the reader a better grasp of the proposed solution. Second, the book will provide a quantitative tool, QuickFit, to help assess the specific solution's ability to meet your business needs. The QuickFit methodology presented in this book can also be used to evaluate or compare the "fit" of any other computer solution you may wish to consider.

Finally, the book will provide you with valuable insight into what makes one implementation fail while another succeeds. The intent here is to provide you with practical information to help reduce the risks of the implementation project once you decide to proceed.

We feel confident that this book and the others in the series will help you choose the right computer solution and implement it successfully. We would very much like to hear from you. Please send us your comments on this and any other book in the series.

Best Wishes,

Jim Hoskins
President and Series Editor
Maximum Press

Looking Back at Engineering and ProductManager

From the aqueducts and pyramids of ancient times to the space program and robotics manufacturing of today, engineering and its concepts have played a key role in the advancement of world technologies. In many ways the concepts haven't changed; after all, a right angle has always been a right angle. What *has* changed are the tools engineers use to produce goods. The new tools have made it possible to refine scientific rules and concepts.

Engineering had its beginnings more than 10,000 years ago, when sticks and stones were popular engineering tools. It has only been about 5000 years since the wheel made transportation of people and goods more efficient.

Around 3000 B.C., the early civilizations of Egypt and Mesopotamia produced engineering marvels that included the pyramids, irrigation systems, and roads. In the first century A.D., it was the Romans who continued to make strides in engineering as they constructed a complex series of aqueducts, roadways, and impressive and durable buildings.

Other civilizations had made significant engineering gains by 1200 A.D. The Mongol Empire built massive cities and introduced printing, paper, and gunpowder, while medieval European engineers brought about advances in architecture as they began to apply mathematical and geometric principles.

Modern engineering helped usher in the Industrial Revolution, and as the use of electricity blossomed in the early twentieth century along with Henry Ford's assembly line, it seemed as though the manufacture of goods couldn't be any easier. By World War II another engineering push was under way—the development of the computer. The production and use of sophisticated war machines required more and more computer calculations. At the end of the war, we were in the computer age.

Modern engineering has been through two major stages. The first dealt with discovery and implementation of new technology. This period, when inventors worked alone, started during the Industrial Revolution. Early engineers expanded on the ideas of others and improved them. During the second stage, with the introduction of corporations, engineers began to organize. They began to specialize and form groups that worked together to create new technology. It was the time of serial processing, when brute force pushed products through assembly. Now we are looking at a third stage, when engineers are sharing more information, working in teams, and taking more responsibility for getting a product through design, manufacturing, and distribution and into a maintenance mode.

A lot has changed over the years in the engineering field. Although many of the concepts remain the same, the tools engineers use to design and implement their ideas have changed drastically. With computers, engineering has no bounds.

By the early 1970s, businesses were prolifically developing and releasing new products to manufacturing. Supported by mainframe computers, starting with the IBM System/360 and progressing to the IBM System/370, manufacturers started to control information using the computer as a tool. The online information technology began moving so quickly that it was hard for industries to keep up with the changes. Just managing information about part numbers became an overwhelming job. Similar parts were being produced around the world, and tracking the information was becoming unmanageable.

During this period, industries were becoming bogged down with their development and production records. By the early 1980s, there was a massive amount of information that controlled design and manufacturing. **Information systems (IS)** groups, which program and maintain computer systems for user groups, struggled to keep up with the growth. Along with product information, other programs that managed parts, release, and plant/floor operations appeared. They ran independently of the original products and drained IS resources to maintain them.

In 1986 a team of IBM representatives began gathering information from around the world about manufacturing, to see what industry needed to address the growing pressures of information management. They looked at all the processes of running a manufacturing company, starting with computer-aided design and computer-aided manufacturing (CAD/CAM), engineering release management, material requirements planning, and plant operations. The outcome of the study indicated that businesses were in need of engineering data management and engineering release tools that could support new integrated development concepts. It took too long to get products to market, and global competition was increasing.

In 1987 IBM began developing a family of application programs to address these data management needs. Although several smaller programs existed at the personal computer level, there were no programs that could be used by large organizations with development and manufacturing sites throughout the country and around the world. Nor were there programs that provided an overall architecture that a company could easily tailor to its way of doing business. Evaluation of the program requirements was completed with input from customer groups around the world, including Japan, Korea, Australia, England, the United States, Germany, and France. They all voiced a need for software that would help manage product data and that could be used to release new products and product changes to manufacturing. Their design and manufacturing engineers were struggling with the control of information.

Validation sessions with additional customers in 1988 finally gave IBM the details it needed to define an engineering release and product data management program. A team began work on the program called "ProductManager: Engineering Management Edition." It employed object-oriented programming concepts and hoped to provide a solution to engineers' needs with a technology that would carry a manufacturing company forward. ProductManager was first announced in 1989 as a mainframe product. ProductManager customers continued to drive the development and direction of the program, and in 1992 ProductManager was made available in the Multiple Virtual System/Time Sharing Option (MVS/TSO) mainframe environment, to complement the CAD/CAM capabilities already used by companies in this environment.

IBM also recognized the need for ProductManager capabilities on smaller computers in a distributed data environment. In mid-1992, IBM formed a team to look at what was needed and how long it would take to meet industry demands for a system that wasn't dependent on a mainframe, but still had the same capabilities and functions for managing product data. Meanwhile, early in 1993, Version 2 Release 1 of the ProductManager mainframe program was released, with more functions and capabilities. By employing the reuse capability of object-oriented technology used in the mainframe version of ProductManager, the team was able to develop, by mid-1993, a version of ProductManager that could be used on smaller computers called workstations. Made available in June 1993, ProductManager/6000: Engineering Management Edition brought engineering needs to the workstation level on the IBM RISC System/6000 platform, under IBM's Advanced Interactive eXecutive (AIX) version of the UNIX operating system. Now businesses had the option of managing complex product data at a fraction of the cost of purchasing and maintaining a mainframe computer.

Along with the mainframe version of ProductManager, ProductManager/6000 continues to grow in functionality. At the end of 1993, document management facilities, computer-graphics design, and manufacturing integration functions, along with configuration management enhancements, were announced for ProductManager. Early in 1994 the system was made available on a wider range of hardware products, operating systems, and databases, including popular workstations from Hewlett Packard and Sun Microsystems. According to CIMdata Inc., a leading product data management consultant, ProductManager, through its basic functionality, has the potential to become a market-leading product.

CHAPTER 1

An Overview of the Engineering World

This chapter takes a brief look at the responsibilities of a variety of engineers involved in designing and producing goods. The chapter examines the roles of development engineers and manufacturing engineers. Based on interviews with engineers in a variety of industries, the chapter also looks at current engineering trends and what the future holds for product development and managing product information.

Introduction to Engineering

In the business of making things, we need people who understand how and why things work. Called *engineers,* this group of people applies the rules and concepts of science to produce goods in the most efficient way. The engineering profession covers a wide variety of fields, ranging from chemical and petroleum engineering to electrical and mechanical engineering. For every branch of science, there's an engineer who has studied and trained to bring the science to its most useful stage.

Each major engineering field, including mechanical, electrical, and chemical, has a set of **branches.** Each of these branches focuses on a specific discipline within the field. For example, the bioengineering field includes specialized subfields such as medical, bionics, and human factors engineering, while mechanical engineering branches into aeronautical and automotive engineering groups. In addition to the major engineering fields and their branches, engineers can be classified into **functional** groups. Functional groups are defined by the scope of their work, which spans the major engineering fields. Research, design, and manufacturing engineers fall into the functional aspects of engineering. Figure 1.1 shows how an engineering field branches into other specialized fields of engineering and some of the functional groups that cross all engineering branches. The lines that separate engineering groups are not drawn in black and white. Often there are crossdisciplinary engineering groups that could fall into several branches. The figure shows only partial fields, branches, and functions.

In most cases, engineers from different fields, branches, and functional groups combine their talents, share information, and work together to develop or change a product to meet a variety of consumer needs. For example, it's not unusual to see a human factors engineer working with a design engineer to create an ergonomically correct chair or to ensure that a human hand can reach and adjust a setting on a tight-fitting engine. If the hand can't make the adjustment, another engineering skill is called upon to produce a tool that can make the adjustment. This combining of skills can also be seen when an electrical engineer works with a construction engineer to create the safest and most efficient wiring scheme for a new building. Engineering today is an effort by engineering groups to develop and produce products together.

The importance of engineering has never been greater, as businesses around the world compete to make better products while using fewer resources. Businesses need an effective and efficient engineering team to meet the demands of a quality- and cost-conscious consumer world. And regardless of how you put it, everything businesses do is geared to cost, quality, speed,

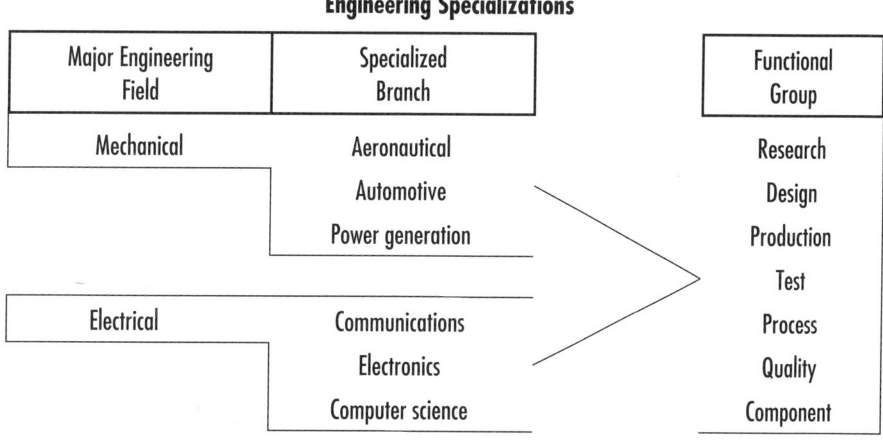

Figure 1.1 Functional engineering groups perform development or maintenance work for each specialized branch of engineering.

and innovation. Make the product as economically as possible, with the best quality possible, and as quickly as possible, and at the same time create new products and develop new techniques to improve existing products. Engineers across all industries continue to bear the responsibilities of reaching these objectives.

The goal of meeting standards of revenue and quality is present from the beginning of the development cycle. Whether it's designing a new product or improving an existing product, the engineering profession is responsible for taking that product from an idea to a manufactured commodity.

Engineers come into play when the requirements for a new product or a product change are identified. The requirements can come from the marketing area, quality groups, or an assembly worker who has identified a problem with the material used in a product. Once the problem is identified, whether it be a marketing need, safety concerns, or incompatible parts, everyone knows what has to be done, but not how. Where do they turn? Without the technical ability to design or fix the problem, they turn to engineers who have the skills to tackle these requirements.

When a car manufacturer sells 3000 units that have a problem with the braking system, it's the engineer who must determine the cause of the problem and come up with the solution. When environmental standards are raised, it's the engineers who must go to computers to work on solutions that will bring a product in line with the standards. For example, in the wood and pulp industry, converting engineers who oversee changing pulp into paper strive to keep low chlorine levels in water used to make paper. The residual chlorine in the water that is discarded can have a negative impact on the environment. It's the responsibility of the converting engineer and the chemical engineer to keep the business in line with environmental requirements.

Engineers operate in a continually changing environment. Thanks to new tools and technologies, they are achieving more and more, helping businesses meet the challenges of change and competition.

Today's Engineers

Faced with the challenges of adapting to new tools and technologies, ongoing international business competition, information management problems, and engineering cultural changes, today's engineers are under the gun to bring products to market within the constraints of the four driving business factors mentioned earlier: cost, quality, speed, and innovation. Many of these problems are not new or unique. Engineers faced similar challenges during the 1940s when they worked on war projects. Every project has deadlines and pressures. The difference with today's engineers is the global aspect of doing business.

Businesses once had the luxury of absorbing extravagant development costs. Manufacturers had the time and resources to allow their engineers to design a product and then "throw it over the wall" for manufacturing to build. If the product couldn't be built as designed, it was thrown back over the wall for design changes. In some cases, when pieces and parts didn't fit just right, they were classified as "off-specs" and used anyway. Large manufacturers had the resources and time to do it their way. Without stiff international competition, they were able to conduct business as they had in the war years, living with flaws and lengthy cycle times. Times have changed.

While many U.S. industries were "throwing it over the wall," other countries moved in on the manufactured goods market. The United States and Europe were leading manufacturers in the 50s, 60s, and 70s. Japan led the way to a rise in global competition in the late 1970s, appealing to consumers with quality products at reasonable prices. This is where today's development and manufacturing engineers are needed. Businesses want to maintain and expand their share of the market. Engineers are searching for any advantage that is going to better meet those business needs. Whether it be a prototyping tool or a better way to manage product information, today's engineer is pressured to look for ways to maintain and expand that market share.

Our focus in this chapter is on engineers who work in the manufacturing business--the ones who are responsible for taking an idea and transforming it into an assembled product. It's certainly not a one-person show. Just like the design engineer who needed a human factors engineer to work out the tight-fitting adjustment on the engine, so do engineers in a development and manufacturing environment work together to meet consumer needs.

Businesses are realizing that the challenge to compete lies at the front end of the development cycle, where designs can trim manufacturing costs and time. Whereas it may have taken a company years to design and build a product in the past, with new technologies that cycle time has been significantly reduced. Today's engineers are stepping up to the challenge of increased competition. With advancing technology, it's becoming possible for engineering groups to design, test, and produce a product with less rework time, with greater quality, and at less cost.

Generally, these engineering groups can be divided into **development engineering** and **manufacturing engineering**. Development engineers are the ones who come up with the methods to make an idea work. In larger companies, they work in research or development laboratories. In smaller companies, development engineers may be hidden behind a stack of drawings next to the vice president's office. Manufacturing engineers take what development engineers have designed and produce it. Unlike the trend of the last 50 years, manufacturing engineers are now more involved in the development of products.

There are specialized branches of engineering in development and manufacturing engineering. Depending on the product, a wide range of engineers can be involved in its production. The grouping of engineers in this section highlights functions engineers are likely to encounter in producing a product. In many businesses, there are not hard-drawn lines between engineering responsibilities. You may find a design or test engineer performing responsibilities of other engineers and vice versa.

Engineering Basics

Engineering begins with a problem or need and ends with a resolution. Problems can be raised through a variety of channels. A common one is the marketing channel. Salespeople listen to the needs of customers every day. Customer concerns and requests need to be transformed into new products and improvements for existing products. By the time the request gets to the engineer, it comes as a business need and, yes, a problem for the engineer to solve.

Engineering proceeds in three phases: the initial design, design integration, and final design. The **initial design** begins with the engineer looking at the new product or problem. An agreement has been reached that the problem needs to be fixed and the engineer's responsibility is to fix it.

The initial design phase is when engineers roll up their sleeves and put together a plan for creating a new product or changing an existing product. The problem is analyzed, resolutions are considered, and a final direction is agreed upon. During this phase, engineers arrive at the basic design to fix the problem. If a car manufacturer has a problem with windshields that allow moisture to seep in, the engineers have to determine the weak spot in the windshield and develop a rough idea of how to fix it.

The **design integration** phase is where the fine-tuning of the problem comes into play. Engineers will look at the windshield and, using computer tools, come up with a solution and evaluate the best way to apply the new design to the product. Then, working with other engineering groups, they will look at how the new windshield will be manufactured and installed.

The **final design** takes into consideration the input from all areas of the manufacturing and designing groups. This is the last stage before the design is **released to manufacturing,** which is when design engineers first relinquish their control and turn a design over to manufacturing for production. All groups involved in the final design agree on an effectivity. When the design goes into production, it's complete--at least for the moment. As the product goes through its life cycle, there are going to be changes to the design and the process starts over again.

Engineering groups vary from industry to industry and business to business. It's an ever-evolving field that one day may have an engineer as part of a **systems group** and the next day part of a functional group. A systems group is a group pulled together to work on an entire project from beginning to end. The systems group is often called an integrated product team. The functional group is a static group of engineers that work on a variety of projects at the same time and belong to the same organizational group. Let's take a look at the engineers involved in producing a product and what they add to the process. These engineering titles are generally functional, meaning that they may apply in any specialized branch of any engineering field. The titles will vary from business to business, but here's the list we will concentrate on:

- Design
- Detail
- Prototype
- Test
- Component
- Process
- Manufacturing
- Facilities
- Quality

Design Engineer

Design engineers are responsible for the initial design of a product. They also are responsible for making changes to a product. Design engineers work to bring a concept to reality, or what is referred to in the engineering business as bringing the "art to a part." They analyze requirements, often write specifications, and then draw plans that resemble the product as they envision it. After the design is created, design engineers work to resolve problems that arise from the design.

Design engineers are the first engineers to work on a product, but they often consult and work with other engineering groups to complete the final product design. They consider ways to reduce the time it takes to build a product. Look at the cover on a telephone. Instead of using a screw to hold it in place, a design engineer would consider snapping the cover in place using one or two fewer parts. Instead of using several plastic parts, design engineers look at ways to produce the parts as one unit, again reducing the number of parts used in the phone and reducing the time it takes to assemble.

Design engineers are also concerned with quality. They have to understand what the actual requirements are. They have to make design decisions that recognize the real cost of the design while at the same time meeting the real requirements of the design, adding quality to it.

Detail Engineer

Detail engineers are responsible for fine-tuning the work of design engineers. They look at the feasibility of a concept, gather information about the design, and study how the product is going to be put together. Detail engineers work closely with design engineers to determine product specifications, what holds the product together, and how it's going to be built. Often, design engineers work as detail engineers. Both groups of engineers do similar work.

Prototype Engineer

Prototype engineers are responsible for creating a working model of a proposed new product or a proposed change to an existing product. A **prototype** is a *working* model, whereas a model is only a suggested design. Early prototypes help engineers see how a product is going to perform. Using prototypes, engineers can test tolerances, stability, durability, and reliability of parts. It's a way to catch design flaws or bad components before the product goes into production.

These working models can be used in everything from software production to aircraft production. With the use of new technology, model testing can now often be simulated without building a prototype.

Test Engineer

Test engineers are responsible for making sure the product will work. They design and develop manufacturing test equipment. Once a prototype is established, this group of engineers looks at ways to test the endurance, tolerance, and quality of the proposed product. In today's economic environment, it's especially important that products and their designs work as called for by the requirements and specifications. To make sure the product or product change can stand up to its challenge, test engineers work on procedures and requirements that test products to their limits. They develop stress tests that simulate the life cycle of the product.

An aircraft propeller that contains titanium must be tested in the early stages of development to determine whether the material can withstand the stress of pulling the plane off the ground. Testing can also be considered an analysis stage in the development of a product.

Component Engineer

Component engineers are responsible for determining the components used in a product. They must determine which components are used, where they come from, how many are required, and how effective they are. Electronic components, for example, are used in many products. A component engineer looks at the components and decides which ones meet the product's quality standards, where they will come from, and which ones can be replaced by another component. The component engineer, along with a quality engineer, makes the decision about which component has the right quality at the right price for the product.

Component engineers also assist in sourcing parts. They work with purchasing and material requirements personnel to find suppliers for the parts. They deal with a variety of suppliers. First, there are **off-the-shelf** suppliers, who provide products on demand. From electronic components to roll-sheet steel, off-the-shelf suppliers can quickly provide parts, already built, that meet manufacturing needs.

The next type of supplier is the **build-to-order** supplier. Build-to-order suppliers take engineering specifications from a business and produce a part that meets the business's needs. When purchasing locates and contracts with a supplier that can provide the part, specifications are sent to the supplier, who builds the part from the specifications. Another type of supplier is the **specification-buys** supplier. This type of supplier provides the engineering expertise to create the specifications and part required for the product. A business can use the expertise of another business that has more qualified engineers to create a part using metals, plastics, or chemicals.

The final type of supplier is the **assembly contractor**. These suppliers do not build or design parts; they simply put them together based on the specifications provided by the business. Assembly contractors can normally put parts together more economically than a larger business with more overhead. Working with suppliers and deciding on the best supplier for a part keeps component engineers active in all stages of development and manufacturing.

Process Engineer

Process engineers determine how a product goes through the manufacturing cycle. They are responsible for providing the tools used to manufacture a product. Tools can range from punch presses to plastic-injection molds. This group of engineers is involved with minute details of how a product is put together. Process engineers determine how to get the space shuttle from its refitting building to the launch pad, which tools assemblers will use to bolt a motor to a frame, and what molds will be used to produce a plastic cover.

Process engineers also work closely with facilities engineers to make sure a building is properly suited for manufacturing a product or even testing it. How do you put a product through environmental conditions it may be exposed to during use? Process engineers work with other engineering groups to ensure that appropriate conditions are established for testing the product.

Manufacturing Engineer

Manufacturing engineers generally "own," or oversee, the production of a product. They work closely with process and design engineers to get a quality product out the door. Whereas process engineers determine the requirements for moving a product through manufacturing, manufacturing engineers make decisions on how products are put together. They follow the product through the entire manufacturing process.

Manufacturing engineers are usually attached to a specific product or set of products and determine how the product will go through the manufacturing process. Working closely with other engineering groups, a manufacturing engineer determines the most efficient way to build a product. They get involved when a problem arises from something like an "off-spec" tolerance. They question the elements that make up the product if a problem occurs. Manufacturing and design engineers work for businesses that cover a variety of manufacturing techniques. The basic categories of manufacturing are described below.

Push and **pull** are contrasting manufacturing concepts. The push concept starts with buying raw materials, then transforming them into a final product, and finally selling the product. The concept is that you build a product on a planned schedule that dictates what you are going to build. On the other hand, the pull concept starts at the other end of the process. You make only products that have been asked for by distribution. Your schedule is driven by what customers are requesting.

The **make-to-stock** manufacturing concept is one in which schedules are dictated by forecasts and marketing promotions. Typically, customers order from a catalog and require immediate shipment. Manufacturers must maintain inventory, equipment, and labor based on marketing projections. The **make-to-order** concept deals with customizing products to meet customer requirements. The term **job shop** represents make-to-order manufacturing very well. This type of manufacturer normally doesn't make the same product twice, but uses an inventory of components to make different versions of the product.

Assemble-to-order manufacturers partially build and store products before receiving orders. When orders are placed, the manufacturer completes the final product based on the individual customer's requirements.

Finally, there are **discrete** and **process** manufacturers that take into consideration the nature of the products. Products of a discrete manufacturer are entities that are distinct from each other, such as automobiles, appliances, and computers. The discrete manufacturer can be driven by customer orders or can base production on a convenient batch size. Process manufacturing products are not as distinct as those of a discrete manufacturer. Paint products, for instance, are produced by mixing components to produce the product. The containers are distinct objects, but the paint inside is not. Process manufacturing systems run continuously, shutting down only for maintenance, as in paper mills and refineries.

Depending on the type of manufacturing a business is in, the relationship between design and manufacturing engineers can vary.

Facilities Engineer

Facilities engineers ensure that a building or manufacturing area is arranged for the maximum efficiency in producing a product. When a business creates a new product line, it could easily require a new building or the refitting of an existing building to adapt it to manufacturing requirements. If a business is producing a complex product that may take weeks to go from one end of the floor to the shipping area, facilities engineers have to determine the space required to handle overflow, parts, and production requirements. Such details as where large pieces of equipment will fit and how conveyor lines from one production area to another are installed are the facilities engineer's concerns.

Consider the facilities needed to mass-produce cars. Facilities engineers have to determine which buildings are suited for which production operations and work with process engineers to determine locations of subassembly areas, such as chassis, underbody, and tire-and-wheel assembly. Add to that the painting, final assembly, and test areas and you can see it's a massive job.

As businesses attempt to get more out of their production facilities and meet the bottom line for revenues, facilities engineers are busy refitting buildings and planning to meet space requirements at the right cost.

Quality Engineer

Quality engineers look at how the product works and how it performs. In manufacturing environments, quality engineers oversee the quality standards expected of the product. Not enough can be said of what we expect from this group. They, too, are customers. They look at the product and determine whether it meets customer requirements. Quality is a driving factor in today's engineering environment. Some companies will spend \$1 million on producing a product and another \$150,000 on checking to see that the product is built right.

The role of the quality engineer is drastically changing. While quality programs are not the direct responsibility of a quality engineer, the quality-improvement group will be a focal point in making sure the programs work. With the implementation of quality programs such as **Total Quality Management (TQM)**, businesses are taking product quality more seriously. TQM is a process for managing and measuring quality. Along with TQM, you hear such terms as "quality circles," "continuous improvement," and "Six Sigma." No matter what terms you use, business today is serious about improving the quality of its goods.

Since the U.S. government has adopted TQM, a TQM program is required of industries doing business with the government. This move affects not only large companies, but smaller companies that do subcontracting as well. It's not a concept that's going to drift away. TQM may evolve into other forms, but the drive for quality is a way of life in engineering. Quality engineers will play a key role in measuring the success of a TQM program, but all engineers on the plant floor and in development labs are constantly under pressure to ensure that quality programs are monitored and quality goals are met.

How Engineering Changes Fit into the Process

Once a product has been built and introduced, a business wants not only to get a return on its investment, but also to continue to sell and improve the product, rather than create a new product to replace it. That's where **engineering changes (ECs)** play a key role. An EC is the formal method for introducing a new version of an item or product. By reacting to consumer needs and improving its product, a business can keep the product profitable for years. We've looked at a variety of engineering responsibilities that go into producing or changing products. Let's see how they work together in a manufacturing environment to release an engineering change to manufacturing.

We're going to look at how a more complex piece of equipment is designed and built. While the wing of an airplane is extremely complex in design, the same principles apply to building a stapler, although the latter wouldn't call for as much engineering involvement. Also, remember that the three phases of engineering (initial design, design integration, and final design) can be interpreted differently by different businesses.

The **engineering cycle** for making a change to an airplane wing starts with a contract. A company's finance department issues the work order and a product manager takes control of developing the product, starting with a master schedule and the assignment of responsibilities. A team is formed and a leader assigned to it while facilities engineers start working on where the product is going to be designed and produced. Finding the real estate to produce a product is not always easy. Normally, a business does not purchase land and build a facility to support a new product. It uses existing facilities, so someone has to give up space for the project. Facilities engineers evaluate business needs and cost to help decide who goes where.

Design and detail engineers look at the wing concepts and requirements, then begin creating rough designs and sketches. This is done in the initial design phase and includes input from manufacturing engineers and other engineering groups. Materials needed, subcontracting options, and lead times are considered. A prototype engineer may be brought in at this point if the change requires new parts or significant changes to existing parts. Detailed designing comes later in the process.

After kicking the ideas around and passing them back and forth during the planning stage, engineering goes through a preliminary design review with the customer. The design integration stage for the wing includes basic designs, schedules, concepts, cost predictions, and other aspects such as safety, reliability, and serviceability. Component and test engineers become more involved during this stage. When approval is obtained for the product, the wheels start rolling and teams are solidified. Now the development of the product begins in earnest. Engineers move ahead with the final design and arrange for releasing the product to manufacturing. Process engineers work on the tooling and the steps required to produce the product. In the final design stage, changes to the design are frequent. The customer may change a requirement, or more reliable components or methods may be discovered. Some final touches may be performed on the design even after it is released to manufacturing. Working with quality and test engineers, manufacturing engineers ensure that a good product rolls off the line and continue to work with design engineers to make additional changes as the design matures.

Changes to the product come from all levels and at different stages of its development and manufacture. Even when the product is in manufacturing, a worker in production may find that the sheet metal is not wrapping as it was designed to, or the customer may encounter unexpected problems in the finished product. These situations come back to the design engineer, who initiates another engineering change, and the release process starts over again.

To bring about engineering changes, engineers use a variety of processes for working with items, information, and changes. We'll briefly discuss some of the processes used for building and changing products. These processes provide control and organization for making changes. They round out the daily routines of engineers and are based on design and release management principles that bring together the processes used in a development and manufacturing business. The key processes are the following:

- Item definition
- Design review
- Request for engineering action
- Engineering change
- Release to manufacturing

Item Definition

We'll begin our discussion of these processes with the item definition process. This is also known as the part or product definition process in many manufacturing environments. The difference between the terms is the context in which they are used and depends on what area of manufacturing you work in. Generally, you can say that a part is a good that can be stocked on a shelf, while an item may or may not be a physical part. Item is the blanket term that covers any information about a part or a product. For example, an item can be a specification or a grouping of other items or parts.

An item is also any part, subassembly, or product that can be manufactured or purchased as a part or assembly. The assembly can be an end product or a raw material such as a plastic product. Items make up a product and can be defined for a variety of assemblies, from an engine in a lawn mower to an airplane wing or a truck wheel assembly. Engineers establish and maintain information that describes and supports an item. This information makes up the definition for the item.

Item definition encompasses a wide range of information. Engineers have to maintain this definition data, keeping it current by updating it when the item changes. It defines everything a business needs to know about an item, such as where it is used, how it is used, and who supplies it. Items can also have codes and statuses that track and control them as they go through a change. For example, an item type code describes the type of an item, for example, a detail part, which is not made up of other parts or is purchased as a complete part. Or an item can be a reference item, meaning that it is not a physical part but rather a set of specifications or a drawing, for example.

When an item starts through a change process, engineers must protect their work. **Product data management (PDM)** systems help them in this endeavor by tracking and managing the item. Product data management systems are electronic means of handling information related to product development. The systems track and manage the information and provide security measures to protect the information as it goes through the development cycle. With a paper trail, information and business processes cannot be automatically protected. Without strict enforcement of business processes dealing with change and rework, mistakes and miscommunication are more likely to occur, resulting in the need to redesign an item, even after the design is released.

Another part of the item definition process is the creation of a **bill of material (BOM)**. This is a listing of all raw materials, subassemblies, and parts that go into an item. A BOM can also show how an item is built; and thus it is like a picture of the item. It is used to manage and work with complex levels of information about an item. Engineers create BOMs for development and manufacturing that can be associated with new items or engineering changes to existing items. Design engineers may produce a BOM that only lists items necessary to produce an assembly, but it may not describe the manufacture of the part. Manufacturing engineers use the same items from the design-engineering BOM, but structure their BOM to reflect the manufacturing process. Figure 1.2 shows examples of a BOM and how it is used. The top BOM is a simple design BOM for a lamp as a design engineer may view it. The lower BOM shows how a manufacturing engineer may view the same lamp.

Engineers have to maintain BOMs for a variety of uses, from planning to design and manufacturing. When a change is made to an item, the BOMs for the item are changed as well. It's not an easy task to keep all BOMs up to date as an item is changed. If the change processes and BOMs are not closely controlled, costly errors will be introduced into the manufacturing process. For example, if a manufacturing group is working with a different level of a BOM than the design group, a product could be produced using the wrong items. **Revision levels** associated with BOMs make it easier to work with changing item data. These revision levels identify an item at a particular point of time in development or manufacturing.

Another part of item definition is **configuration**. Because the term can change meaning with context, let's first establish a framework for discussing configuration. While the term can be applied to anything in the engineering field, it generally applies to a complete product. A configuration is what a specific product unit is made up of and is used to group products. A BOM shows what goes into a product configuration. If a single item in the product has changed, it produces a different configuration for the product. Engineers normally call each different configuration of an item a **version**. Figure 1.3 shows two BOMs for a lamp. The top BOM shows the configuration of the lamp before EC 101. The bottom BOM shows how the EC changed the configuration of the lamp. In this case, the lamp knob was redesigned as a result of the engineering change, resulting in a new configuration for the product.

Product configuration can be assigned by serial numbers or by dates of manufacture. The configuration of a product is affected by the engineering changes that have been applied to the product. Each time a change is applied, a

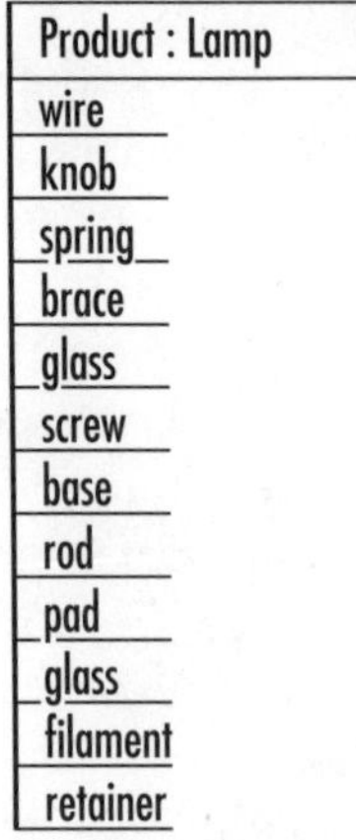

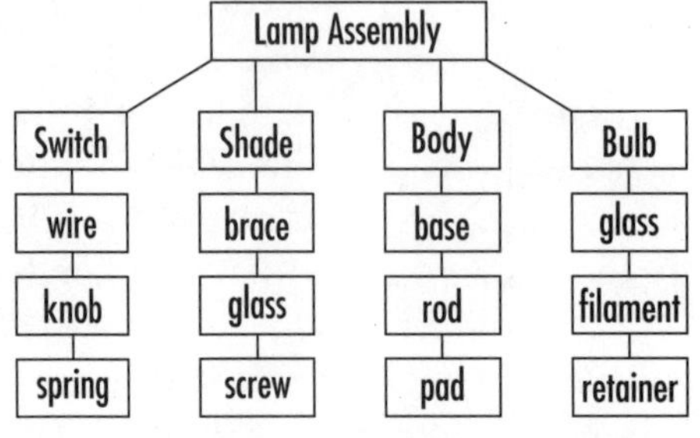

Figure 1.2 Design and manufacturing engineers look at products from different perspectives. Manufacturing engineers place more emphasis on how the product is assembled. The bottom BOM represents how a lamp could be built.

new configuration is created. Throughout the life cycle of a product, depending on its complexity, the product can go through thousands of changes.

Managing product configurations takes patience and time. When engineers complete work on a product change, they can't just pack their bags and go to the next project. Information concerning what the changes were, along with their history, has to be maintained for service and maintenance reasons. This is especially important in industries that are required by safety and legal standards to conform to certain guidelines. Information pertaining to a specific change, such as who initiated it, who reviewed it, what process was followed, and when it was implemented, must be documented, stored, and

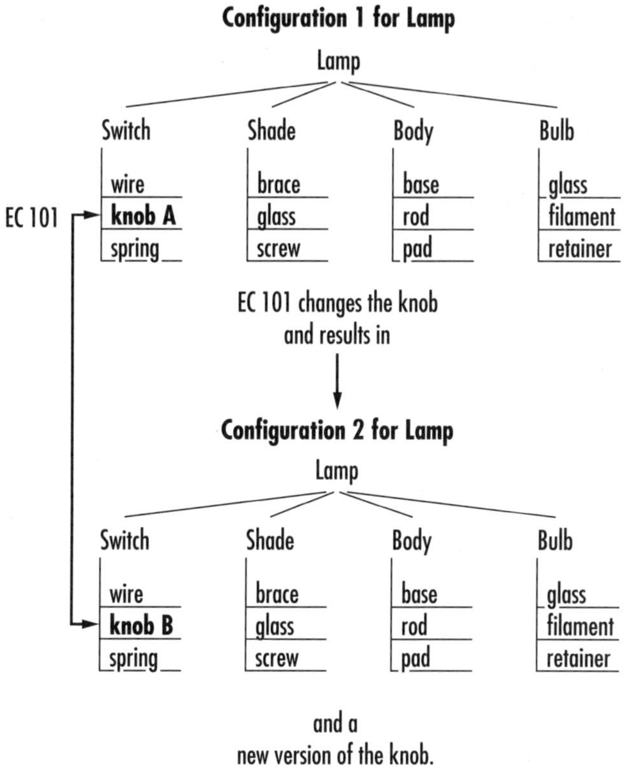

Figure 1.3 A configuration shows how a product is built. When changes are made to the product, it creates another configuration of the product. EC 101 results in a change to the lamp knob and a new configuration of the lamp.

readily available when needed--sometimes many years later. Tracking and maintaining information about a configuration is another task that falls on the engineer's shoulders. If a company is building a special line of products and has good configuration control, engineers will spend more time producing a good design and less time reinventing the wheel to make additional changes to the product.

Being able to define multiple representations of a design structure is also important. This is called a **view**. Views are different representations of BOMs that show the same design data from different perspectives, such as the contrast between design and manufacturing items. The design view may list all of the parts in an item structure, whereas the manufacturing view may define the items used to build a part in their order of assembly on a manufacturing line. Parts of the structure for an engine may be restructured in a manufacturing view because they are assembled in a different order than the design engineering structure shows. Views can also be used for different locations, plants, or even assembly lines within a plant. One manufacturing location may build an item differently than another location does. If a component can be purchased for less in one geographic region than in another, then the manufacturing plant in that region may choose to use the optional component rather than the component defined in the design BOM. Component engineers look closely at various BOM views in their search for ways to reduce cost or lead time and improve yields for components.

Design Review

The next engineering process is the **design review.** The purpose of a design review is to examine each detail of a design, whether it is a new item or a change to an existing item, and to expose any errors or problems before the design is released to manufacturing. These reviews examine every aspect of the design, including conformance with specifications, standards, and business practices. After an item's definition has been completed or changed, the new item data is typically assembled into a package or **folder**, which can then be hand-carried, mailed, or distributed electronically to other engineers for information purposes or for their review and approval. The reviewers examine various item definition data such as specifications, drawings, BOMs, and configurations.

While the manual distribution of folders is a common practice today, many businesses are looking at computerizing the design review process in order to reduce cycle time, save money, and provide a comprehensive audit trail. If the folder is stored in a computer in electronic form, it is often easier to control and tailor the review process to meet business needs and to conduct a review in a more efficient and timely manner.

Request for Engineering Action

A **request for engineering action (REA)** is the initial stage of an engineering change. It is used to request a change, define a problem that needs fixing, or initiate a new requirement. Other terms to describe the change process include "change request," "design change request," "problem report," and "engineering report," to name a few. The REA is a method of obtaining a preliminary review and approval to continue with a formal engineering change, but is not a required step for an EC. An REA removes some of the barriers to adopting and implementing an EC by flushing out problems that the requesting engineer may not be aware of. Many businesses do not use this process, but it has proven to be an effective method for removing obstacles before the initial design phase is started.

REAs are similar in theory to the engineering change. They both use a design review package that can be distributed manually or electronically, and they both contain justification for the suggested change. The main difference between them is that the EC becomes the final authority for implementing a change.

Engineering Change

The engineering change (EC) represents another engineering process. It is the formal method for modifying an existing item's definition. An EC process identifies the method by which the newly modified item definition data is packaged for release to manufacturing, and contains the specifics of the change. The engineering change process can be either a manual or electronic operation. In either case, the justification and documentation for the change are included in the design review folder that is distributed for review and approval. The **EC review** is a review folder associated with an EC. It contains all the information about the change, including BOMs, **affected items**, drawings, reviews, and **deliverables**. An affected item is an item affected by the EC, while a deliverable is an activity that has to be completed before an EC can be released. The deliverable concept supports the assignment and control of tasks such as creating a BOM or a set of specifications.

Manufacturing engineers can also originate an EC that changes an item in another EC. This is often called a **manufacturing engineering change (MEC)**. MECs can be used to add manufacturing data to an EC, initiate a manufacturing change, or change material requirements planning data such as supplier information.

The EC is a key process in controlling the release of items into the manufacturing environment. **Effectivities** are used to bring order to releasing changes to manufacturing. Generally, an effectivity is the date an EC advances from one stage to the next. Most businesses use the effectivity as the date an item on an EC goes into manufacturing, but the term can apply to a number of status changes in an item or EC. An effectivity can be when a change is going from design to prototyping or testing, or when one is going from design to manufacturing. Engineers must coordinate effectivities. This makes scheduling, lead times, and coordination major factors in meeting effectivities. Effectivities can be managed manually or with a computer. However, the more complex effectivities, where several engineering changes are being coordinated and numerous items are being introduced at different times into the manufacturing process, make controlling the effectivity of an EC for a complex product a logistical nightmare, especially if it has to be manually managed. Again, it takes close coordination between multiple engineering groups.

How an effectivity is used varies from business to business. For example, an effectivity can be based on a product unit, serial number, lot or batch number, or a date. **Date effectivity** indicates the date a change will be implemented, while the **product–unit effectivity** is the unit number of the product in which you implement the change. In the aircraft industry, the product–unit effectivity could be assigned as a tail number of an aircraft. **Batch** and **lot number effectivities** apply mainly to the process industries. Batch effectivity indicates when a standard run or lot size is implemented. It can be determined by container size, line rates, or standard run length. Lot number effectivity is assigned to a homogeneous quantity of uniquely identified material such as paint, oil, or wood. For instance, when paint is produced, the lot number is determined by the specific batch in which the paint was produced.

Release to Manufacturing

Before an EC can become effective, both design and manufacturing engineering must agree on the design. The formal method for obtaining this agreement is through the release to manufacturing. In this process, the design BOM, specifications, and product definition data (item data) are turned over, or promoted, to manufacturing for production.

The release of a design covers a wide spectrum of activity. Along with being released to manufacturing engineering, the design may also go to other manufacturing groups, including costing, inventory control, and scheduling. If manufacturing has been involved in design of the item, there will most likely be less need for redesign when the design is promoted to manufacturing. On the other hand, if it's the first time manufacturing engineers have seen the design, the promotion of the item could be considered the **initial release to manufacturing,** and the design may not be accepted by manufacturing, resulting in redesign or negotiations. When manufacturing accepts a design, the release to manufacturing is complete.

There are two ways to release a design and its information to manufacturing. The first is releasing the design to manufacturing computer applications such as **material requirements planning (MRP)** or purchasing applications. MRP is responsible for ensuring a steady supply of raw materials, purchased items, and supplies needed to maintain production, while purchasing is responsible for obtaining the materials and items. If manufacturing and other support organizations are involved in early design efforts, the item may already be established in the system. The second way to release a design is an organizational release, where one organization makes the design information available to another, for example, when design engineering turns the design over to manufacturing engineering and purchasing.

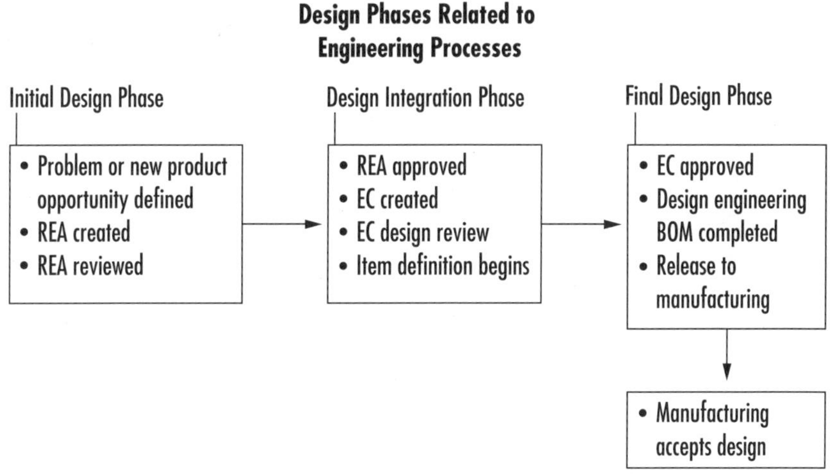

Figure 1.4 This figure shows the basic engineering processes and how they relate to the three engineering design phases. It's a flexible scheme, and if manufacturing doesn't accept the design, the whole process could start again.

The only step left for placing the design into actual production is promoting the design to an effective status, where the design can be phased into production. Figure 1.4 shows how the preceding engineering processes, from item definition to the design's release to manufacturing, relate to the design phases discussed earlier. It's important to remember that each business has a different set of processes for placing a design into production. The figure represents a general guideline for engineering processes during the initial design, design integration, and final design phases of engineering.

Engineering Today

Concepts in engineering are the methods engineers work with to produce a product. The concepts can range from methodologies to electronic aids, and vary from business to business. If you ask ten people about the current concepts in engineering, you will get ten different answers because each business operates differently. Basically, the discussion of engineering concepts focuses on how a business manages the development and manufacturing process.

Cost, quality, speed, and innovation are the driving forces behind all concepts in the engineering field. Of course, the primary objective of all businesses is to meet a need and make a profit. When a business looks at using technology to help manage product data, it's not the technology itself that's of interest but rather improving the bottom line of the business. We'll look at the following concepts:

- Computer integrated manufacturing
- Concurrent engineering
- Integrated product and process development
- Product data management
- Design for manufacture
- Modeling

Computer Integrated Manufacturing

A much-discussed concept that has been implemented at varying levels in different manufacturing companies is **computer integrated manufacturing (CIM)**. Ultimately, CIM intends to use computer technology to streamline the entire manufacturing business by optimizing a company's use and management of information. With CIM, computer systems act as repositories for many different types of information, ranging from supplier lists and inventory levels to engineering drawings and the **numerically controlled (NC)** programs used by sophisticated machine tools to cut parts.

The advantage of computer integrated manufacturing is that it ties together two or more operational areas in a business. This ensures a smoother flow of information between groups, resulting in easier and immediate access to information, more accurate information, better communications between development and manufacturing groups, and, ultimately, improved profitability. The level of use for CIM can be between groups within manufacturing or it can be used between development, manufacturing, and purchasing groups. Computer integrated manufacturing is a slowly but steadily maturing technology in most companies. Companies that have completely implemented computer integrated manufacturing are rare, or may not exist at all. That is, they do not purchase and bring in raw material, design and make the product, then sell and distribute the product effectively using computer systems in every facet of their operation.

A true CIM business has little human intervention. For example, when a design engineer produces specifications for a supplier, they generally mail the specs to the suppliers and, most likely, the suppliers mark up the blueprints and mail them back. That's a lot of human intervention; it's not computer integrated manufacturing. What is more typical in industry is what has been termed **islands of automation**. These are pockets in a company that use computers to do one somewhat independent thing, such as to control sophisticated machines or robots, schedule product flow, or track inventory. These "islands" are self-contained; their computers do not communicate or share information with other areas.

The ultimate CIM solution addresses a business's information requirements from developing the business plan and design through shipping the product and providing customer support. It involves the integration of all the information systems in the business, not just the ones in manufacturing. Businesses are finding that CIM is not a solution that can be implemented overnight. It's a gradual process that will take years to phase in and requires constant evaluation and improvement. While the development and manufacturing organizational areas are generally making great strides in CIM, other areas that use the same information, such as purchasing and financial operations, have not kept up.

With the rapid pace of technological change, it is often difficult to introduce a CIM product and not have it outperformed by another technology within six months. Then businesses start looking at the whole process again. This is causing a delay in the adoption of CIM programs by manufacturing industries. So many companies offer so many development and manufacturing solutions that businesses often find it difficult to choose the product that best suits their needs. While they may find a good program for managing specific organizational needs, few packages provide cross-organizational functions that can be tailored to meet all their unique needs. The net result is that a business may start a CIM program, only to have it derailed when one of its organizations finds a newer technology that works better for its group but doesn't fit in with the company's overall CIM plan.

Concurrent Engineering

Leading the way in current engineering trends is **concurrent engineering**. Concurrent engineering is when the designers of an item work closely with their counterparts in other areas of engineering to release or change a product. The concept brings engineering groups such as manufacturing, process, and quality engineers, along with material requirements management, into the product cycle at the beginning of the design process, when changes they recommend can be more easily accommodated, rather than having them wait until the initial design is complete. Concurrent engineering allows a process engineer, for example, to influence the initial design in ways that will make the eventual manufacturing process flow much more smoothly. Some businesses are not at the concurrent engineering stage, while others have been practicing and refining the concept for years.

Traditionally, there has been an organizational boundary between development and manufacturing. This boundary resulted in the phrase, "design it

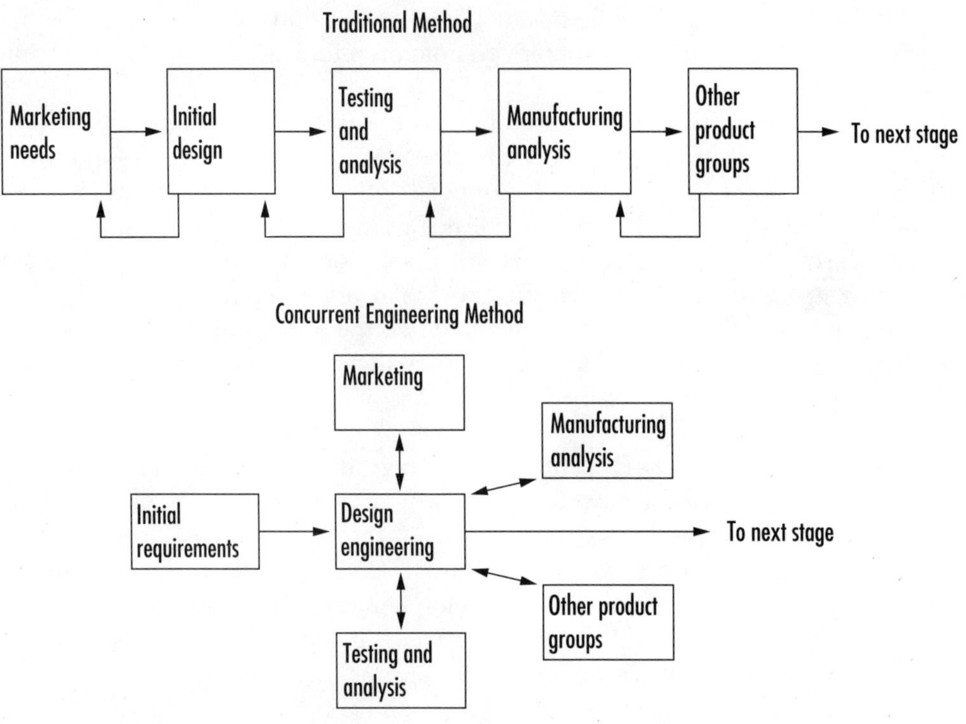

Figure 1.5 Concurrent engineering brings all groups associated with the development of a product into the review process at the same time. The traditional method of product development passes the review from group to group.

and 'throw it over the wall' to manufacturing," which describes a practice that has become costly. Concurrent engineering takes some of the guesswork out of design. Before the product gets to manufacturing, it has been studied by engineering groups that traditionally saw it only after the initial or even final design stages.

Concurrent engineering is applied in a variety of ways. It blends into different scenarios of development and manufacturing so smoothly that it often is not even recognized as a distinct method by those who use it. Regardless of the application, the result is a design that is more suited for manufacturing when it gets to the final design stage and is ready for the production line.

While concurrent engineering has been facilitated by improved technology, some engineers who have been around a while say that it has actually been practiced for the past 40 years. One engineer said that in the old days, before businesses expanded across states and countries, design and manufacturing engineers all worked in the same area. As businesses grew, the engineering areas grew apart. Figure 1.5 shows the differences in **traditional methods** of introducing changes and the concurrent engineering method. The concurrent method gets everyone involved in the early stages of development.

Concurrent engineering is driven by information sharing. Unless there's a commitment throughout the business, the team effort, which was strong at the beginning of the product cycle, can be weakened as the product goes through manufacturing. Successful implementation of concurrent engineering concepts keeps the expertise of these teams available so that the actual manufacturing of the product continues to have the same support as the design efforts had at the beginning of the development cycle.

Integrated Product and Process Development

Integrated product and process development is a concept that most government contractors are familiar with because of its popularity in such environments. It takes concurrent engineering a step further, bringing a dedicated team to a product that stays with the product through its life cycle, whereas with concurrent engineering, there is a team, but team members may report to different organizations within the company.

The secrets to integrated product and process development are accountability and "ownership." Program managers are held accountable to meet project goals and needs. Organizational boundaries are completely removed, and design, test, component, and manufacturing engineers work on the same team in the same organization. Integrated product and process development brings full design support to the product after it rolls off the production line. The concept is also flexible: A full team is in place at the beginning of the cycle, but the team size can fluctuate as needed. The responsible engineers are always available, however, to meet production or maintenance requirements.

Product Data Management

According to a description from a CIMdata Inc. (a worldwide consulting firm) report, "Product data management involves a software management system that organizes, accesses, and controls information related to a business' products. The management system also manages the life cycle of the products." A PDM system makes it possible to manage information among a variety of hardware and software applications in a heterogeneous environment. And, when necessary, the system can be integrated with paper processes. The big advantage of PDM is that it protects business information and processes by automatically controlling how information can be used and changed. PDM allows all users of the system to share a single copy of product information. When portions of the information, such as a drawing, are to be updated, PDM allows for a **three-tier architecture** of use.

Also called **distributed data,** a three-tier architecture is a hierarchy of development wherein information can be maintained at the organizational or

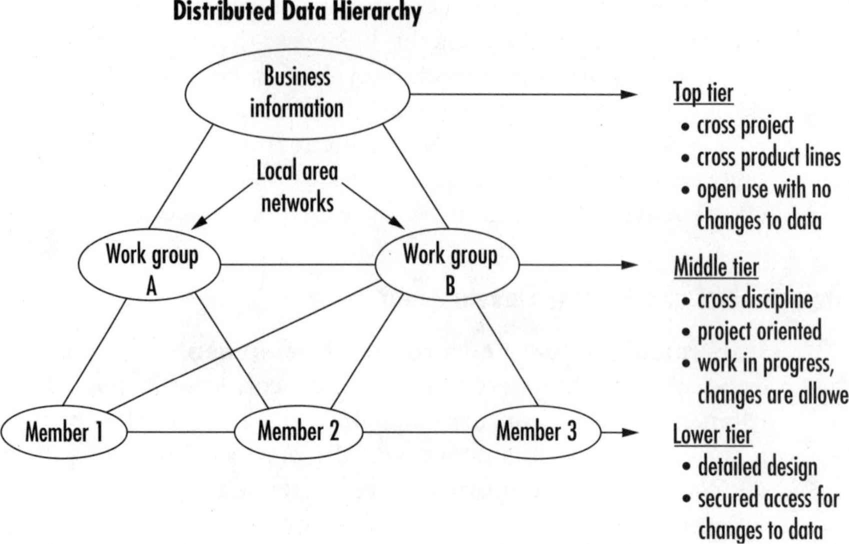

Figure 1.6 When a product is undergoing change, the information associated with the change can be accessed by the groups or individual users making the changes. Distributed data protects against unauthorized changes during the development cycle and, at the same time, maintains existing product information for the entire organization to use.

business level for all authorized users to access while it is undergoing design at lower tiers. Figure 1.6 shows the architecture. When product information needs to be changed, for example, after redesigning a fuel tank for an aircraft or a door on a refrigerator, the responsible engineering group extracts a copy of the item from the top tier of the hierarchy (business information) and takes it to the next lower tier (work group) to perform the changes. From the project, or work group, level, individual group members can work on their portions of the design. While the wing or door is being redesigned at the work group and member tiers, the remainder of the organization can still use the current information at the top of the tier. Product information may also reside permanently at the work group tier.

When individual engineers complete their work, the redesign is sent back up the tiers for the remaining organization to use, but not to change. With these tiers, the design remains intact for the rest of the organization to use while engineers are working on a design change.

Many times, computers are linked to a server in a **local area network (LAN)**, which makes up the middle tier in the PDM hierarchy. A LAN is a data network that allows a group of computers and their users to communicate and share programs, data, and equipment. A **server** is a computer in the LAN that shares resources, such as item definition data, with others in the LAN.

Design for Manufacture

Design for manufacture is a growing theme in industry. The goal in engineering is to design or change a product in such a way that it is ready for production when it hits the manufacturing floor. Designs that do not achieve this goal often result in higher manufacturing costs, and delay the introduction of the new product. While designing for manufacture may require more time during the initial design phase, the lost time--and more--is typically made up when the product enters the manufacturing stage. In addition to saving time, engineers are interested in reducing the number of parts used in an item. Thanks to improvements in PDM software, engineers have the capability to look at the structure of parts as they relate to each other. In many cases, a redesign will reduce the number of items in a product.

A product that has been designed for manufacture can begin realizing benefits of the design even before it leaves the development area. A good design reduces analysis and testing time. Like passing a design back and forth with manufacturing, designs are passed back and forth between design and test engineers. At this early stage of product development, it's less expensive to make changes.

Modeling

Modeling is the technique used to graphically display an item, enabling engineers to work with its dimensions, sizes, and components. A model is an abstract representation of an item that gives engineers the opportunity to see how the item is put together without reviewing drawings. Most modeling is still performed using two-dimensional views, but three-dimensional modeling is growing in popularity and certain to become the standard. Seeing the actual layout helps engineers to better understand all dimensions of the product and assembly and to more easily work with the components that go into it. However, it requires time and resources to convert three-dimensional models to two-dimensional drawings that will be used in manufacturing. Rather than reengineering the entire business to work with three-dimensional drawings, however, most businesses still choose to invest the time and expense to convert three-dimensional models to two-dimensional drawings.

Rapid prototyping is an offshoot of modeling. Engineers spend a significant amount of time prototyping product designs. With rapid prototyping, engineers can more quickly build models, which helps reduce product cycle times. A rapid prototyping tool takes a three-dimensional CAD drawing and analyzes it a slice at a time. From this drawing analysis, a tool reproduces each slice of the image and physically builds the part in a matter of hours. This bypasses the traditional method of manually producing clay or plastic models, which often take weeks to complete.

Manufacturers are also using rapid prototyping to create molds of parts in a matter of hours rather than weeks. They then use these molds to manufacture plastic or metal parts. Rapid prototyping is a particularly good solution for make-to-order businesses, where there may be only a one-time need for a part. Rapid prototyping is a practice that is gaining momentum, saving millions of dollars in design work and reducing the time required to get a change into production.

Future Directions in Engineering

There are many outside factors that, while not directly related to engineering, are driving the direction of businesses, which, in turn, drive the direction of engineering. We will examine the following examples of such factors:

- Industry standards
- International implications
- Competition
- Advances in technology

Industry Standards

What lies ahead for development and manufacturing engineers? Rest assured that the exchange of information within and between PDM systems is going to drive the future of releasing and changing products. How information and processes are managed will set the pace for development.

For more than a decade, U.S. groups tried to standardize how product data is exchanged between computer systems and environments. Then a worldwide group called **STandard for the Exchange of Product data (STEP)** teamed up in an effort to share information. Their goal is to establish a universal language for sharing information between businesses. They want to develop architectures that reuse, regroup, and modify existing product data management programs. The U.S. group that is working on implementing STEP is **Product Data Exchange using STEP (PDES)**.

For STEP and PDES to be truly successful, industries must be willing to share detailed information about technologies they have created. This means that after industries have put millions of dollars into the development of a particular technology, they will share the basics of the technology with the rest of the world. Some industries are not willing to do this and, for this reason, STEP and PDES have some obstacles to overcome before universal information sharing is a reality.

Along with information standards, the drawing engineers also have a standard. **Initial Graphics Exchange Specification (IGES)** deals with computer-aided design systems. The objective of IGES is to take a geometric layout and convert it into a standard form so that multiple CAD tools can use the same output. Being able to do this is a benefit. Information in a drawing can be lost in converting it to another system. Using IGES standards, models can be produced in standard form so that groups, other engineering areas, or suppliers can take the initial drawing and convert it to the system they use to reproduce the drawing.

Another standards classification is the **International Standards Organization (ISO)**. This is an international set of standards for establishing and maintaining a quality management system. The **ISO 9000** series is a standard that businesses are not only trying to attain, but will be looking for in their suppliers as well. The series is a quality management and tracking system for product development. In many cases, it's a condition for doing business. If a company is not ISO 9000 certified, customers may go elsewhere to purchase goods.

ISO 9000 compliance means businesses can define, document, and repeatedly activate business processes to produce a product that conforms to specified requirements. It ensures consistency in performance, which indicates a supplier is credible and reliable. ISO 9000 credentials are good for a business when it wants to gain customer acceptance and confidence.

International Implications

Today's marketplace certainly extends beyond any set of national borders. Except for trade regulations, which are becoming more and more forgiving over time, it's becoming as easy to trade between countries as it is between cities. The global marketplace is upon us. Not only do we trade between countries, we develop and manufacture around the world. Design engineers in Detroit are working on designs that will be manufactured in Mexico. An aircraft manufacturer may use five subcontractors in five countries to design and manufacture an engine.

What is driving this global economy? The emphasis is on cost and quality. First comes the cost factor. A business may be able to build some products at half the cost in another country. Now add to that the quality factor. When U.S. manufacturers first started looking overseas, they found a labor base that lacked skills needed to perform the job and thus required significant training. Today that's not the case. Countries that manufacture for a low cost have developed a skilled work force that brings quality to the product.

Many businesses involved in worldwide manufacturing are finding that when a deal is struck with a foreign country, an **offset program** plays a role in getting the contract. Here is how an offset program works: When a country buys a technology from the United States, it often asks that some of the manufacturing take place in the purchasing country. For example, if South Korea agrees to buy a technically advanced product from a firm in the United States, they may request that a portion of the product be built in their own country. This gives them a chance to generate money in their own economy and, at the same time, provide a cost-effective product for the manufacturer. Everyone benefits.

Along with economic factors, technology gains for the purchasing countries are valuable. The transfer of technology helps a country not only make a better product but also use the new technology in other industries. This sharing of information is widespread, taking place in Europe, Southeast Asia, and Latin America. The former Soviet Union is also a prime target of joint design and manufacturing projects. Sponsoring companies handle joint development and manufacturing by assigning staff members to the manufacturing site in the purchasing country.

Jumping cultural barriers is another international challenge engineers face. Engineering practices are requiring more interaction, not only between countries and design laboratories but between cultures that speak different languages, have different forms of government, and have different social values. The engineering profession is being dispersed throughout the world and its different cultures. When businesses relocate engineers and their families to a different culture to carry out projects, they must consider the cultural impact on the engineer and the family and help them to cope with it to make the venture successful. Furthermore, to succeed, products must be designed for use across cultural and language barriers. Software programs translated into the languages of the people who are going to use them can facilitate the international development of a product. Software with built-in translation features provides the flexibility to communicate across language barriers and gives businesses a head start in dealing in the international arena.

What It Will Take to Compete

As we head into the twenty-first century, manufacturers must seriously consider three major factors to survive:

- Automation in design and manufacturing
- Product data management across systems
- Flexibility in the engineering force

These are the three components that are going to make a manufacturer more successful. Before we begin our discussion of these factors, let's consider one other point: No matter how a business automates, people are the key to making it work. The spirit and dedication of the workforce can help drive the success of the company. People are the foundation for making the success factors come to life. Without their enthusiasm for their jobs, their support of new technologies and processes, and their dedication to do the best they can, progress in improving a business can certainly be curtailed. Whether it is the design engineer, parts assembler, or a manager, people play a vital role in the success of a business.

Automation in Design and Manufacturing

Today, automation is driving the biggest changes in the design and manufacturing processes, and it will continue to do so at an increasing rate in the future. This is because the design cycle is being significantly reduced by advances in these automation tools. Complex parts lists, advanced wiring schemes, and model production are being automated to enable engineers to perform certain design tasks at a quicker pace. Engineers are using **knowledge-based design** software that allows them to enter requirements and receive an automated design that suggests such features as fastener spacing, joint design, preferred parts, and recommended tolerances. An engineer can take this design and refine it to meet product requirements. What once took a design engineer three days to do can now be done in three minutes.

Three-dimensional design is definitely gaining importance as a tool for engineering. While some companies have had success with complete three-dimensional design, it is still a theory with most businesses. Businesses have a problem converting standard engineering organizations to three-dimensional design organizations. Unless all groups are using the same level of data, there's going to be a problem converting one form of data to another. When one group uses three-dimensional techniques and another group is still using two-dimensional programs, the integration from one level to the other is time consuming and costly. Businesses will have to evolve into the three-dimensional environment.

Product Data Management across Systems

Product data management systems are needed to organize, access, and control data about products throughout their life cycle, from development through modification and, finally, retirement of the product. PDM systems are becoming more important because product data is becoming more complex and changing more quickly. Businesses are turning to PDM systems to help control costs associated with managing product data. A system to manage product data can include a variety of software and hardware products, but the secret is to make the use of these different PDM products easy and seamless for the users. Today's growing use of various PDM products has made managing and sharing information between PDM products the number one priority with engineering groups. As businesses begin purchasing more and more PDM products, they will be increasingly looking for off-the-shelf PDM products that fit into their overall automation strategy. This will help them reduce maintenance and support costs for their automation projects and move them closer to their CIM goals.

One of the success stories for computerizing the design and manufacture of a product from beginning to end is the Saturn project in Tennessee. The plant was built from the ground up to include computer-aided design and computer integrated manufacturing technologies. Most of today's large manufacturers are not equipped to completely automate the manufacture of goods. The complexity of tying product data management programs together with automated manufacturing tools isn't complete. However, the Saturn plant was built to facilitate just such a venture.

Having access to accurate and up-to-date information is an important consideration for an engineer. In most businesses, the information exists, but is not easily accessible. When requirements or specifications change, engineers must have immediate access to the changes, even if the design engineer is in Detroit and the manufacturing engineer is in Mexico. When you have to move information from one application to another, it takes time and can result in lost information. Furthermore, if you have to recreate the information, it may not be accurate. How businesses manage product information is going to determine their ability to produce a product within cost, quality, and time constraints.

Flexibility in the Engineering Force

Finally, a flexible engineering group is an important success factor because they can adjust quickly to change, work more effectively together, and adapt to new technologies. This group must be strong, as pressures to meet business objectives will continue to grow. Tomorrow's engineers are also facing cultural changes in their profession. They will have to work smarter and more closely with each other and have a thorough understanding of the tools and the business around them. With the power of new technologies, an engineer will be responsible for the complete design of a product. It's going to require education, motivation, and determination to stay on the leading edge of technology. At one company we examined, a manager had to let an engineer go because he did not know how to use CAD tools. This engineer had drawn designs all his life, but he had not kept up with the influx of new technologies and methods. Technology finally caught up with him and he found his skills outdated in a changing engineering environment. His situation reflects the cultural change in the engineering world.

Engineers will have to be more in tune with the environment. That is, they will have to be more aware of how their design and manufacturing decisions will affect nature. Just like the engineers who must monitor the levels of chlorine in paper, so are tomorrow's engineers going to have to look at what they put in products and how it's going to fit into our environment. Developing with the environment in mind means considering the materials that go into a product, any effects those materials or their byproducts may have on the environment, and even how the product looks. Also included in the environmental aspects of engineering is the reuse of products. Recycling is not just a trend, but an upcoming way of life in product design. After a product has completed its life cycle, engineers must analyze ways the depleted product can be used in a new product. This analysis can lower the costs of production, save natural resources, and help protect the world's environment. This concept has been applied for years in plastic, metal, and paper products.

The pursuit of automation and product data management means that more of today's and tomorrow's engineers will be more accountable, and often solely responsible, for product design. At the same time, they will interact more with other engineering and manufacturing organizations. They must continue to break down the organizational walls that have historically impeded engineering progress.

Advances in Technology

Along with being a more flexible group, engineers can expect other initiatives from business that will drive down cost and time factors in making a product. The **intelligent manufacturing system** is a program and agenda first introduced by the Japanese in 1989. Billed as the next level of computer integrated manufacturing, it is supported by many major U.S. companies and the Department of Commerce. The goal here is a manufacturing system made up of a number of autonomous, intelligent modules that merely have to be connected and they will work together. There is a major initiative in the United States, Japan, and Europe to bring this billion-dollar concept to life.

Another technology, **Mechatronics,** is essentially the integration of sensors, actuators, computers, and control. The belief here is that electronics will be woven into all aspects of a business and will control and drive the business, with much less human interaction than in today's manufacturing environment.

Agile manufacturing technology leads to a type of manufacturing where businesses rapidly form alliances with suppliers and customers to quickly bring mass-produced, customized products to the market. One of the main focuses of the process is the ability to reconfigure machines and software quickly to meet changing needs of customers. It may provide a future in manufacturing where businesses, their competitors, and their suppliers are linked to the same system so they can quickly respond to customer needs. We'll discuss agile manufacturing further in Chapter 4.

CHAPTER 2

The ProductManager Solution for Engineers

This chapter introduces the applications and features of ProductManager, explains how they are used in the design and manufacturing engineering environments, and discusses how they can help a business manage product information. The discussion also includes information about the AIX- and UNIX-based computer systems, object-oriented technology, and the basic architecture of ProductManager.

What Is ProductManager?

ProductManager is a product data management system designed to manage information associated with a product or line of products. It is the management framework for combined repositories, work-flow managers, and drawing and document systems. It provides for the implementation of electronic, integrated processes for managing product development and manufacture. Using ProductManager, engineering changes are created, tracked, and controlled; item data and bills of material are created and maintained; and design information associated with the development or change of a new part, such as an item or bill of material, is packaged and distributed for review and approval. In addition, ProductManager is used to identify, locate, and manage product-associated documents such as spreadsheets, drawings, and publications.

ProductManager is made up of four application programs that work with each other to provide data management capability. Here's a brief description of each application:

- **Application Services Manager (ASM)** serves as an enabler that drives the system, interfaces with other programs, provides administrative services for users, and contains a comprehensive electronic folder capability. ASM can be used as a stand-alone product with its folder and **logical data reference object** capabilities. It also provides the building blocks necessary for developing your own custom application programs to meet specific needs.
- **Product Change Manager (PCM)** controls product information while it is being changed. PCM both identifies the processes for making changes and provides the functions to help manage those processes.
- **Product Structure Manager (PSM)** maintains information about all items and products, such as their design attributes and suppliers. PSM is also used to define bills of material and product structures for engineering and manufacturing organizations.
- **Document Control Manager (DCM)** serves as a **logical repository** for product documentation. A logical repository is a listing of product documents that shows where the documents reside, what the documents are, and how to get to them. If the documentation is in an online library or file, ProductManager may also be used for viewing or changing the document. The application provides functions that register, control, and store document information as if it were in an electronic vault.

Why IBM Created ProductManager/6000

As product information grows in volume and complexity, computer systems are increasingly necessary for controlling the massive flow of information between development and manufacturing organizations. Such a system is needed to remove the traditional barriers between engineering and manufacturing groups.

IBM first developed ProductManager for the mainframe environment to help solve product data management problems faced by large businesses. Despite any doubts about the future capabilities and usefulness of the mainframe, it is still a powerful and essential tool for controlling massive amounts of information. For example, ProductManager applications on the mainframe are currently used in the space shuttle program, in worldwide development of aircraft engines, in chemical processing, and in facilities and architectural change management. However, the mainframe is not an option for many small and medium-sized businesses. Although the products of such businesses may be fewer and less complex, product information is just as vital to their success. Their product data management needs are not very different from those of larger businesses. In fact, product data management in small and medium-sized businesses is one of the fastest-growing and competitive sectors in industry today. These businesses are realizing that a poorly planned data management process can contribute to failure in reaching business goals.

Computer size and environment are the main differences between small or medium-sized businesses and large businesses. The kind of information an aircraft manufacturer manages on a mainframe may be better stored and managed by the manufacturer of a stapler on a desktop computer. To provide an integrated product data management environment for small businesses, IBM moved ProductManager to the small and mid-range computer environment.

A team comprised of specialists from each ProductManager application area was assembled to develop a workstation version of the product for smaller but still powerful computers, called **workstations**. Building on ProductManager's object-oriented implementation significantly reduced the development time, and less than a year later, IBM introduced ProductManager/6000, its first UNIX version of ProductManager. In many cases, ProductManager, with its complete product data management process, can be used as it is shipped, without alteration. In other cases, it can be tailored to meet individual business needs. In summary, IBM introduced ProductManager/6000 to do the following:

- Support the expanding trend toward using smaller computers for product data management
- Reduce the cost of purchasing and implementing ProductManager
- Address customer need to downsize from the mainframe environment
- Meet customer requirements for a workstation product data management system
- Provide a comprehensive system for customers to build a PDM solution

ProductManager/6000 also provides worldwide development and manufacturing support through translation. In addition to American English, ProductManager/6000 is available in Canadian French, Chinese, Dutch, French, German, Italian, Japanese (Nihongo), and Spanish.

A Look at ProductManager

As yet, a sole computer program does not exist that can meet the needs of all areas of development and manufacturing. We find that some products perform certain tasks better than others or are easier than others to adapt to the existing products in a business. Product data management systems, including ProductManager, still depend on an assortment of tools and programs to communicate. The secret of product data management is to develop a complete solution, by which different groups can work in an environment using different tools while having a seamless interface between those tools.

In the next several sections, we will discuss how ProductManager can help engineering organizations manage product information more effectively. As we examine ProductManager, we will discuss the workstation version. Although PDM functions of both the mainframe and workstation versions are similar, and much of the discussion can be applied to both, we will concentrate on the workstation version, which runs in a different computer environment than that of a mainframe, and with a different user interface. First, let's look at some important aspects of ProductManager:

- Architecture
- Platforms and operating systems
- Database
- Object-oriented technology
- User interface

Architecture

The **architecture** is a high-level description of the model of a system. It describes how the parts of a system fit and work together. The architecture of a software product is not apparent to the user. It is woven into the functionality of the system. ProductManager's architecture is geared toward **code reuse** and maximum flexibility for the user. Code reuse, which enables a single piece of **code** to perform similar actions on different objects in the system, is discussed in the **object-oriented** technology section later in this chapter. Code is a system of characters and rules for representing information.

You cannot select a software product based only on today's needs; you must consider its ability to meet both present and future needs. The implementation of software products to manage product information is an evolving process. The software you select for your business must be capable of growing with your business and must be a part of your long-term business strategy. The purpose of the ProductManager system is to handle product information. Considerations involved in designing this kind of software include an analysis of the life cycle of the product data, including where the data is first entered into the system, everywhere it is to be used, and what happens when it is no longer needed. As you plan the data objects, platform, functionality, and repository support for your system, the product's architecture and its future effectiveness are important considerations.

A PDM system based on the architecture of ProductManager can be visualized as a pyramid. Figure 2.1 shows the architecture for the ProductManager system in the form of a pyramid as viewed from above. The bottom layer

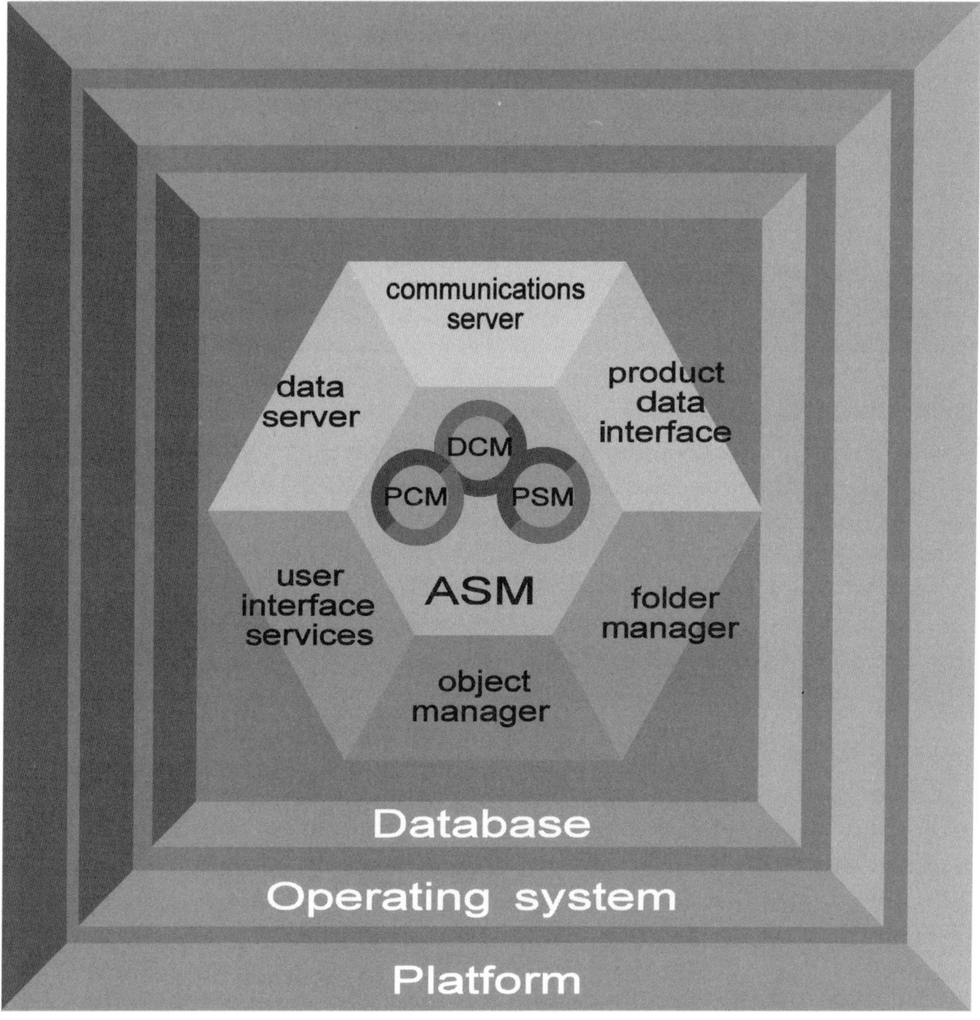

Figure 2.1 Looking down on a layered pyramid of the ProductManager architecture. The platform, operating system, and database make up the lower layers, while the ProductManager applications make up the top of the pyramid.

of the pyramid is the **platform**. The platform is the configuration of hardware that comprises a general purpose computer system. The next layer is the **operating system**. The operating system manages the hardware resources of the computer system and provides the environment in which the application programs execute the tasks requested by the user.

The next layer of the architecture is the **database**. The database houses and organizes the information maintained by the ProductManager applications. Resting on top of the database layer is ASM, the foundation of ProductManager. ASM is commonly referred to as the system **enabler,** but is actually a set of several enablers. Its role is to integrate ProductManager into a business's existing system environment. It also provides enablers that do logistic functions for ProductManager, such as exchanging and managing information. The six most important logistic enablers (shown as trapezoids in Figure 2.1) will be discussed later in this chapter.

The peak of the pyramid, resting on the ASM layer, is made up of the PCM, DCM, and PSM **applications**. Applications are computer programs that provide specific user functions, such as producing reports, creating engineering changes, changing item data, or controlling documentation.

Platforms and Operating Systems

ProductManager code runs on several computer systems, or platforms, based on the **Reduced Instruction Set Computing (RISC)** architecture. Platforms that implement a RISC architecture use a simple set of programming instructions to perform work. The simplicity of the instructions allows the machines to run at a high speed, providing an efficient platform for engineering and scientific applications such as computer-aided design, computer-aided engineering, computer-aided manufacturing, and product data management. The computers come in a variety of models ranging from desktop and deskside units to large, floor-standing racks.

Companies offering hardware for ProductManager platforms include IBM, Hewlett Packard, and Sun Microsystems. All these platforms provide similar capabilities. You must evaluate performance and cost to decide which can best meet the data management needs of your business. Figure 2.2 lists some ProductManager platforms, their operating systems, and their databases.

Any of the platforms listed can be obtained with the particular main memory size, disk storage, and **input/output adapters** needed for your business. Input/output adapters manage data transfers between such devices as disks and communications programs. Most models also offer upgrade opportunities. Chapter 3 of this book offers some pointers for evaluating which platform might best meet your particular business needs. Figure 2.3 shows a desktop

ProductManager Hardware and Software Options

Operating System	Platform	Database
HP-UX UNIX	Hewlett Packard HP Apollo Series 700 HP Apollo Series 800	Oracle
Sun Solaris 1.X UNIX	Sun Microsystems SPARCserver 10 SPARCstation 10	INGRES
Sun Solaris 2.X UNIX	Sun Microsystems SPARCserver 10 SPARCstation 10 SPARCserver 1000 SPARCcenter 2000 SPARCcluster 1	Oracle
AIX	IBM RISC System/6000	DB2/6000 Oracle

Figure 2.2 ProductManager is compatible with a variety of hardware. The figure shows some of the different platforms, operating systems, and databases on which ProductManager can run.

Model 370 of a RISC System/6000, while Figure 2.4 shows a Sun Microsystems SPARCstation 20. Both pieces of hardware run ProductManager.

All of these ProductManager platforms are **multiuser** computer systems; that is, their hardware and software share a single computer system among many users at the same time. For higher performance, you can install many computer systems, all running ProductManager. All terminals provide windows into the computer system or systems and allow users to perform tasks independently of one another. As many businesses are discovering, this is a step in the right direction for managing product information. All engineers on the systems share a single, up-to-date copy of product information that may have changed a few minutes earlier. The systems can span a building or the world.

Another option for working in a multiuser environment is an **Xstation**. Xstations are pieces of generic hardware available from a variety of suppliers. They provide a low-cost means of working with graphics. Rather than providing each user with a more expensive, fully capable computer system attached to a LAN, Xstations can be substituted. An Xstation is a cross between an

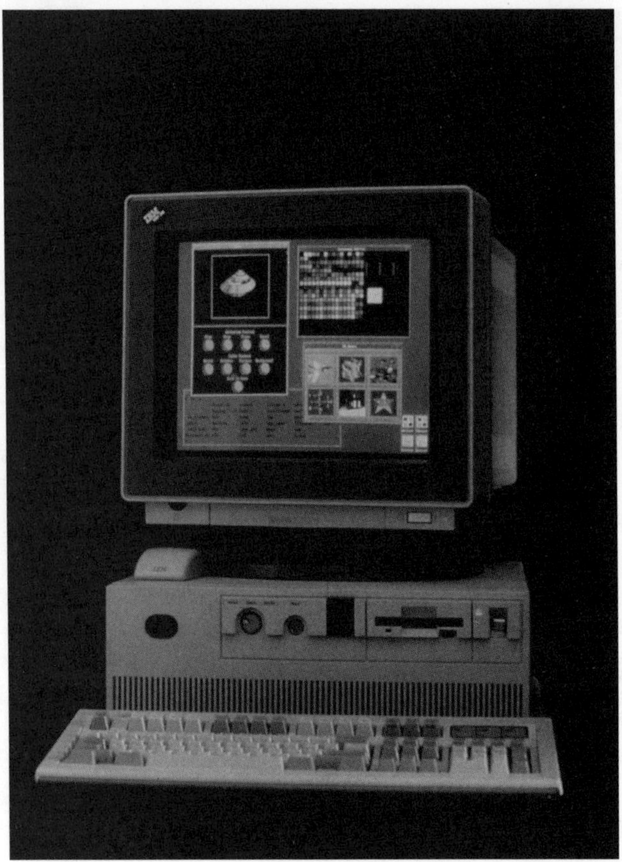

Figure 2.3 The RISC System/6000 desktop Model 370 runs ProductManager.

intelligent and a dumb terminal. An intelligent terminal includes a keyboard from which users can send information to the system and a display screen on which they can see the information sent to or received from the computer. You cannot run ProductManager on an Xstation, but you can display and work with ProductManager information on an Xstation attached to a computer running ProductManager. Any properly equipped computer can be used with the platforms and operating systems. Intelligent terminals and PCs have computing and graphical user interface power of their own, while nonprogrammable (dumb) terminals do not. Using a PC as an intelligent terminal, an engineer can pull a specification from a mainframe server through the operating system to the PC, where it can be edited using a preferred editor.

Along with multiusers, the systems support **multitasking**. This is the ability of a single user to run two or more independent application programs

Figure 2.4 The Sun Microsystems SPARCstation 20 is another platform on which ProductManager can reside.

simultaneously. Multitasking allows users to switch back and forth between active programs. This is called a **windowing** environment. Most open systems use the **X Window System**, developed by the Massachusetts Institute of Technology. Using this standard protocol, users can manipulate information across applications and systems. For example, by switching between the windows on a display terminal, an engineer could be writing or reviewing specifications while at the same time working with a drawing. Figure 2.5 shows a display screen with several applications running.

In addition to its compatibility with different platforms, ProductManager can run on any of three operating systems in the workstation environment. All these operating systems are modeled after AT&T's Bell Labs **UNIX** operating system. The first is the **Advanced Interactive eXecutive (AIX)** operating system from IBM. The second, from Hewlett Packard, is **UX,** and the third is **Sun Solaris** from Sun Microsystems. All three systems are **open systems,** meaning that they conform to industry standards defined by independent groups rather than to the standards of any single company. These standards regulate aspects of how the system works, such as its programming interfaces or communication protocols. A protocol is like a programming language in that it is an information package containing data that can be transmitted between systems. In other words, the AIX and UNIX operating systems can

Figure 2.5 Multitasking enables users to go from one computer program to another on the same display screen. This figure shows several programs that a user could be working with.

interact with a variety of products and software programs. They can be used in a mainframe environment or they can stand alone. Using emulation programs, you can extend systems to work with larger systems such as the **IBM System/390.**

A typical setup for a ProductManager installation can include one or more local area networks. A LAN allows a group of computers and their users to share information and to communicate efficiently and quickly. For example, a design engineering department or organization could be connected to one LAN, while another group across town is on a different LAN. By linking the LANs together with available communications equipment, both the groups can have access to the same data. Each computer that is part of a LAN is called a **node** in the network. Any properly equipped computer can act as either a **client** or a server node. In the client/server scheme, the clients in a network use information, whereas servers provide it. If an installation of ProductManager and its database reside on a RISC System/6000, for example, that system is a server. But if ProductManager is installed on another computer, then the RISC System/6000 becomes a client by accessing ProductManager on the server. Figure 2.6 shows the RISC System/6000 being used as a server in a LAN environment. The server provides the database (DB2/6000), as described in the next section, as well as the applications and the table support for the LAN. Figure 2.7 shows the ProductManager applications being stored on one server with the database and ProductManager tables stored on another. Both servers share information with each other and provide information to clients hooked directly to the system or to the LAN.

ProductManager supports both **Ethernet** and **Token-Ring** LANs. Ethernet is the most popular LAN protocol used in open-system environments. Ethernet can run on a variety of cabling schemes shared by host systems. The Token-Ring Network is a popular IBM-designed LAN.

Database

ProductManager uses the services of a separate database management system to store product information. With the RISC System/6000, ProductManager can use the IBM Database 2 AIX/6000 (DB2/6000) or Oracle as its database system. This **Distributed Relational Database Architecture (DRDA)** provides support across the distributed data development structure discussed in the Product Data Management section of Chapter 1. With Sun Microsystems computers that run the Solaris 1.X operating system, ProductManager uses an INGRES database. For those that run Solaris 2.X, and with Hewlett Packard computers, ProductManager uses the Oracle database.

All these databases are **relational databases.** A relational database stores product information in **tables** with rows and columns, where each row is a record and each column contains pieces of information, or fields, for each record, as shown in Figure 2.8. The term "relational" pertains to the relationship between the columns of different tables. For example, if an engineer wants to work with an EC review folder that was created by Mary Allen on January 20, 1994, the engineer can type in criteria for the search. Using a

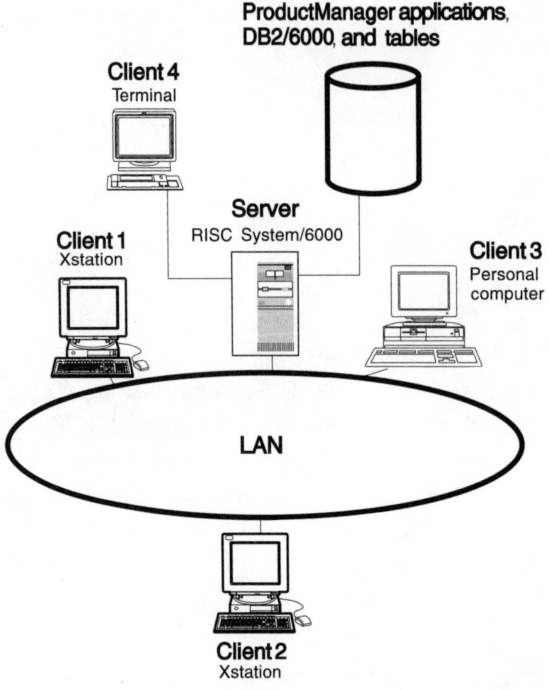

Figure 2.6 The RISC System/6000 used as a server. Like the Hewlett Packard and Sun Microsystems machines, it's a single piece of hardware capable of providing complete product data management services.

search of tables, the relational database lists the folders created on that day by that person. Figure 2.8 shows how the relationship is built between tables. Based on the object ID for the person who created the folder, the person and folder database tables are searched for matches. Each user in the database has an ID in the person table that corresponds to the originator field in the folder table. In this case, the object ID for M. Allen is matched with the folder originator in the folder table, and the folder is flagged as meeting the **search criteria**.

Relational databases use **Structured Query Language (SQL)** to access information stored in the tables. SQL minimizes duplication of information by using "where clauses" that specify the exact pieces of information to be included in a data search. In ProductManager, each **persistent class** such as a user or a request for engineering action (REA) is represented by a table. A table cannot be searched, but instead is matched to another by defined criteria

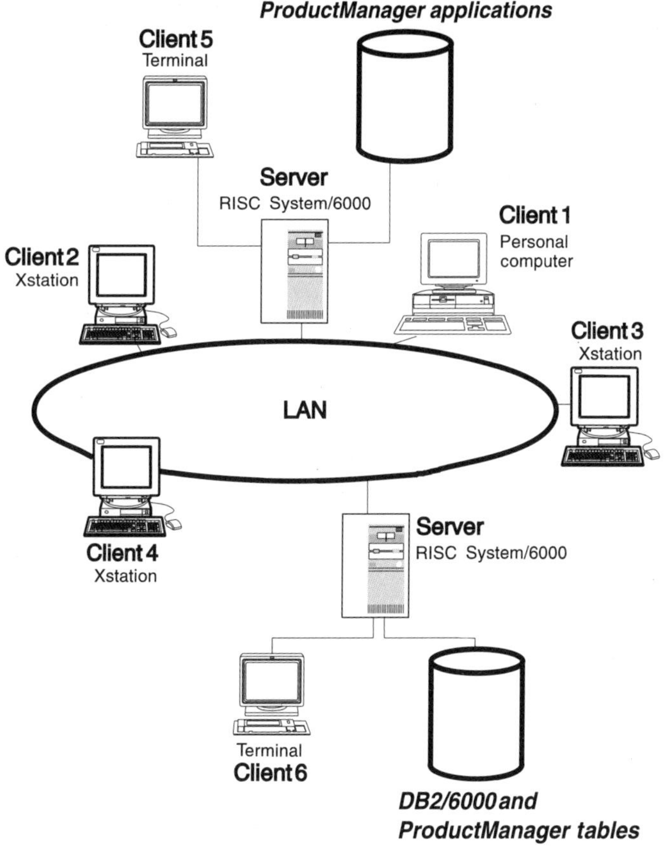

Figure 2.7 Two RISC System/6000 machines used as servers. The ProductManager applications reside on one machine, while DB2/6000 and ProductManager tables reside on another server on the LAN. Additional machines enhance the performance of the system.

that relate the two. Then, as represented in Figure 2.8, a complete object definition can be made. In addition to accessing data, SQL can be used to insert and update information in the tables and provide authorizations to the data.

The Oracle, INGRES, and DB2/6000 databases also have the capability of communicating with **remote databases**. A remote database is another installation of ProductManager with a database that runs on another software system or another operating system. Each database has its own way to access remote data. The DRDA is used to interact with any DRDA database using SQL

Person Table

	Object ID	Name	Person #	User ID	Network	Node
Records	**PER222**	M. Allen	433556	AJ340	L230	10
	PER375	R. Jones	699349	AJ520	L230	10
	PER942	N. Lutz	249839	AJ344	L230	10
	PER465	J. Olson	298484	AJ699	L230	10
	PER132	J. Smith	489384	AJ423	L230	10

Folder Table

	Object ID	Folder ID	Description	Originator	Status	Date
Records	FF5466	AJRE02	Review	PER822	Complete	12/28/93
	FF8603	AJRE10	Review	PER465	Defined	02/15/94
	FF1285	AJRE17	Review	**PER222**	Defined	01/20/94
	FF3433	AJRE62	Review	PER673	In-Review	03/05/93
	FF5987	AJRE77	Review	PER132	Complete	04/04/94

Figure 2.8 Relational databases use tables to create a relationship between two objects. The highlighted fields show the objects that are related when the system looks for the person who created a folder.

across different operating systems, including MVS. If one database "knows" the other exists, they can communicate with each other.

A variety of administrative tools can be added to the databases to control user access, maintain system statistics, back up and recover data, and log events such as changes to data.

Object-Oriented Technology

ProductManager is an object-oriented product. "Object oriented" does not mean that it is a programming language. It is a concept around which programming languages and programs are designed. Object-oriented programming builds **objects** within the computer system, making it easier for people to separate different items and functions. Objects are usually discrete, well-defined entities, such as bolts, folders, or system users. We think of objects in terms of what can be done with them. The characteristics of an object determine the actions users can choose to perform on that object. For example, a car is an object. Actions you can perform with the car include starting, driving, stopping, and parking it. If you produce it, there are even more actions you can perform. You can design, build, ship, and sell it. The same can be applied

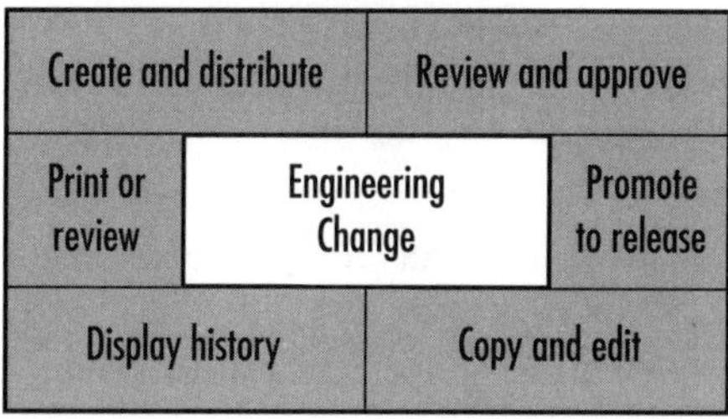

Figure 2.9 An engineering change object is surrounded by the actions that can be performed on the change. The engineering change can, for example, be created, copied, or reviewed.

to an engineering change. You can create, route, approve, and implement it, as shown in Figure 2.9.

Object-oriented technology has several distinct advantages for businesses. First, the technology can be used to more accurately reflect business requirements and processes because the software is designed to work as we think. Business requirements can be mapped more easily using objects in place of traditional and more abstract data structures. Second, object-oriented programming lends itself to change. When business requirements or processes change, object-oriented programs can be more quickly adjusted to meet those changes. Finally, objects and the information associated with them are more readily available for programming use in an object-oriented environment than in other, more traditional environments. That is, information is easier to access, use, and understand, making it more suitable for cross-business application.

A big advantage of object-oriented technology is the reuse capability of its programs. Reusing is simply using the same code to perform similar actions on a variety of objects. The code that makes ProductManager's folder feature work also drives the requests for engineering action and engineering change reviews. It is the **inheritance** nature of the code that permits reuse. Inheritance is an object-oriented property in which a child class has all the data attributes and methods of its parents. Inheritance provides a means of creating specific classes from generic ones.

Let's take a closer look at how object-oriented design works. Object-oriented design uses **data abstraction** to extend the use of software. Abstraction separates out the common parts shared by different objects. For example, all manufacturing items have identifying numbers, suppliers, and bills of materials. These are abstracts, and they are central to object-oriented design. They allow engineers to manipulate the parts rather than manipulating the programming language to work with the parts. Object-oriented technology manages the complexity of information by using **classes** of objects that contain similar data elements. For example, all items in a given class of objects share a particular set of **attributes** such as size, length, and weight. The attribute values will differ for each item, but the set of attributes is always the same. A specific object existing within a given class is called an **instance** of that class.

A class also has a set of **methods** that are used to manipulate the objects, or instances, of that class. For example, a specific folder is an instance of the folder class. Methods in the folder class might be used to create, change, or copy a folder. Methods are carried out by the sending of **messages**.

Figure 2.10 shows a bearing with the attributes of weight, yield, length, type, and status. The attributes are stored with the object but are not seen by the user unless they are requested. In object-oriented programming, these attributes are **encapsulated** so that only the attribute against which an action is performed is affected. To change the weight of the bearing in Figure 2.10, the user would send a message from the change method to open the encapsulated weight attribute.

Object-oriented programming is not a new concept, but its technology is still relatively young. It was introduced by the Norwegian Computing Center in the late 1960s as the **Simula programming language**. While the tools and programmers that work with the technology are not as common as those in other established technologies, their numbers are growing.

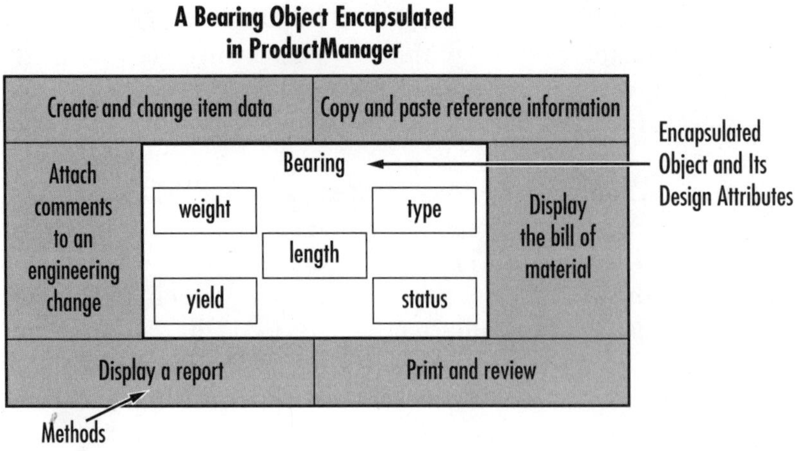

A Bearing Object Encapsulated in ProductManager

Create and change item data
Copy and paste reference information
Attach comments to an engineering change
Bearing
weight
type
length
yield
status
Display the bill of material
Display a report
Print and review
Encapsulated Object and Its Design Attributes
Methods

Figure 2.10 An encapsulated bearing with its attributes waits for a method to send a message that initiates an action to be taken. An engineer can select to change only the status attribute of the bearing.

The programs' capability for reuse makes object-oriented technology attractive. Although establishing an initial **class hierarchy** is difficult, and making changes to the structure is time consuming and expensive, once the basic hierarchy is defined, changes are made much more easily than with more structured programs. A hierarchy is the relationship between objects or groups of objects that implies a ranking. It involves a complete understanding of all the components of a business and how they relate to one another.

Users can get ProductManager with a ready-to-use default hierarchy in place that is geared toward the manufacturing industry. This saves time and money in tailoring the product. This hierarchy of objects reflects the requirements of typical users, but if changes are needed, ProductManager code can be tailored to meet different development and manufacturing needs.

User Interface

The user interface is the part of a program that users see on the computer's display. Users work with the user interface to perform tasks. The workstation version of ProductManager provides a **graphical user interface (GUI)** that enhances productivity for users of the product. A GUI uses pictures that are called **icons**. Icons and words that identify them appear on **panels** to assist users in making quick selections. A panel is the complete set of information that appears on a computer screen. The GUI allows for direct manipulation of screens. Figure 2.11 shows how icons for nine sample functions would look on the ProductManager Menu. The GUI created for ProductManager conforms to the guidelines established by **Open Software Foundation/Motif (OSF/MOTIF)**.

The Open Software Foundation is a group of companies dedicated to consistency in styles and principles of user interfaces. Their guidelines are intended to make movement between systems easier and to facilitate multisystem use with enhanced consistency and connectivity. Users are able to navigate through and manipulate panels using a mouse to select the objects they want to work with from menus.

The ProductManager interface works with X Windows, an environment that can provide windows into applications and processes that may not reside on an individual user's console or computer system. Windows are portions of a computer screen that permit a dialog between a user and a specific application. X Windows makes it possible to perform multitasking functions. Using ProductManager, an engineer could be reviewing design specifications in one window and working with item data in another.

ProductManager's user interface is task oriented and works the same way throughout the product. The available objects and the actions that the user can perform on them appear on the display at the top of the panel. The interface

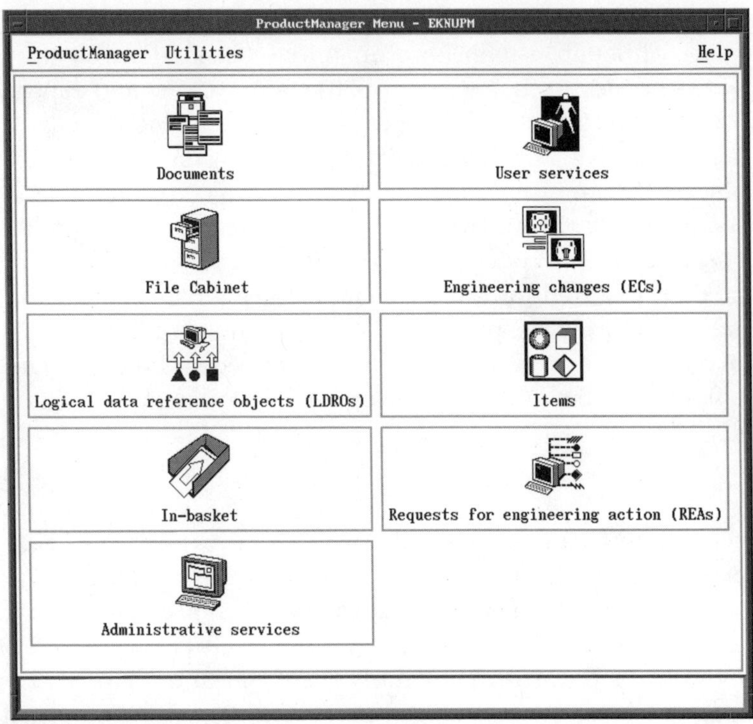

Figure 2.11 An example of the ProductManager Menu with an icon for each available application.

provides icons for each task that can performed from that screen. It also contains a fast-path menu that you can pull up from anywhere in the program, saving navigation time. Users can select a variety of objects from the ProductManager Menu, including engineering changes, items, and folders (File Cabinet). The panel flows are the same for each object, making the system easy to learn and use. Using the drag function of a mouse, users can **cascade** icons to make a selection that lies several layers below the ProductManager Menu. For example, Figure 2.12 shows the path a system administrator could take to change information about a security group. By selecting Administrative services from the ProductManager Menu and holding the mouse button down, the administrator can drag the cursor directly to the Groups folder instead of clicking on three separate icons.

When an engineer wants to create or work with a request for engineering action (REA), the icon for REAs can be selected from the ProductManager Menu. After the engineer has made this selection, a selection criteria panel appears that is used to define search criteria. Search criteria limit the amount of information that is displayed to that which is of interest to the engineer. By

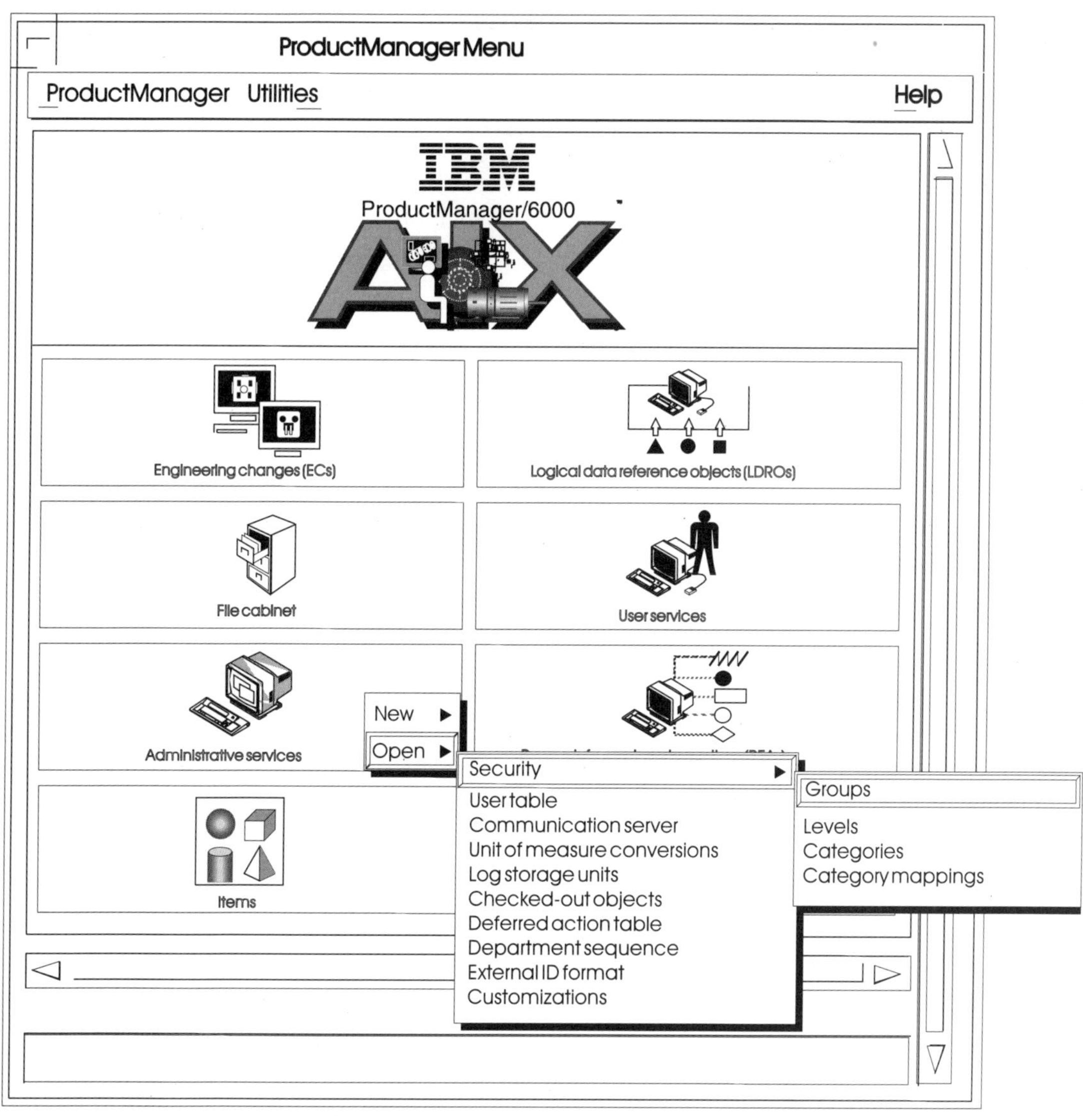

Figure 2.12 A cascading panel in the ProductManager Menu.

defining search criteria such as dates, originators, or statuses, engineers can eliminate the need to search through REAs that are of no interest to them at a particular time. For example, engineers can review REAs they created during the past three months by specifying the dates and their user IDs as the search criteria. The ability to define criteria for a search reduces the need to develop custom reports and streamlines the capability of an online design review.

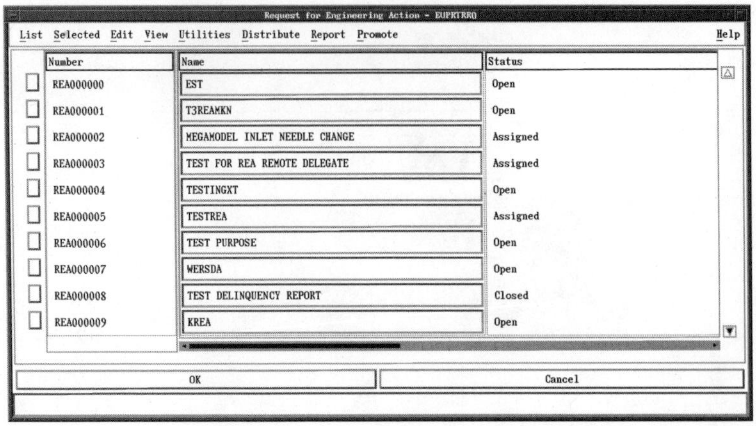

Request for Engineering Action - EUPRTRRQ

List Selected Edit View Utilities Distribute Report Promote Help

Number	Name	Status
REA000000	EST	Open
REA000001	T3REAMKN	Open
REA000002	MEGAMODEL INLET NEEDLE CHANGE	Assigned
REA000003	TEST FOR REA REMOTE DELEGATE	Assigned
REA000004	TESTINGXT	Open
REA000005	TESTREA	Assigned
REA000006	TEST PURPOSE	Open
REA000007	WERSDA	Open
REA000008	TEST DELINQUENCY REPORT	Closed
REA000009	KREA	Open

OK Cancel

Figure 2.13 A Request for Engineering Change list panel is used to work with an REA or access an REA's object detail panel. Changes can be made on on this panel or a specific REA can be selected for more detailed work.

The next panel in the flow is a list panel. Figure 2.13 shows how an REA list panel might look. It contains a list of REAs that meet the defined search criteria. An engineer can either select an REA to work with or make changes to it from the list panel by tabbing to the fields to be changed. After an REA is selected, an object detail panel appears. This panel contains information about the REA and a list of subobjects the engineer can work with. Engineers can work with some of the fields on this panel by typing over the existing information.

ProductManager provides **online help** for all panels and entry fields. Online help is information made available by pressing a key or clicking a mouse. The advantage of online help is that users can access it immediately. Instead of searching through a book to find an explanation of a term that appears on a panel, users can ask for help while the cursor is positioned on the term. Additional information can be accessed by selecting extended help for the field. ProductManager online help provides general information about the panel; it does not provide in-depth discussions of terms and concepts. For more detailed information, the ProductManager reference library is also available through **AIX BookManager Read/6000**, which gives users online access to documents associated with the product. The UNIX operating system version of ProductManager does not have an online reference library, but it does have online help.

ProductManager also provides online messages for error conditions or warnings. The severity of the message is color coded. There is also help for these messages, which provides suggestions for correcting the error condition.

A Closer Look at Each ProductManager Application

Four applications make up the ProductManager program. Application Services Manager (ASM) serves as the base application, supporting the other applications. Product Change Manager (PCM) and Product Structure Manager (PSM) are the engineering application **towers** that work together to manage product data. Towers are applications that rest on the base application. The final tower, Document Control Manager (DCM), is used to manage and control documentation associated with products.

Each application contains unique components that are required for complete control of product information. ASM contains distribution lists used by PCM for reviews, and PSM contains information about items used by PCM for engineering changes. DCM manages the documentation associated with an ASM folder. Only the ASM application can stand alone as an application. The other applications require ASM to run. Figure 2.14 shows how the towers and base application are organized to form the ProductManager system.

Now let's look more closely at each of these ProductManager applications.

Application Services Manager

The base application for ProductManager, Application Services Manager, contains the components that drive ProductManager. ASM controls how the ProductManager applications interact with one another and with other

ProductManager Application Overview

Product Change Manager	Product Structure Manager	Document Control Manager
• Requests for engineering action	• Product data	• Tool management
• Engineering changes	• Bills of material	• Central repository
• Process control	• Views	• Version control
• Deliverables	• Effectivity	• Document check-in and checkout
	• Initial data load	

Application Services Manager

• Folder management	• Personalization	• Object management
• Administrative services	• Distributed resources	• User interface
• Product data interface	• Application model	• Data communications

Operating System

Figure 2.14 The ProductManager applications and their functions. Application Services Manager is the base application. The remaining applications are considered tower applications.

programs. The enablers for the performance of the other applications reside in the ASM application. When you send an REA to a review team, for example, the folder management functions of ASM are what enable the folder to be packaged and electronically distributed.

ASM is a stand-alone application. That is, it can be used by itself as well as in conjunction with other applications. The application has three general uses. As an enabler, ASM provides a set of tools that perform tasks for the other ProductManager applications. ASM drives such functions as communication services, data management facility, user interface, and presentation services for all the ProductManager applications.

ASM also provides administrative functions such as units-of-measure conversion and network configurations. Security controls; information about system users; and number generation algorithms for automatically numbering items, REAs, and ECs reside in ASM.

Finally, ASM provides end-user functions such as the In-basket and electronic folder features. Figure 2.15 shows the breakdown of the enabling, administrative, and user-functional aspects of ASM. These groups interact with the other applications to perform all system tasks.

First we'll discuss the enabling aspects of ASM as they relate to the system. Then we'll discuss the administrative and end-user functions of the application. The functional aspects of the system are the menu options available to users for performing tasks in ProductManager.

Primary function: ASM serves as the base application and provides enabler services that control how the product interfaces between applications and other products. ASM also provides a variety of administrative functions for system users.

Enabler Functions	Administrative Functions	End-User Functions
• Product data interface	• Security controls	• User services
• Communications server	• User table	• In-basket services
• User interface server	• Deferred-action table	• Folders
• Object manager	• Communications server	• Distributed resource management
• Data server	• Unit-of-measure conversion	
	• Log storage units	
	• Checked-out objects	
	• Automatic numbering	
	• Customization features	

Figure 2.15 An overview of Application Services Manager (ASM) functions, broken down into three general categories.

Enabler Functions Supported by ASM

Product Data Interface Communicating across systems and products is one of the greatest challenges facing small and large businesses today. It is difficult for a single data management product to meet the expectations for data management unless it can be linked to other products and tools the business may use. For this reason, ProductManager has built-in methods for exchanging information with other systems. There are also various tools to enhance these methods. The **product data interface (PDI)** component of ASM provides the means for moving information between ProductManager applications and for exchanging information with other ProductManager systems. PDI also provides a way to exchange information with other computer integrated manufacturing programs and **legacy systems** (older programs still in use). PDI provides for the **import** and **export** of data from and to other systems, respectively. The ProductManager PDI format is aligned with PDES/STEP standards.

A **product data interface format (PDIF)** file is the standard form of data exchange between ProductManager and other systems. A PDIF file contains ProductManager objects such as folders; bills of material; reviews; engineering changes; requests for engineering action; and referencing objects, which reference drawings and documents outside of ProductManager's database.

Communications Server ASM's **communications server** is a collection of objects that provide the services for transferring information in PDIF between the ProductManager system and other systems. The communications server works with the product data interface to send and receive information. These systems can be other ProductManager systems, other CIM programs, or legacy systems.

The **asynchronous communications monitor (ACM)** resides in the communications server. This monitor is a continually running, event-driven background process that handles ProductManager processing requests sent from other systems. When a PDIF file, for example, is received by the system, the ACM processes the incoming file for use by ProductManager users.

User Interface Server The **user interface server (UIS)** in ASM manages the interactions between ProductManager applications and individual users at terminals and workstations. The server is used to manage panels and provide support for the translation of various types of data entered through panels and stored in the database.

ProductManager uses the X Windows System commonly found in the UNIX environment to provide a **point-and-click** interface. "Point and click" means placing the mouse cursor on an icon and pressing the mouse button to select the icon. The user interface server is also structured so that menus;

panels; online help; online messages; and data-element names, lengths, and values can be easily changed without using programming language.

Object Manager The **object manager** component of ASM controls the object environment for the system. It loads and manages objects, passes messages between objects, controls access to data, and controls the actions a user can perform on the data. Using the object manager, programmers can manage instances of class, or objects. When a user logs on to ProductManager, a class initialization module makes all valid classes known to the object manager. This causes the object manager to load classes into memory and **materialize** instances of the classes so that these objects can receive messages. Materialization is an object-oriented process that obtains a persistent object instance from the database and transforms it into a nonpersistent object in memory.

An instance is a single occurrence of a particular object. Any level of the object class hierarchy can have instances. For example, an EC is a class of object. When an EC is created and a number is assigned, it is considered an instance, or object, of an EC. Object manager copies the object and transfers the information to an EC object.

Data Server ASM's **data server** provides the interface between ProductManager and the database management system, which manages, stores, and retrieves the information in the ProductManager database. The server also maintains data integrity and logs system actions by providing services that control access to objects in the database and by converting objects between memory and the database. The data server also provides the capability to log security violations.

Administrative Functions Supported by ASM

The next set of ASM functions are those that **systems administrators** normally work with through the user interface to manage the ProductManager system environment and perform PDM tasks. Systems administrators are people who maintain system information, whereas end users are the engineers, analysts, and support personnel who use the system to manage product information.

Figure 2.16 shows how a panel may appear after an administrator selects Administrative Services from the ProductManager Menu. Administrative services are functions that allow administrators to do their jobs. For example, they can define security for individual users and groups of users or create distribution lists for use by all ProductManager users. Other functions are available by selecting lower-level administrative services icons.

As we discuss the functions, we'll explain how they are used in a fictitious company called ABC Stove Company. A medium-sized company, the ABC Stove Company makes stoves and refrigerators and has design and manufacturing engineering locations in two cities.

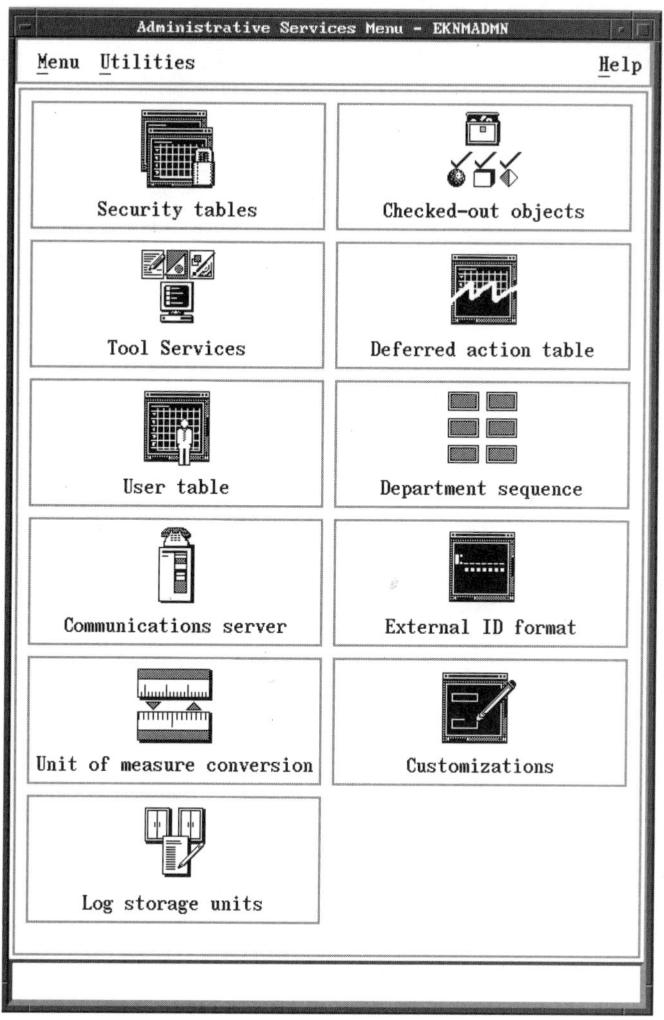

Figure 2.16 The ProductManager Administrative Services Menu is used to select from a variety of administrative functions.

Security Tables **Security tables** are used in ProductManager to classify and protect information. After information is classified, users of the system are given access authority to information based on their needs. Administrators can set user security according to levels, categories, groups, and methods. **Security levels** are assigned to information on the basis of its sensitivity. They determine the level of authority required to view or work with the information. The **security groups** feature is used to assign authority levels to groups of users. A group can consist of all business engineers across departments, for example, or of a department of engineers. An engineer may be a member of several groups. **Security categories** are used to classify data by project, by department, or by other groupings. Security groups and categories are used together to define who can access and work with what data. ProductManager functions can also be secured. **Secured methods** prevent users from performing specific actions against objects, such as releasing an EC, for example. At ABC Stove, the lead engineer has the authority to perform any action on any object, while other members of his department have the authority only to work with but not to delete objects. Authorities can be designated for creating, viewing, changing, and deleting objects.

Security category mapping is also available with ProductManager. This protects product information while it is in development, but removes the protection when the status of the information changes. As an example, when an REA and its affected items are promoted to an EC, security conditions for the affected items are applied automatically. With the security conditions in place, the item design and its definition data remain available for authorized engineers to work with while the EC is being worked through the system. After the change is released to manufacturing, the security conditions are removed so that the entire organization can work with the items again.

User Table

The **user table** manages information about users on the ProductManager system. The table is used to identify the **network** and node for each user. A network is a specific group of connected computers that exchange information, while a node is a computer connected to a network. The node specifies the location or address of the computer attached to the network.

Complete and preferred names of users are defined in the user table along with each user's security group level, employee number, and other identifications. The table also controls processing information for users. Users can have more than one ID specified in the system. For example, an administrator can work as a lower-level user on a second ID. A user can specify one ID for receiving messages and notifications. Through the user table, users can do things like delegate reviews to other users or assign alternates for reviews.

Deferred Action Table

The **deferred action table** is used to identify the objects and actions that can be transmitted between nodes and networks through **background** or **interactive** modes. Interactive processing requires a user to monitor and interact with the system to perform a task. Background processing executes a predefined series of actions with little or no input required from the user or the system. Using the deferred action table, an REA review class with a distribution method as the action can be predefined as an object that is sent or received in either background or interactive mode.

There are two types of background functions in ProductManager. The first controls the order in which a ProductManager application processes information it receives from *other applications or systems*. The second controls background jobs submitted by *users*, and is performed using a **shell script**. A shell script is a simple, macro-like program that guides the automatic execution of system and environment functions. Along with supporting the background environment, shell scripts link users to specific product libraries.

Communications Server We discussed the communications server earlier as an enabler for the system. However, the communications server also provides administrative functions that identify all systems that are connected to the network. It has two administrative components: the **application ID** (identifier) and the **network control table**. The application ID contains information that describes a unique ProductManager environment on a local or remote computer. These IDs are assigned by IBM to reduce the likelihood of conflicting IDs.

The network control table describes the network; the node; and the person responsible for the drivers, the security levels, and the operating system. Records that can be sent or received directly by the asynchronous communications monitor are also defined. When a record is too large for the ACM to process directly, a new background process is created to handle the request.

Unit-of-Measure Conversion In a worldwide development effort, it is important to be able to use measurement systems that differ from those used in the United States. ProductManager has built-in conversion routines that automatically convert, as an example, gallons to liters or yards to meters. **Unit-of-measure conversion** is useful when you run reports that are to be converted to another country's standards. You can enter the U.S. standards and then specify the measurement system to which you want the information converted. ProductManager's built-in conversion routine will make the change automatically. Using these conversion factors, an engineer in the United States can convert a measurement in yards to its equivalent in meters for use by engineers in Europe. ProductManager allows for measurements in several units, including pairs, carats, volts, kilos, atoms, revolutions per minute, and density.

Log Storage Units **Log storage units** contain messages about database and security errors. Administrators can use the information in the logs to monitor, analyze, and resolve system problems. Log storage units produce and log messages, create message objects, and assign log entry types.

The ProductManager system creates log entries to record certain actions performed on certain objects. It also identifies the files that contain the log storage unit and gives the status of the files.

Checked-Out Objects When a system has a number of users, it's likely that more than one user may attempt to make changes to a particular file at the same time.

ProductManager protects objects that have been opened by more than one user. When a comment is checked out by more than one person, the user who selected it first can change the comment. Other users can make changes after the first user checks the object in.

Department Sequence and External ID Format The **department sequence** and **external ID format** functions are used to automatically generate ID numbers for items, ECs, REAs, EC deliverables, and EC reviews. The format for the numbers is maintained using administrative services, but the numbers are generated using the other ProductManager applications.

ABC Stove tracks 100,000 items that make up their line of products. Last year, they applied 750 ECs to new and existing products and added 2400 items to their database. It took three people working with department coordinators to control the numbering for items and change requests throughout the company. Using ProductManager has reduced the coordination and paperwork required to number the changes and parts.

ProductManager generates numbers automatically by tracking and controlling the ranges of numbers for each object. An **external ID** is the number created by the user or the system. ProductManager users have the option of including a department sequence number within the external ID. The sequence is the portion of the external ID that identifies a department or users within departments. It is easily located, which facilitates tracking.

Also included in automatic number creation are options that delimit the length of a number and allow text to be included in the number. The text included in a number indicates the number's type. Engineers can select one or all of these options for creating numbers. External ID formats and department sequencing pinpoint the creation and control of information associated with products. Using ABC Stove's numbering scheme, a department manager can access information produced by any of 10 engineers in the department who create items and ECs.

While automatic number generation is one of the least-standardized capabilities in the product data management industry, an item's number happens to be one of its most important pieces of data. Having a system that allows you to define, control, and automatically assign this data, without the risk of manual transposition errors, is very helpful.

Customization Features ProductManager can be tailored to meet different business needs. Customization of ProductManager is performed at different levels using different means. Tailoring at some levels, such as the creation of a new object, must be done by a programmer. Other changes, such as changing the behavior of a panel, can be made by administrators. Sometimes it takes both programmers and administrators to make a change. End users normally do not tailor the behavior of panels or define new object classes in ProductManager. They can, however, personalize certain parts of ProductManager, such as distribution lists, nickname files, national language preferences, and types of keyboards.

Programmers can work with the **application program interfaces (API)**. An API is a functional interface that allows an application program written in a high-level language to use specific data or functions. With ProductManager, programmers access the API information by using the **application model** function in ASM. The application model is the online interface between the user and the functions and descriptions of ProductManager object classes and their methods and attributes, which were discussed in the object-oriented technology section.

The application model shows each class's place in the inheritance hierarchy as well as its corresponding attributes and methods. It also shows how the class works within the system and what parts can be tailored to meet specific business needs. The extended description is displayed in a text editor format to make it easier to view and manipulate. Programmers can click on the menu selection, go to the API information, and change the behavior of the program using the interface.

We'll discuss more about what can be tailored and by whom in "Tailoring ProductManager" in Chapter 3. That chapter also explains the user groups and how they usually work with the ProductManager system.

End-User Functions Supported by ASM

The final of the three sets of ASM functions is that of the end-user functions. All of these functions can be selected from the ProductManager Menu.

User Services

The **user services** component of ASM provides a way for users and administrators to work with product information and internal company information. User services allows users to interactively manipulate personnel, company, and location information. Personnel information enables administrators to define or change a person's name, department, user ID, number, node, or network. **Company information** includes business addresses, contacts, phone numbers, and supplier codes for companies that provide products or services. **Location information** describes remote office networks and nodes. Nodes can be maintained in user services along with codes designating them as design or manufacturing locations. Users can also list the contacts at each location and specify the currency and number-rounding techniques used by locations in different countries.

The user services option also allows system users to maintain nickname data. User-defined nicknames can be used instead of cryptic ID numbers in distribution lists, making it easy for users to share information. User services also provides flexibility for background processes, allowing users to specify whether they prefer batch or interactive processing for different files.

Other features in ASM's user services support the exchange of information across cultural and language barriers. **National Language Support (NLS)** lets users select the national language preference for date, time, and integer formats. Character set descriptions provide character sets and their attributes for different language groups. ProductManager has **coded character set identifiers** that distinguish between alphabetic and numeric characters.

In-basket

The **In-basket** utility of ProductManager is an electronic version of the "in basket" that sits on your desk. It contains mail and work items, such as requests for engineering action and engineering change reviews, that are waiting for your review or response. It also receives and stores notification messages related to the status of an item that you have sent for review. For example, when a reviewer or **recipient** approves an engineering change, a message is immediately sent to the In-basket of the review's originator. If a reviewer is late in responding to a review, the system automatically sends one message to the **originator** and one to the delinquent recipient. The originator of a folder is the person who created it. A recipient is anyone to whom the folder is sent. Figure 2.17 shows how notifications and messages are listed in the In-basket.

When a review is sent to your In-basket, the ProductManager In-basket icon illuminates to let you know you have mail. At that point, you become a recipient of the review. Depending on the type of recipient you are, you may

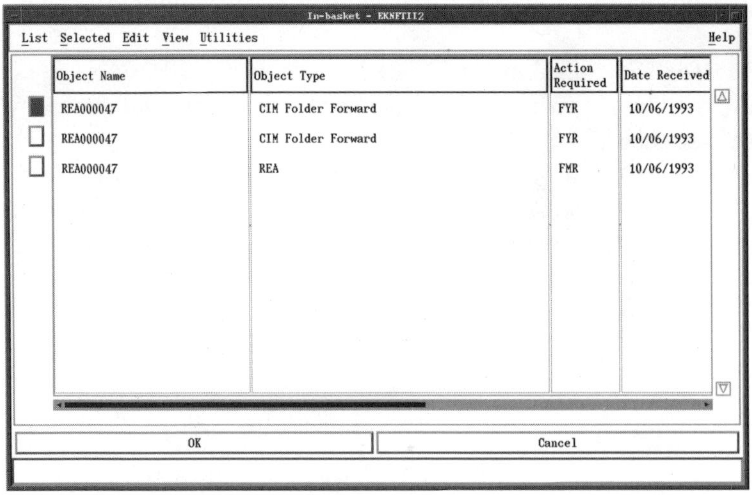

In-basket - EKNFTII2

List Selected Edit View Utilities Help

Object Name	Object Type	Action Required	Date Received
REA000047	CIM Folder Forward	FYR	10/06/1993
REA000047	CIM Folder Forward	FYR	10/06/1993
REA000047	REA	FMR	10/06/1993

OK Cancel

Figure 2.17 The ProductManager In-basket panel is used to view incoming reviews, messages, and notifications. New messages are highlighted.

then make comments about the review, approve it, disapprove it, or specify conditions that must be met before approval. You can merge the comments from your review into the original review and return it to the originator. If you want to distribute the review further, you can work with the folder from your In-basket to create your own distribution list and send the review to everyone on the list.

Folder Distribution A folder in ProductManager is conceptually the electronic equivalent of a paper file folder you maintain in a file cabinet or desk drawer. The folder contains information associated with a particular review or action. The information can range from specifications or drawing references to comments about the review or other folders. A folder can also include BOMs, spreadsheets, product documentation, ECs, and item information. Folders and In-basket processes are related. The folder is used to collect and route information, whereas the In-basket is used to view and respond to folders that you receive. The folder concept is used by ASM and all other ProductManager applications to control review and approval processes.

Each folder has a **header** that describes the folder, a table of contents that shows what's in the folder, a **distribution list,** and a **history**. Public distribution lists are predefined electronic mailing lists that are available to all ProductManager users for electronic folder distribution and other folder-based processes. Users can also create private distribution lists that are unique to individual folders or various reviewer lists for things like ECs or REAs. For example, ABC Stove engineers can create a review folder for a burner and then hand-pick the reviewers for that burner. By handling the reviews electronically, ABC Stove engineers save time in copying folder contents, putting together physical packages, and mailing the contents to various reviewers. In addition to saving handling time, electronic reviews save time in the development cycle by getting the package to reviewers immediately, receiving comments as soon as reviews are complete, and reducing the need for meetings. The electronic folder provides for a more complete and timely review process. Furthermore, when you eliminate shipping and handling costs as well as salaries for mail room personnel, the direct cost savings are significant.

Using ASM distribution functions, folders can be distributed to a sequence of reviewers, distributed to all reviewers at the same time, or both. **Serial distribution** is used to send a review from one person to the next in a specified sequence. The advantage of serial distribution is that each reviewer can review the comments of the previous reviewer. Important comments about a design that the originator did not include can now be part of the review and decision-making process for subsequent reviewers. With **parallel distribution**, folders are sent to all reviewers at the same time. This speeds the review process, but doesn't allow reviewers to see one another's comments. However, if

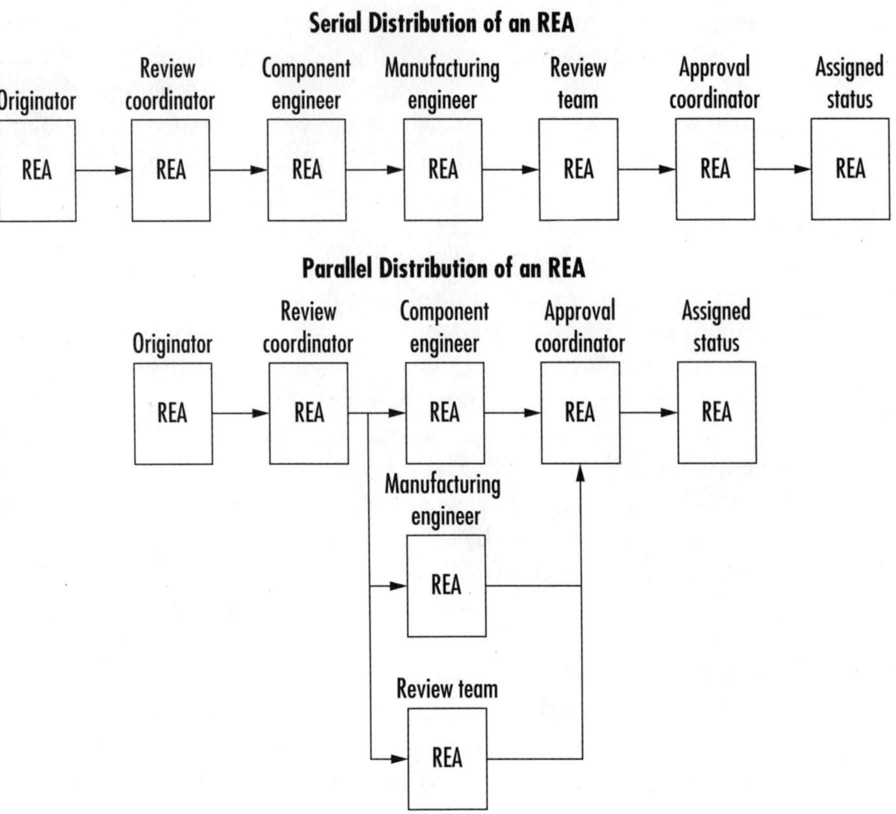

Figure 2.18 A serial distribution path is shown for the top REA. The bottom REA is sent to all reviewers at the same time in parallel distribution. Engineers can modify review processes.

they have the appropriate security authorization, they can view the comments of others after the comments have been added to the review. Figure 2.18 shows the differences between serial and parallel distribution.

When Sam Wallace, ABC Stove's lead design engineer for ovens, opened a new REA that appeared in his In-basket from marketing, he saw a request to design a new plug to meet 120- and 220-volt requirements. Sam worked up an initial design and added the specifications and his comments to the REA. Using ProductManager, he sent his design and recommendations to the review coordinator for further review. After the coordinator had reviewed the design, the review was continued in serial distribution to the remaining organizations, as shown in the top portion of Figure 2.18.

Sam selected the participants in the review when he created his serial distribution list. He also could have used parallel distribution for his REA. The bottom portion of Figure 2.18 shows how the same REA would go through parallel distribution. After the review coordinator approves the REA, it is sent to the component engineer, manufacturing engineer, and review team at the same time. As they complete their reviews, they send the REA to the approval coordinator, who then assigns it to an engineer. In this case, it goes back to Sam Wallace, who will take the REA through the EC process as well.

Included in ASM's distribution functions is a **delegate feature**. If users indicate that their distributions should be delegated to other ProductManager users, the folder will automatically be rerouted to the person specified as the alternate. If an engineer plans to be out of the office for several days or weeks, this feature ensures that the alternate person can respond to the folder, reducing review time. Once distributed, folders can still be **transferred, forwarded,** or **recalled**. When they are transferred, the original recipient is no longer responsible for responding to the folder. If the folder is forwarded, the original recipient remains responsible for responding to the originator of the folder. Only the originator of a folder can recall it. For instance, if Sam Wallace sent an REA and left out a specification, only he could recall the folder, add the specification, and distribute the folder again. Oversights do occur, so having a system that lets you adjust the process for deviations is important. **Delinquency reports** are also available for distributed folders. These reports show which recipients are late in responding to folders containing REAs or EC reviews.

Distributed Resource Management The distributed resource manager in ProductManager's ASM application works with **logical data objects.** These are drawings, documents, specifications, numerical control programs, or any other information not created within ProductManager. For example, many drawings are created by the computer-aided design program CATIA. The resource manager defines CATIA as the environment in which such a drawing is managed. An engineer can use the resource manager to indicate whether a drawing or other logical data object resides in a drawing library, in a filing cabinet, or on another computer system.

The resource manager provides a link to such an object through a **logical data reference object.** This is a referencing object that points to a logical data object but is not itself that object. Referencing objects are sometimes referred to as **metadata**.

When an engineer creates a logical data reference object, ProductManager associates that reference with the real logical data object. Reference objects refer to originals or copies of objects such as BOMs, test results, specifications, or drawings, which can be created as new objects or included in folders. Reference objects allow the logical data objects to which they refer to become part of a folder without being "physically" (electronically) present in that folder.

Complete libraries of logical data reference objects can be listed on the ProductManager system. ASM supports the distribution and management of CIM Data Services, CADAM, CATIA, CATIA Data Management, and UNIX file objects.

Product Change Manager

ProductManager's Product Change Manager (PCM) application is designed to help manage the processes and flow of information necessary to create new products and release design changes to manufacturing. PCM is used to initiate, track, and release ECs for new or existing products. It gives engineers control over changes as they go through review processes. Manufacturing engineering changes (MECs) can also be controlled using PCM. Figure 2.19 summarizes the functions of the PCM application.

Together, PCM and ASM provide the functions necessary to control the release-to-manufacturing process. However, this pair of applications will not maintain and track individual item information. Extra efforts are needed to manage each item separately, ensuring that it is protected from unauthorized changes and that it progresses to release along with the EC that affects it. In some cases, the less stringent control afforded by the PCM and ASM combination is wanted, since it allows engineers to move changes through the process by pointing to affected items (items that will change as a result of the EC or MEC) rather than making them a part of the EC folder. When

Primary function: PCM manages and controls product changes. The application provides process and release controls, "takes items from non-EC control to EC-controlled status," and defines date, batch, lot, unit, and serial number effectivities.

- Initiates informal change request through request for engineering action.
- Provides mechanism to make formal change request through engineering change.
- Ensures that business procedures are followed during the development cycle.
- Assigns statuses to items during the development cycle.
- Maintains a history of all change activity for an engineering change.
- Takes an item to effective status and secures access during development.
- Provides for effectivities for a variety of manufacturing scenarios.
- Relates engineering changes to one another for release sequence.
- Provides a distribution package with all affected items, related ECs, deliverables, and reviews.
- Manages product configurations.

Figure 2.19 An overview of Product Change Manager (PCM) functions.

more stringent control is wanted, PCM and ASM can be used with the Product Structure Manager (PSM) application of ProductManager. The link between PCM and PSM is the EC affected item. When PSM links the affected item to an EC, ProductManager takes over the tracking and management of the item information, just as it does with the EC. The item can now be attached to the EC and can progress automatically with it.

Now let's take a closer look at the two things PCM works with: requests for engineering action (REAs) and engineering changes (ECs).

Requests for Engineering Action

A request for engineering action (REA) can be created to initiate a change to an existing product or to introduce requirements for a new product. Building on the folder structure provided by ASM, the REA component of PCM automates the REA process. Any authorized user can initiate an REA. The REA can then be routed for management review or routed directly to an REA coordinator for evaluation. The coordinator can then distribute the request to a review team for further evaluation. During this process, PCM tracks the status of the REA and sends warning messages when reviews come due. The system also sends delinquency messages when reviews are late. The message intervals can be custom tailored.

Using the ASM folder concept, an REA can be distributed by serial or parallel distribution to review team members. The manager or review coordinator may also terminate the REA. An REA can be delegated to other reviewers, transferred to other reviewers (which takes the person who transferred it out of the process), or recalled by the person who originated it. Reviewers who sent the REA to another group for review can merge that group's comments back into the original REA.

After an REA is approved, its status is changed from "approved" to "assign" and it is sent to an engineer, at which point it becomes an EC. The assigned engineer usually manages the EC and the design change. Thus, a request for engineering action is the forerunner of an engineering change. Figure 2.20 shows an object detail panel for an REA. System users will work with this panel to create, review, and add comments to an REA.

Let's briefly discuss the elements of an REA.

Header Provides a brief overview of critical information associated with the REA. The header appears on the screen when an engineer opens the REA. As shown in Figure 2.20, the header occupies the upper portion of the panel, and the icons from which actions can be selected appear in the lower part of the panel. Additional header information is revealed by scrolling. Scrolling is using the mouse on scroll bars along the edges of a display to reposition the information that appears in a display portion of the panel. Briefly, an REA

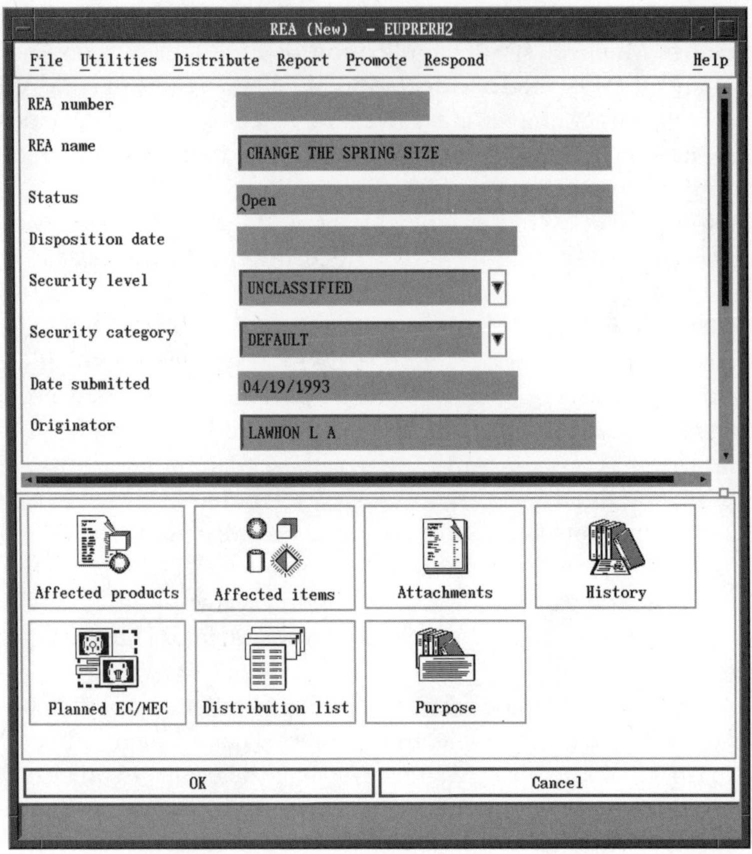

Figure 2.20 A Request for Engineering Action object detail panel. An engineer can select an icon to work with the different objects of an REA.

header shows information such as the REA number, name, originator, and date of submission.

Purpose Describes the nature of the REA, such as changing the design of a metal cover to keep it from rubbing against a pulley. The online editor used to create the purpose allows the user creating it to provide as much detail as is needed. The online editor is a program for creating documents that can be accessed through ProductManager.

Affected Items Items that will change as a result of the REA. If the metal cover in the previous example is changed, it becomes the affected item. The dye that forms the cover will also change, a consideration for the process engineer, so the dye also becomes an affected item from the manufacturing viewpoint.

Attachments The supporting information that goes with the REA. Attachments include reports, reference objects, comments, and folders. The information in an attachment provides details that help reviewers determine whether or not to approve the REA. Any object that can be placed in a folder can be an REA attachment.

Distribution List A system-maintained list that contains the user IDs for a selected group of ProductManager users. A user creating an REA can select user IDs from the master list to create a distribution list of recipients of the REA. Recipients can be managers, coordinators, review teams, or approving engineers. When an REA is distributed, it goes to the In-basket of each recipient, who then uses the In-basket to work with the request.

Affected Products The end products assembled from the affected items as described in the bill of material. If our example of an improved metal cover is an affected item in a business that makes engine assemblies, the **affected product** is the engine assembly. If the business produces entire engines, the affected product is the engine itself instead of a lower-level assembly.

Planned ECs and MECs The formal change processes that will result if the request for engineering action is approved. The REA is only the beginning of making a change. Once the request has been approved, it goes to a more formal stage of change in which engineers must complete designs and plan for implementation.

History The **history** shows the activities that have been performed with an REA, such as when it was created and who has responded to it.

As discussed earlier, in the "Folder Distribution" section, users can use the distribution list to define the reviewers, the folder, and the distribution method (serial or parallel). While the REA is tightly integrated with the EC process, it can be customized and used in other facets of the business, such as requests for work, procurement, travel, or facilities. Any process that begins with a request and concludes with a review or an acknowledgment is a candidate for the REA process.

Engineering Changes

An engineering change (EC) identifies the method by which product definition data is packaged for release to manufacturing, and manages the specifics of the change. The EC contains all the information about the change, including BOMs, affected items, drawings, reviews, and deliverables. ProductManager also supports change from the manufacturing perspective. Manufacturing engineering changes (MECs) include ECs and BOMs (MBOMs) released from manufacturing.

After an REA is approved, an EC is created, and the change process then follows a set of formalized steps. PCM uses its EC functions to control all aspects of the change. The system tracks and logs significant activities in the change process. An engineer can open an EC and view the progression of the change. Before the change goes to production, the EC function runs tests to verify that all work required for the change has been completed according to the business's rules.

When ProductManager users want to create or work with an engineering change, the Menu provides direct access to the EC list. Figure 2.21 shows how an object detail panel may appear for working with ECs. The initiator is the person who creates the EC.

As an EC advances through the process, it goes through several statuses, including "prerelease," "received" (for ECs from remote locations), and "release." The statuses can be renamed to match a business's terms. The status

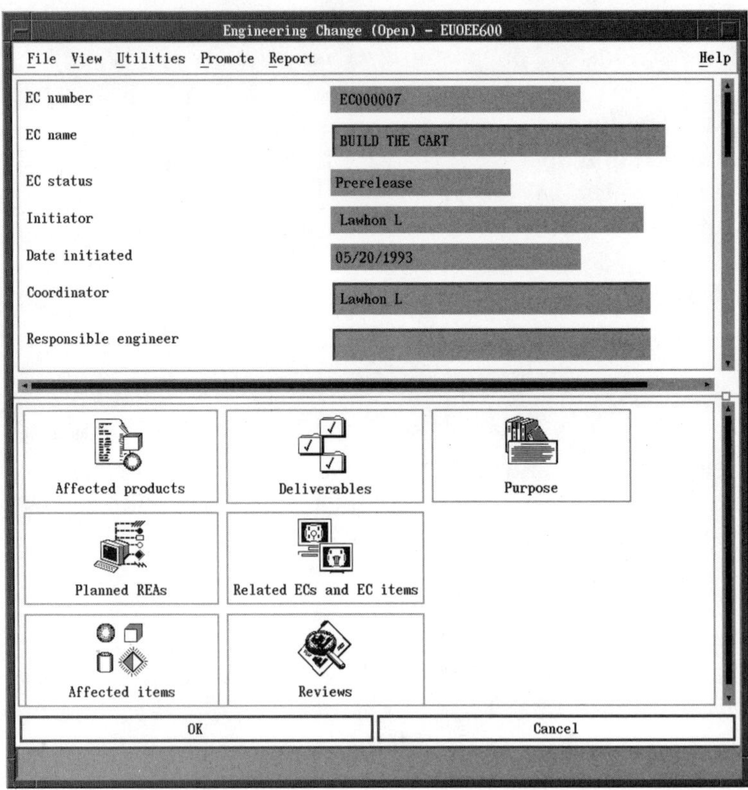

Figure 2.21 An Engineering Change object detail panel. The header in the top portion of the panel provides basic information about the EC.

of an EC determines when it can be changed. For example, when an EC reaches the "release" status, the system automatically prevents changes to the items associated with the change. During the change process, security authorizations control who may view and alter the change data. Before being promoted to manufacturing, the EC, with its affected items, is automatically tested by the system for release readiness. The system checks for conditions such as completed deliverables and reviews. Engineers can also test the EC for release readiness and preview it for any problems before promoting it.

The EC header indicates the locations of control and design, the status, and the planned due date, and specifies whether the change is an EC or an MEC. The **location of control** indicates the ProductManager system on which the EC is stored and controlled. An EC can have only one location of control. The **location of design** is where the EC is being engineered. The location of design is used to determine the location of control, the type of EC, and the EC's status. Between them, the locations of control and design help determine who is responsible for which designs. This ensures that only authorized persons change the EC or MEC.

The location of design provides additional product data management functions. The design location indicates whether an EC is local or remote. For a local EC, the location of design is the same as its location of control. For a remote EC, the location of design is within a location of control that is not on the same ProductManager installation from which the EC originated. If a manufacturing location engineer creates an EC, the location of control for that MEC is the ProductManager installation used to create it.

Suppose a company has two installations of ProductManager. Each installation has a location of control. Within each location of control are locations of design and manufacturing. When the future-products laboratory engineers create an EC and distribute it to groups within its location of control, it is considered a local EC. But when the same laboratory creates an EC to an existing product that resides on the other ProductManager system, the EC is considered a remote EC. ProductManager controls the processing between the installations, ensuring that only authorized users work with the changing information.

In addition to the basic administrative control information given in the EC header, the EC has other optional objects that let you use ProductManager to manage product changes using either simple or sophisticated processes.

Let's briefly discuss each object of an engineering change in PCM.

Affected Items The affected items object controls the changes to specific information on an item. PCM applies processing rules that guide the item through its release. Items that are created in the system by ECs are also considered EC-controlled items. Affected items have change actions, previous change numbers that can be associated with issue numbers and statuses, revision levels, and item and engineering effectivities. When an EC is complete and ready for release, engineers can share the new item information with other manufacturing locations. PDIF files (described earlier) can be produced, containing the changed and new data associated with the EC. That data can then be distributed to other ProductManager systems and non-ProductManager systems.

The status of each of an EC's affected items is also tracked during the EC process. ProductManager assigns the following statuses as the item moves through the EC process:

Prerelease This is the stage at which an engineering-affected item is created on an EC. During this stage of development, design engineers can make changes to the item and its BOM.

Received A remote item is created.

Release Design engineers have completed the EC work and cannot make further changes to an item without creating another EC to do the work.

Accepted The version of the affected item that is accepted into the manufacturing location that accepts the EC. At this point, the item can progress through the manufacturing process independent of other affected items of the EC.

Effective Manufacturing has completed the changes to an affected item they have accepted. The affected item is promoted to the "effective" status after the type of effectivity is specified, such as date, lot, serial number, or batch.

Closed All changes have been made to the affected item data, and the effectivity has passed.

Purpose The next EC object, the EC purpose, is text written by the EC initiator describing information about an EC. The purpose usually explains why the change is being made and what the change is.

Related ECs and Items Using **related ECs and items,** engineers can define a sequence in which ECs or EC-affected items are to be released or made effective. For example, if one EC changes the size of a rivet, the next EC in the sequence might change where the rivet is inserted. **Prerequisite and corequisite ECs** identify dependencies between two ECs that must be introduced into the next development or production stage in a specific order. A prerequisite EC is a change that must be implemented before another defined EC. A corequisite EC means that there is another EC involved in the change. ProductManager builds and manages the relationships between ECs. At ABC Stove, engineers in the product-planning area develop the product release plan. They identify the ECs that will be used to release the product and input the data to ProductManager from their project management software. From there, ProductManager controls the release of the changes.

Deliverables A deliverable is an item such as a drawing or certification that must be produced during the processing of an EC before the EC can be released. For example, if a deliverable such as an updated drawing is not complete, the EC cannot be released. Deliverables are managed by PCM. The deliverables process, like the REA, uses folders for distribution. A deliverable is electronically packaged and contains a header, attachments, affected data, and a history.

EC Review An EC review establishes an electronic process for distributing, reviewing, and approving an engineering change. The EC review functions of PCM provide a method of controlling the process for reviewing product data changes. Since it is often not necessary for all engineers to review all of the information associated with an EC, users can tailor folders and distribution lists to the varying needs of reviewers. For example, you can create a separate safety review folder that is independent of the EC folder for a product. Or all reviews can be grouped within one EC folder. You can elect to have one review, many reviews, or no reviews of an EC, depending on the merits of that EC.

After an EC review has been distributed, recipients of the review can add their comments, add other review attachments, and approve or disapprove the EC. If an EC review is disapproved or conditionally approved, the PCM application requires the recipient to add a comment explaining that decision. Elements of an EC review include the following:

Header Contains descriptive information about the EC review and is used to establish the review folder and due dates for the review. The header is also used to indicate that distribution of the review is being stopped because it was disapproved.

Review attachments An index of the documents or drawings that are included in the review. These can include REAs, reports, comments, and logical data reference objects. Engineers can open and review the attachments.

Distribution list Defines the recipients and their actions, due dates, due time, and sequence levels. EC reviews can be distributed in parallel distribution, serial distribution, or both. The order in which recipients receive the review is based on the sequence level they are assigned.

Review history Lists the activities that have been performed on the EC review. Engineers can review the history online. Included in the history for an EC review are the originator's ID, the dates of its creation and distribution, and the IDs of those who have responded to it.

Product–Unit Effectivity Effectivity controls the release of items and products into the engineering or production environments. Product–unit effectivity is the range of units for which a change is implemented on a specific product. ProductManager uses effectivity to control when specific changes to items are placed into production. Product–unit effectivity takes some of the complexity out of managing multiple products with multiple configurations. Using an EC and its effectivity, a business can more smoothly phase in and phase out the manufacture of different product configurations. With some manufacturers such as make-to-order manufacturers, even if a configuration of a product is phased out, it can be phased back in if the customer makes another order.

When ABC Stove engineers create an EC to change the handle on a refrigerator door, they also include the effectivity. This helps them plan for depleting the stock of existing handles before the new handle goes into production. ABC Stove normally uses a date effectivity in its mass production operations, with little or no differences from one stove to the next. But what about the big products that may take months to build, such as airplanes or missiles? How does a business manage the effectivity? Using product–unit effectivity is the answer. When an airplane manufacturer receives orders from three airlines for different seating schemes, the manufacturer relies on product–unit effectivity to track the configurations. The seating-design EC and any items required to complete the design are assigned a product–unit effectivity. This becomes the mechanism for tracking the configuration of the airplane.

Using ECs and affected items, PCM tracks and manages the configuration of products. The product configurations and item versions are created in the Product Structure Manager application of ProductManager. The product's version is defined through the EC to which the item is attached. The effectivity assigned to the item specifies the right version of the item to be used in the product. In ProductManager, a version is created when an item and its BOM are defined at a given EC level.

PCM requires each affected item on an EC to have an item effectivity type. ProductManager supports these item effectivity types:

Product–unit Defines effectivity using the product and unit in which changes to the item will be implemented. Items with a product–unit effectivity type cannot have a date effectivity.

Date Defines the date a new change is implemented. Items with a date effectivity type cannot have a product–unit effectivity. The date effectivity supports batch and lot effectivity.

Date and sometimes product–unit (DASPU) Defines the date effectivity as the base effectivity type, but product–unit effectivity can be defined as well.

Effectivities in PCM can also be assigned at different levels when an EC is created. First, the effectivity can be assigned at the EC level. When the EC level is assigned, any effectivity assigned to the EC is automatically assigned to the EC's affected items. Engineers do not have to assign the same information over and over for affected items. This step is performed in ProductManager using **propagation**. The effectivity information is automatically copied to the affected items on the EC. Once an affected item is assigned EC-level effectivity, it cannot be changed unless the EC effectivity information is changed.

The second effectivity level is the affected item level. This effectivity level provides more flexibility in assigning effectivities for specific affected items. Since engineers work with individual items, the EC effectivity information does not have to be propagated across affected items. An advantage of affected item effectivities is that they can precede the EC-level effectivity. If an affected item has to be produced before the EC is implemented, that item can have an earlier effectivity than the overall EC.

When a product–unit effectivity is created at either the EC or affected item level, it indicates the unit numbers for a specific product in which the changes are to be implemented. Only items that are classified as a product item type can be assigned as a product-affected item when product–unit effectivity is used. At ABC Stove for instance, motors used in refrigerators are classified as product items. They are used as replacement products. The business's engineers can use product–unit effectivity when they define the motor as an affected item on an EC to change the refrigerator, because the motor is considered a product item. The items that make up the motor, however, are not considered product items and cannot have a product–unit effectivity assigned to them.

PCM supports effectivity in design and manufacturing views. In the design view, before the item is released to manufacturing, engineers can control whether a planned effectivity is required if the item effectivity type is date or DASPU. They can also control whether the item's product–unit effectivity is required if the item effectivity type is product–unit. The system defaults to requiring either a planned effectivity date or item product–unit effectivity, depending on the item effectivity type, before an EC can be released. The effectivity for all items on an EC is verified to ensure that the effectivity for a BOM component exists on a BOM item at the current EC level. PCM also allows engineers to secure the effectivity information at "Release" status.

In the manufacturing view, after the item is accepted by manufacturing, the effectivity can be changed or removed. PCM provides manufacturing engineers with the option of controlling whether product–unit effectivities can be defined for items that did not exist in the design view. The system default is to not allow new items to be added. Manufacturing engineers can also control whether an actual effectivity date is required for items with an item effectivity type of date or DASPU before the item can be promoted to "effective" status, and whether the date or product–unit effectivity is secured after an item is promoted to "effective" status.

Regardless of a business's method of manufacturing, efficiently controlling product configurations and effectivities can make a significant difference in the efficiency and profitability of the business.

Affected Documents The **affected documents** function is used to link documentation and ECs. An engineer can create new documents for an EC or select a document and link it to an EC. By using the affected documents function from within the EC to link documentation to that EC, the engineer can avoid navigating to the DCM application in order to perform the task.

Product Structure Manager

The Product Structure Manager (PSM) application of ProductManager is used to define **product definition data** and maintain BOMs. Product definition data consists of the item information that makes up a product. Whereas PCM manages the change and release processes in ProductManager systems, PSM provides the means for creating and working with item information. PSM can be used to define product definition data with or without implementing the rest of the EC-control processes. If EC control is a part of the development process, PCM is the application that manages it. If EC control is not a part of the process, then PSM can be used to control ECs. When a new item is added to the database or information about an item changes, PSM is used to work with the item or input the change. Figure 2.22 summarizes the functions of PSM.

PSM also incorporates several concepts that help control information. We'll first look at the main functions of PSM and then discuss how PSM helps control information. Our discussion will include the following:

Product definition data

Non–EC-controlled data

EC-controlled data

Multiple views

Product Definition Data

The product definition data function of PSM is used to create and maintain the basic information about items that go into products. The information includes, as an example, supplier information and physical characteristics of the item. Authorized users have unrestricted access to the information. Product definition data is created and a number is assigned to the item when it is initially added to the database. As long as the item is not under **EC control,**

Primary function: PSM is used to define information about all items and products. The application is also used to create ProductManager reports and works with PCM to take items to EC-controlled status. Along with maintaining BOMs, it works with ASM in number generation.

- Manages item data not under change control.
- Provides multiple views of item BOMs.
- Creates a variety of reports used to work with item and BOM information.
- Updates BOMs automatically, using information from drawings.
- Defines substitute, optional, and operation information for BOMs.
- Identifies supplier and routing information for items.
- Maintains item ownership.
- Shows where and how an item is used at different locations.
- Maintains item codes and statuses for design and manufacturing engineering.
- Displays a product structure.
- Tracks locations of design and control.
- Identifies item documentation and its location.

Figure 2.22 An overview of Product Structure Manager (PSM) functions.

it can be manipulated, but once an item is placed under EC control, it becomes an affected item and is protected by the ProductManager system. This keeps the item stable for the work that has to be done to it or any of its components. Affected items on an EC are EC-controlled in the PCM application.

Items can be assemblies, end products, parts, or raw materials. ProductManager users access the Item Engineering Data panel shown in Figure 2.23 to work with product definition data. An ABC Stove engineer who wants to input an alternative supplier for a heating element selects Suppliers from the menu.

While an item can have extensive data defined for it, it is not necessary to define all of the types of data for every item. Businesses have the flexibility to determine the type of data that they use with an item. The following types of data can be associated with an item:

Engineering data

Manufacturing data

Location usage

Design attributes

Item comments

Association data

Reference documents

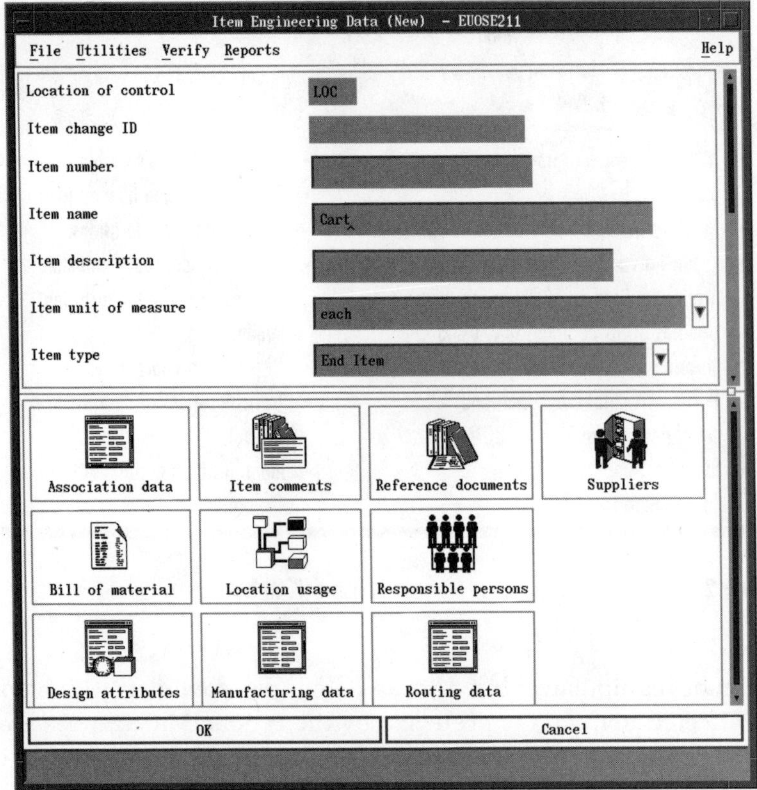

Figure 2.23 An Item Engineering Data object detail panel. Additional header information and icons can be viewed by scrolling the panel.

Responsible persons

Supplier data

Routing data

Bill of material

Engineering Data Item **engineering data** defines the basic characteristics of an item from a design engineer's perspective. This data is important in determining how ProductManager processes the item as it goes from design to manufacturing. Item engineering data covers areas such as the locations of control and design. The location of control identifies the ProductManager system on which the item design originated. Location of control enables a business with several installations of ProductManager to verify that only authorized users within the location owning the item can change the item. Any changes to the item must originate from the location of control that owns the item design. The location of design indicates the design group, laboratory, or plant that controls the design. This location of design function of PSM allows you to define independent engineering groups within a ProductManager system or across systems.

Other types of engineering data include the **item type code** and **item-planning code**. An item type code describes the type of item, such as an end item or assembly. ProductManager supports a variety of item type codes, including fabricated, group, document, and detailed part assembly, but you can also define your own item types. The planning code is used by the material requirements department to plan for ordering and stocking an item. An item can be assigned a normal planning code, a reference item code, an "as required" item code, a bulk item code, or any other planning code used by the business.

Finally, the system tracks items and their engineering statuses. This allows the system to control how an item can be used in a product. ProductManager is shipped with predefined statuses that include development, controlled, active, service, and obsolete. When an item becomes an affected item, the system manages it through the EC release process.

Manufacturing Data **Manufacturing data** provides descriptive information about an item from a manufacturing perspective, including item lead time, which is the amount of time needed to procure an item, and the percentage of items that are acceptable as received from the manufacturer. This is valuable information for material requirements planning personnel in manufacturing businesses that must plan and compensate for less than 100 percent yield for an ordered item. Manufacturing data also includes planning codes, sourcing information, and receipt codes for items.

Location Usage Data **Location usage data** shows where an item is used and which engineering and manufacturing locations would be affected by an engineering change to the item. If a business has several manufacturing areas, this information tells an engineer where information about an item or changes to an item should be sent.

Design Attributes This design data describes the physical attributes of an item. It provides businesses the means to group items without creating links between them. Engineers can use **design attributes** to take advantage of previous designs: Instead of completely designing a new bearing, an engineer can copy an existing bearing design and make changes to the copy to create a new design.

Design attributes also include information pertaining to classification codes, product family, item function, and commodity group.

Item Comments **Item comments** give engineers the flexibility to describe items in their own terms. For example, if one supplier makes higher-grade steel for an item than another supplier, an engineer can attach this information to the item as a comment. These comments are created with an online editor accessed through PSM.

Association Data **Association data** is used by engineers to associate the part number they use to numbers used by other groups. For example, the Department of Defense may use a stock number for an item that is different from your company's part number. Association data relates the two numbers to the single item. Other examples of association data include customer part numbers and catalog part numbers.

Reference Documents **Reference documents** contain all technical information that describes or defines an item. Drawings, specifications, and test data are several examples of reference documents. There are three types of reference documents defined in PSM. The first is external documents: documents that are not electronic, but may be housed in a library or drawing box. The next is logical data reference objects: electronic documents that an engineer can view, change, or distribute. Examples can include CAD drawings, CATIA or CADAM models, or technical manuals. These documents can be stored at different revision levels. The last type of reference document is called "documents." These are documents controlled by ProductManager's DCM application.

Engineers can also open other computer-aided design applications while in PSM's reference documents panel. Called **CAD integration**, this function makes it easier to navigate between ProductManager and design applications.

Responsible Persons When manufacturing engineers review a specification that was prepared by a design engineer at another location, questions may arise. The **responsible persons** function of PSM tells the engineer who and where to call and tells what role the responsible person plays in the process. Responsibility data shows who is responsible for the design and manufacture of an item. Other areas of responsibility defined and shipped with the ProductManager system include product analyst, manufacturing analyst, and item initiator. These fields can be customized to specify other areas of responsibility, such as configuration analyst, procurement, or tooling.

Supplier Data **Supplier data** defines the sources from which an item can be obtained. Businesses can use PSM to define both internal and external sources for specific items. Internal sources are manufacturing locations within the business, while external sources are companies outside of a business. Supplier data also provides cross references for supplier part numbers and the source quantity, which is the percentage of the business's total demand for an item that is supplied by a particular vendor.

Our stove company maintains extensive supplier information for many of its electrical components. In some cases, they have identified preferred suppliers because of the supplier's location, prices, or quality. Alternative suppliers are also identified for most of their critical assembly items such as switches and light bulbs.

Routing Data **Routing data** refers to the valid routings or manufacturing process documents associated with an item. It does not, however, include the actual routing. Routings show how an item is manufactured, along with how and where it's used and who uses it. Using routing data, engineers can establish and maintain a where-used list of routings for an item. "Where used" simply specifies where an item is used.

Routing data also identifies the sequence of operations used to produce an item. Master routings show operations for a family of similar items, while individual routings show operations for a specific item. A routing change sequence is also provided to identify the number of changes that have been made to the original routing.

Bill of Material A bill of material is a listing of all raw materials, subassemblies, and parts that go into an item or parent assembly. PSM provides bill of material data and definitions commonly used in design and manufacturing engineering. Businesses can tailor BOMs and the rules that control their processing.

Default BOM information types shipped with the PSM application include the header, components, substitute and optional components, operation data, and comments. Let's take a look at each of these PSM BOM elements.

Header Describes a BOM in ProductManager and is similar to headers used throughout ProductManager. It contains a brief listing of information critical to the BOM. When an engineer requests an item BOM, the header shows her, among other things, the item number, item type, and the item's ProductManager system (location of control). The header also shows the BOM's revision level, **installation type,** and **completion status**. The installation type indicates how the end product will be used, such as internally or by an external customer. The completion status indicates the BOM's degree of completion, such as incomplete or complete. Businesses can tailor installation type and completion status information.

Component An item used within another item. The list of **components** is often called the parts list. The system uses the designation of BOM components to manage the dependencies of one item on another. Items that make up an end product or product item are also stored and managed by the PSM system. Figure 2.24 represents an indented BOM of a bicycle. A BOM displays what makes up a product or part.

Substitute components Components that are not acceptable for one manufacturing location but are acceptable for another. To support this need for

Indented Design BOM for a Bicycle

- Frame
  - Front assembly
    - Fender
      - Support bars
    - Bolt
    - Nut
  - Rear assembly
    - Fender
      - Support bars
    - Bolt
    - Nut
  - Crossbar
    - Bolt
    - Nut
- Seat
  - Cover
  - Cushion
  - Springs
  - Base
- Handlebar
  - Grips
- Light
  - Bulb
  - Wiring
  - Battery
  - Housing
    - Bolt
    - Nut
- Drive assembly
  - Crank
    - Pedal
      - Pad
      - Bolt
      - Nut
  - Chain
    - Link
    - Connector
  - Front sprocket gear
  - Rear sprocket gear
  - Drive box
    - Cover
    - Shim
    - Bearing
- Front wheel assembly
  - Spokes
  - Rim
  - Bearing
  - Lock nut
  - Bolt
- Rear wheel assembly
  - Drive unit
  - Spokes
  - Rim
  - Bearing
  - Lock nut
  - Bolt

Figure 2.24 An indented bill of material.

variation, PSM provides BOM component substitution. The substitute component is listed in the BOM and can be automatically substituted when a manufacturing BOM is created.

Optional components Components that can be used should supplies of the original component be depleted. The BOM specifies an **optional component** to be used in this event. This feature is especially useful to component engineers, who have to make decisions about where and when to use a component and which component to use. Component costs can be a factor when deciding on optional components, but if a less expensive component is not available, the more expensive component may be listed as the optional component.

Operation data Helps the process engineer determine the process steps by which an item will be produced. While the design engineer is concerned more with what the components are, the process engineer is concerned with how they will be put together. By adding component **operation data** to the design BOM, a process engineer tells manufacturing how to disburse the correct components to each manufacturing department at the right time and in the correct quantities, without changing the BOM's component list as described by the design engineer.

Comments Free-form text that lets engineers expand on details about the BOM.

Using the CAD integration functions of Document Control Manager, information in BOMs and product structures can be automatically updated based on drawing changes. Tools are used to translate drawing components into information that can be imported and placed in a BOM or a product structure, saving the time that would otherwise be necessary to rekey the information and update the BOM. We'll discuss CAD integration further in the Document Control Manager section.

Non–EC-Controlled vs. EC-Controlled Data

Placing change control on an item during development is critical. Early in the design stage, before an item has gone to production, engineers will often quickly define and change product structure data. This is the definition data that describes the item and how it's built. The data can be shared and used without the umbrella of a formal process. This is called non-EC control. **Non–EC-controlled data** is item information that has not been assigned to an EC. Once the item is developed to the point where it can be built or the design can be frozen, it can be placed under EC control to ensure that all the necessary people are involved in any decisions on design changes. EC-controlled data is linked to an item that is being changed under the EC process.

PSM allows all engineers to start work in a more flexible non–EC-controlled environment and then move to an EC-controlled environment as the design process progresses. When the design moves from a non-EC environment to an EC-controlled environment, the data does not have to be reentered into the system. This is important because it improves the engineers' productivity while reducing the opportunity for errors to be introduced.

When an item is under EC control, it is more secure; the EC has a defined security level that will only permit a certain security group to access it. This is in addition to security authorizations already established in the system. The EC is controlled by the engineering group responsible for completing the work.

ProductManager's PCM and PSM applications control the progression of non–EC-controlled data to EC-controlled data. When a non–EC-controlled item is associated with an EC as an affected item, the product definition data associated with the item is moved to EC-controlled status. Affected items are protected by the system in the same manner as the EC.

Multiple Views

ProductManager's PSM application allows users to define different representations, or views, of a given design structure in order to meet varying needs. Each view is a separate, changeable copy of an item. Normally, there is only one engineering view of an item, but when an EC is released to manufacturing, each manufacturing group or location can create its own view of the item. Views allow segregation and coordination of the design and multiple manufacturing versions of the same data. Views within PSM support configuration management and enable manufacturing engineers and users from other groups such as purchasing and testing to define their own configurations of a product structure. Each manufacturing location can create its own copy of the data within the parameters determined by ProductManager.

Using the EC, the system provides for status control, progression, and distribution to move design information from its initial concept to production. After manufacturing groups receive the design, they can incorporate their own views. PSM supports the creation and maintenance of multiple views of a BOM. For example, a design engineer looks at the parts that make up an item, while a manufacturing engineer creates a view that shows how the parts are used to build the item, and that may include the tools used to build it.

Document Control Manager

Engineers rely on accessible and up-to-date documentation to efficiently introduce product changes or design new products. ProductManager's Document Control Manager (DCM) application serves as a management and control vehicle for critical documents. The documentation can be almost anything,

Primary function: DCM controls the documentation associated with product information. Included in the control are drawings, specifications, and BOMs. The application works with a variety of editing tools and serves as a logical repository for documentation. It also enables CAD integration of information.

- Serves as a logical document repository.
- Protects documents while they are being changed or created.
- Maintains versions of documentation.
- Manages the association between documents and items, EC changes, and BOMs.
- Controls the release of documents.
- Uses check-in and checkout functions to prevent more than one user at a time from updating a document.
- Maintains relationships between documents and the tools used to work with them.
- Enables CAD integration of information.
- Maintains document comments.

Figure 2.25 An overview of Document Control Manager (DCM) functions.

including test specifications, part design, spreadsheets, test and analysis data, manuals, business processes, and instructions.

Electronic management of documentation is becoming more important as the use of workstations, personal computers, and electronic mail continues to grow. DCM processes provide more streamlined electronic counterparts to common information management tools such as paper-filing systems and vaults. DCM provides document administration capabilities including document registration, check-in and checkout features, security, versioning, and change control. Figure 2.25 summarizes the DCM application's capabilities.

DCM manages the associations between documents with different formats and between a document's format and the tool applications used for viewing, updating, and processing the document. DCM does not control or manage the actual design. That's left to the drawing program. Rather, DCM provides a comprehensive system for delivering documentation for designing, producing, and maintaining a product. DCM has an interface with other tools, either purchased or developed in-house, that generate documentation. Figure 2.26 shows the architecture of DCM and how DCM interacts with the other ProductManager applications and other design and editing tools.

Along with managing a document, DCM assigns statuses of the document's distribution and its stage of approval. The application also maintains a history of the document's approval. This is useful for businesses interested in obtaining or maintaining an ISO 9000 certification, which indicates compliance with the ISO 9000 international quality standard. Complete documentation of processes and products is a key requirement for certification.

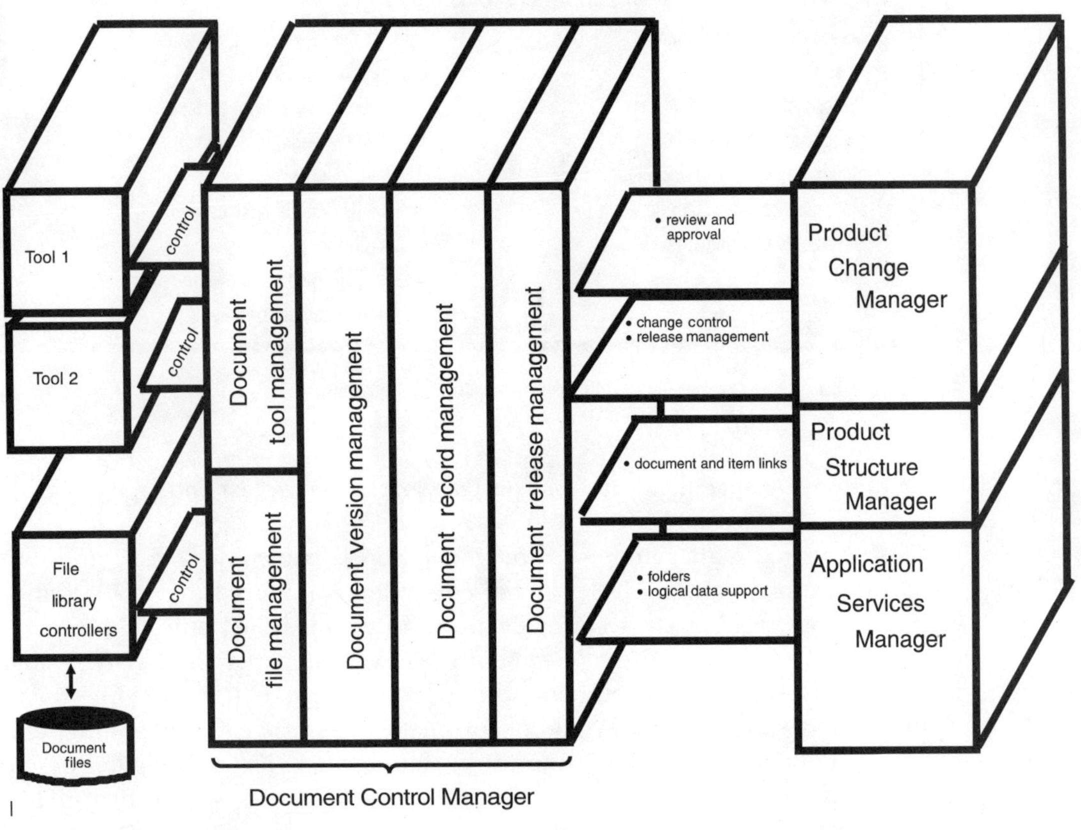

Figure 2.26 The architecture of DCM shows the relationships between the other ProductManager applications and DCM and how tools are used to work with documents files.

DCM is made up of the following management components:

Record

Version

File

Tool

Release

Record Management

The document **record management** component is the primary interface between users and documents. Conceptually, it serves as a vault that holds documents related to BOMs, REAs, ECs, and items. The "vault" is also used to store other documents such as descriptions of specific steps in a development process or a marketing description of a product. It is a distributed vault in that it can either store a document in DCM repositories or point to documents stored outside DCM in user-controlled locations. The record management function serves as a logical repository; any document the business uses can be stored in DCM. Figure 2.27 shows how a list of logical documents may appear in DCM. The panel shows each document's number, revision level, and owner. Users can select a document to work with from the panel.

DCM's record management is used to create, change, search, sort, and delete documents stored in DCM. Document record management is also used to provide a writer with sole access to a document during a document update. This check-in and checkout feature protects the document from being changed by more than one person at a time.

Using DCM, publication writers can maintain new documents for a product and control who accesses the documents by using security controls in the application. When an engineer is working with an EC and wants additional information about the documentation related to it, DCM is used to retrieve the information. This information can be attached to the EC.

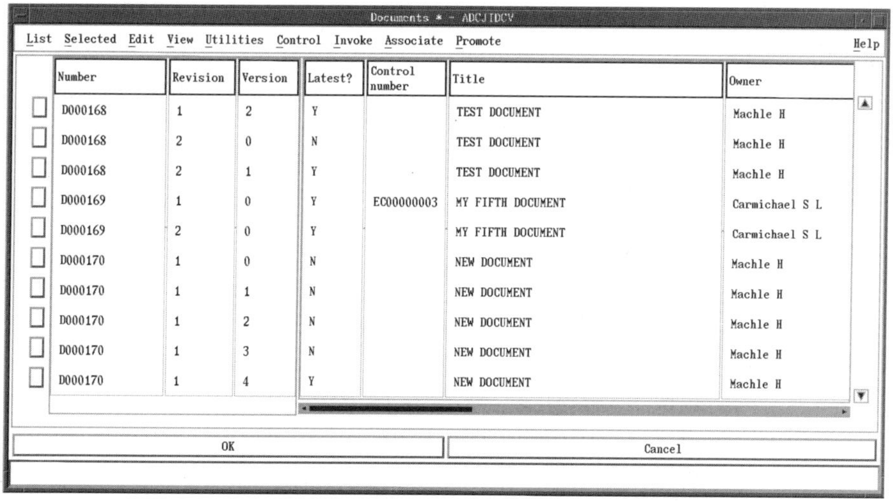

Documents * - ADCJIDCV

List Selected Edit View Utilities Control Invoke Associate Promote Help

Number	Revision	Version	Latest?	Control number	Title	Owner
D000168	1	2	Y		TEST DOCUMENT	Machle H
D000168	2	0	N		TEST DOCUMENT	Machle H
D000168	2	1	Y		TEST DOCUMENT	Machle H
D000169	1	0	Y	EC00000003	MY FIFTH DOCUMENT	Carmichael S L
D000169	2	0	Y		MY FIFTH DOCUMENT	Carmichael S L
D000170	1	0	N		NEW DOCUMENT	Machle H
D000170	1	1	N		NEW DOCUMENT	Machle H
D000170	1	2	N		NEW DOCUMENT	Machle H
D000170	1	3	N		NEW DOCUMENT	Machle H
D000170	1	4	Y		NEW DOCUMENT	Machle H

OK Cancel

Figure 2.27 A Document Control Manager list panel. Using this panel, engineers can open and work with documents associated with product changes.

Version Management

DCM's document **version management** tracks the many different versions of the documents that are typically created during the design phase. DCM also tracks the version of the software release used to create a document. Document version management works with document record management to track changes to each document. It maintains records of documentation revisions along with any comments that were made about the document. When a document is updated, the old version becomes part of the document history records. Users can place a document under change control to take advantage of Product Change Manager's EC-control mechanisms. Document versions can also be grouped into a revision level that serves as a major release, or configuration, of a document.

File Management

When a user wants to work with a document, document **file management** handles the logistics of retrieving and storing the document file. This part of the program receives the request, locates the document, and sends it to the appropriate workstation for presentation to the users. Document file management interacts with a series of file-library controllers, which actually store the documents and control their versions.

Tool Management

Document **tool management** is responsible for maintaining the relationships between documents and applications, or tools, that work with the documents. Most tool selections are identified during setup and are accessed automatically. However, a tool selection capability also exists in DCM. Using tool management, users can select a document and the tool they want to use with it. For example, if an engineer wants to work with a specification, Microsoft Word can be selected for editing the document. Or, if a drawing needs to be reworked, the engineer can select the drawing and CADAM for performing the rework. DCM also provides default **launch** capabilities for CATIA, Microsoft Excel, and other common tools. Launching a tool means being able to open another computer program while working in DCM or PSM.

Another part of document tool management's function is called computer-aided design (CAD) integration. Through CAD integration it's easier for engineers to work with such drawing tools as CATIA while using ProductManager. For example, if an engineer wants to place a CATIA drawing into a ProductManager folder, this can be done from the CATIA program, without opening ProductManager to create the folder. At the same time, engineers can also access ProductManager from other CAD tools such as AutoCAD, Professional CADAM, Pro/ENGINEER, and MICRO CADAM. The reverse is also true: Engineers can access a number of popular CAD engineering applications while working from the reference documents panel in PSM or from DCM.

Release Management

After a document or an item and its documentation are complete, the DCM document **release management** function comes into play. This function relates documents to specific product changes, and after the change is made, makes the document available to all users.

DCM components provide complete document control from the creation of a document to its release. Figure 2.28 shows each of the DCM functions and how they relate to each other.

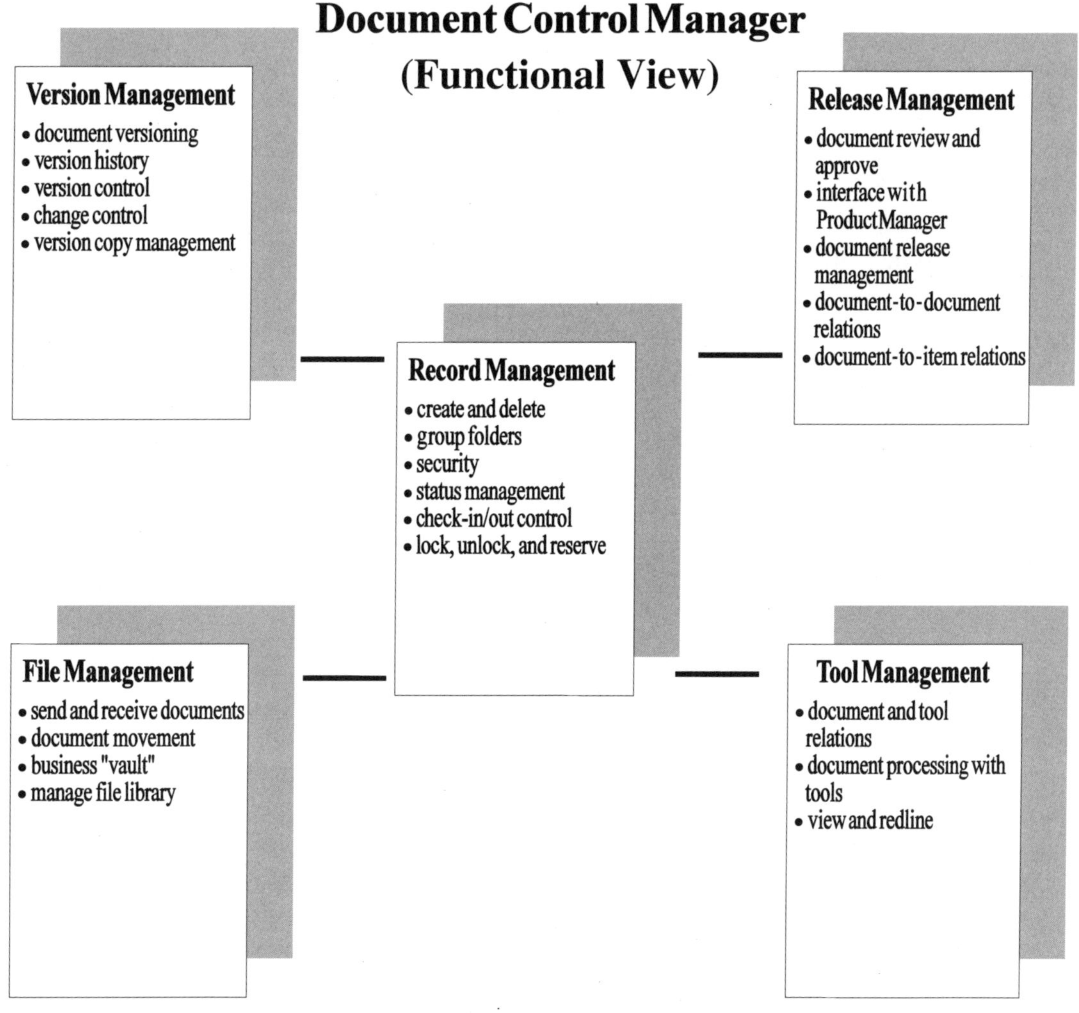

Figure 2.28 A functional view of Document Control Manager, showing which management component performs which function.

Let's see how a business might use DCM with other ProductManager applications through a simple example. When ABC Stove's metals engineer, Karen Sheppard, was assigned to study and recalculate the stress factors for a pin used to hold an oven latch in place, she had to change the spreadsheet on the pin, have it reviewed, and release the pin and documentation to the rest of the company. The current spreadsheet exists in the DCM vault and was created using Lotus 1-2-3. First, Karen reviews the existing design, and after determining that there are stress problems with the pin, she changes the document. Working from a PC, Karen searches the document database for the Lotus 1-2-3 document and checks the document out. The document comes from the file-library controller and is downloaded to her PC, where a Lotus 1-2-3 session is initiated. After the changes are made, she switches back to the DCM session and checks the document back in as a new version. The new version is assigned a "prerelease" status.

Karen now creates a folder, specifies a distribution list, copies the Lotus 1-2-3 document from the documentation list and puts it into the folder, and sends the folder for review. The recipients open the folder from their In-baskets. When they select the enclosed document, DCM retrieves the document from the vault, sends it on the LAN, launches Lotus 1-2-3, and displays the spreadsheet with the changes Karen made. After the recipients have approved the new design, Karen creates an EC, adds an EC review, attaches the Lotus 1-2-3 spreadsheet as an affected document, and sends the review. If changes are made to the spreadsheet during the EC review, she adds the changes and the document is checked in as a new version in DCM. DCM validates that the document version is ready for release, freezes the spreadsheet, and assigns it "new release" status. Now other users who are working on different portions of the project have access to the latest version of the spreadsheet.

A Look at ProductManager Reports

ProductManager comes with a variety of reports. You can view the reports online, place them in folders, print them, or send them to a file. To create reports, an engineer selects Report from the action bar at the top of an object detail panel and then selects the type of report desired. Each report provides a data-entry panel so engineers can specify what type of information they want included in the report.

There are five basic reports: **explosion, implosion, engineering change**, **net difference,** and **item-BOM retrieval.**

Explosion Shows the structure of items that make up a BOM. Indented explosions show the structural configuration of items defined in a BOM and the quantity of each item required at each level throughout the structure. Summarized explosion reports show the cumulative quantity of each item in the BOM, while the indented/summarized explosion report combines information from the indented and summarized reports.

Figure 2.29 shows an example of an indented explosion report as produced by ProductManager. The upper portion of the report shows the BOM header and the lower portion shows the BOM. Engineers can scroll down to the remaining items of the BOM. The Level column indicates the hierarchy of items that make up another item. Level 0 indicates the item that the BOM is for: "robot arm." The two level-1 items represent the left and right clamps for the arm, and the following sets of level-2 items represent the bracket, clamp, pin, nut, and bolt that make up each clamp. The report also shows the part number, the number of the EC that controls the item, the sequence number, how many items are used in each assembly, and the part type for each item.

Implosion Shows all BOMs and products that use an item. If an item is used as an optional or substitute component, this report shows where. Like the explosion report, there are also indented, summarized, and indented/summarized implosion reports. The selection criteria for implosion reports are based on the latest versions of BOMs that exist in either the engineering or manufacturing view.

Figure 2.30 shows an example of an indented implosion report as it appears in ProductManager. The figure shows the implosion for ITM00003, a clamp. The first row of data describes the clamp itself. The remaining rows describe the other items the clamp is used in, such as the right and left clamp of the robot arms. The sequence number indicates the operation sequence in manufacturing.

Engineering change report Shows the information associated with an engineering change, including the BOMs of all affected items. The EC report is created during the distribution process and copied when an EC is forwarded. It also contains review and deliverable information.

Net difference Shows the difference between two different BOMs, two versions of the same BOM, or two views of the same BOM.

Item-BOM retrieval Shows the information that has been defined for an item, its BOM, or both. You can select the way you want to see the report information. Figure 2.31 shows an example of an item-BOM retrieval report for a compact disc as it appears in ProductManager.

Applying ProductManager Concepts

Now that we have examined the four ProductManager applications, let's follow an example EC as it flows through a working ProductManager system. For this, we will revisit ABC Stove.

Indented Explosion **PAGE** 1
DATE 02/24/1994
TIME 02:17:31 PM

Part number.. ITM0000
Product status .... Active
Product description .... Robot arm
Change ID EC00001
Product type.. End product
Location ID...
Structure level .... All
Report format .... Indented list
Explosion method .... Change ID
Product type to include .... All
BOM type.. Engineering
Status.. Release
Effectivity type.....................................
Effectivity start.....................................
Effective date.......................................
Effectivity end product...............................

Level	Part Number	EC Number	Seq	Part Description	Quantity	Part Type
0	ITM00000	EC00001		Robot arm	1.000000	End Item
1	ITM00001	EC00001	1	Left clamp	1.000000	Assembly
2	ITM00002	EC00001	1	Bracket	2.000000	Detail
2	ITM00003	EC00001	1	Clamp	1.000000	Detail
2	ITM00004	EC00001	1	Pin	1.000000	Detail
2	ITM00005	EC00001	1	Nut	1.000000	Detail
2	ITM00009	EC00001	1	Bolt	1.000000	Detail
1	ITM00006	EC00001	1	Clamp base	1.000000	Detail
1	ITM00007	EC00001	1	Right clamp	1.000000	Assembly
2	ITM00003	EC00001	1	Clamp	1.000000	Detail
2	ITM00004	EC00001	1	Pin	1.000000	Detail
2	ITM00005	EC00001	1	Nut	1.000000	Detail
2	ITM00008	EC00001	1	Gear	2.000000	Detail
2	ITM00009	EC00001	1	Bolt	1.000000	Detail

Figure 2.29 An indented explosion report for a robot arm using ProductManager.

			Indented Implosion	PAGE 1
				DATE 02/24/1994
				TIME 02:19:49 PM

Part number.. ITM0003
Product status...................................... Active
Product description................................ Clamp
Change ID..
Product type.. Detail
Location ID..
Structure level...................................... All
Report format...................................... Indented list
Product type to include............................ All
BOM type... Engineering

Level	Part Number	Sequence Number	Product Description
0	ITM00003		Clamp
1	ITM00011	1	Right clamp
1	ITM00001	1	Left clamp
2	ITM00000	1	Robot arm
1	ITM00007	1	Right clamp
2	ITM00000	1	Robot arm
1	ITM00012	1	Left clamp

Figure 2.30 An indented implosion report for a part used in a robot arm using ProductManager.

The ABC Stove Company has manufacturing sites in two states. The company is headquartered in Pittsburgh along with its development and manufacturing organization, and builds a line of refrigerators and stoves. A component manufacturing facility is located in Macon, Georgia. The Macon facility builds motors, wiring assemblies, and heating elements. In addition to manufacturing, the Macon facility has several resident design engineers who constitute a remote development laboratory. They are responsible for overseeing the specifications for the components. The company has a single installation of ProductManager in Pittsburgh, with Macon tied in and defined as a remote location. They share a common ProductManager database. Figure 2.32 shows ABC Stove's ProductManager system layout.

The company deals with constant change as it responds to marketing needs for kitchen appliances. A requirement has been introduced to replace the standard clock on the stove with a more attractive digital clock that has more features. Design engineers in Pittsburgh go to work on the initial design. They want to look at existing items and subassemblies that can be modified to

	Item BOM Retrieval	PAGE	1
		DATE	02/03/1994
		TIME	01:49:07 PM
Item number	:ITM009		
Location ID	:		
Change ID	:EC0001		
BOM type	:Engineering		
Report format	Item data		
Retrieval method	Status		
Status	Pre-release		
Effectivity type			
Effectivity start			
Effective date			
Effectivity end item			
Item name	Compact disc		
Item description	Interactive		
Item unit of measure	Each		
Item type	End product		
Item status	Pre-release		
Location of control	Amsterdam		
Location of design	Utrecht		
Is item precious metal?	No		
Item planning	Normal planning		
Project ID	JR070955		
Item contract number	LL101463		

Figure 2.31 An item-BOM retrieval report for a compact disc using ProductManager.

meet the new requirement. ABC's refrigerator already uses a digital clock, and it's defined in the ProductManager database. ABC Stove engineers feel that by changing several components in the design, the refrigerator clock can be used in the stove.

A few years ago, engineers would have had to scramble to look for drawings that were either in libraries or stored on a floppy disk. They would create specifications and initial drawings, and package them for distribution throughout the Pittsburgh facility and for mailing to Macon. This resulted in expenses for copying, packaging, and mailing. But more importantly, it took time. After initial reviews, a meeting would be called and the resident engineer and a component engineer from Macon would fly to Pittsburgh to meet with process, manufacturing, and quality engineers to work first on initial

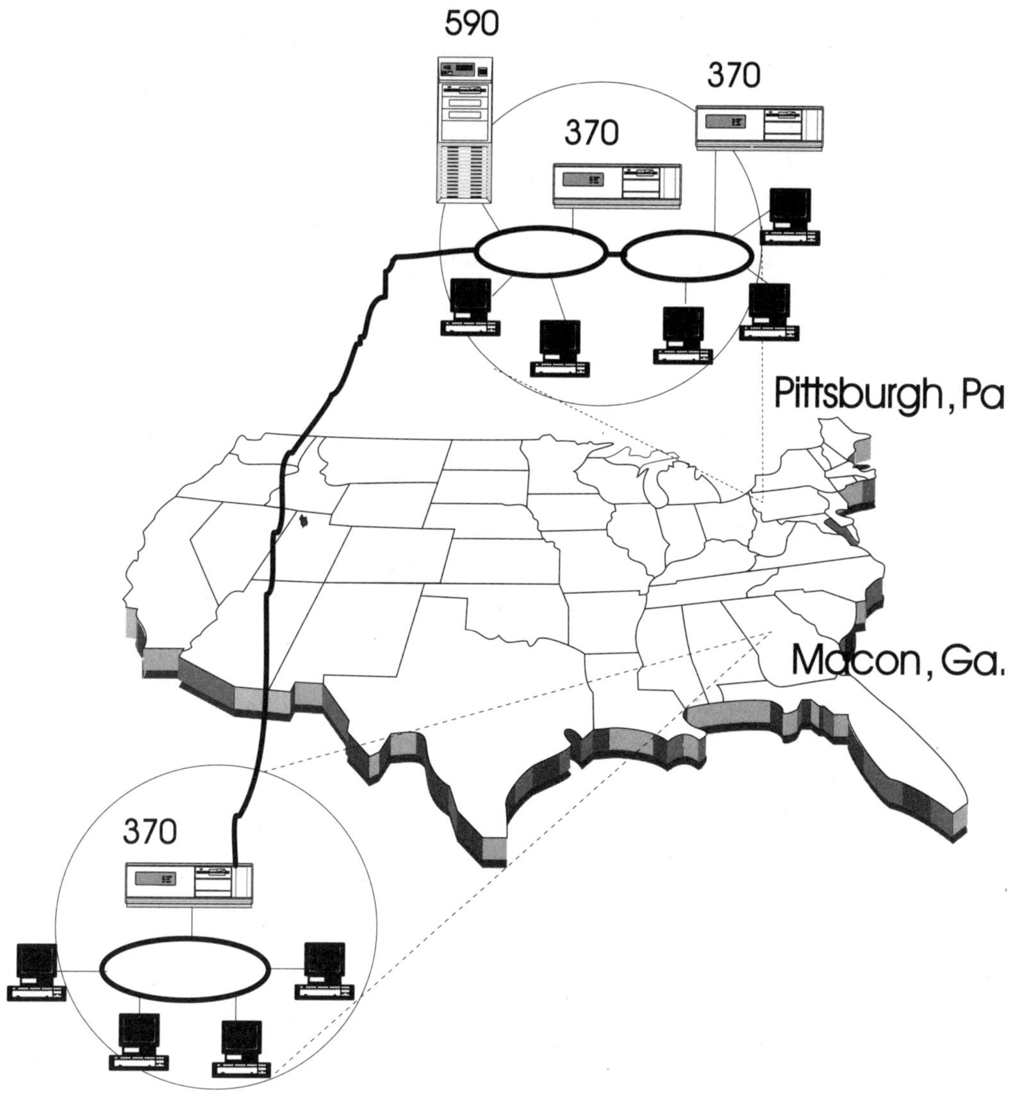

Figure 2.32 The ABC Stove Company ProductManager system for product development and change. All product information is stored on the Model 590 computer in Pittsburgh.

and then final designs. More flights and meetings were needed before an integrated design could be approved. This was a lot of time and effort to get the product changed, not to mention expense. They might even have looked at producing a new clock, because it would be faster than redesigning the existing one.

Things have changed at ABC Stove. With a product data management system like ProductManager, a design engineer in Pittsburgh creates an REA with the initial design that includes a CAD drawing, specifications, and comments. The REA is sent for review with the click of a mouse. A few minutes later, engineers in both Pittsburgh and Macon are scanning the package and sending out their own distributions. The design engineer in Pittsburgh has a materials specialist, who knows the capabilities of the metal, looking at the stress tolerances. The Macon manufacturing engineer already has the component team looking at the specifications. If there is a real time factor, those reviews can be sent back to Pittsburgh the same day. It would have taken at least a day just to get the package in the mail several years ago.

After an REA is created and approved, it's assigned to an engineer, who creates a formal engineering change. The process starts over, but this time ProductManager is going to become more involved in controlling information. In addition to using folders to take the EC through the process, the system is going to start managing the information associated with the stove and the clock and its items. The responsible engineer assigns Pittsburgh as the location of control and design. Later, a manufacturing engineer in Macon, where the clock will be assembled, will create a manufacturing view of the clock based on the original EC and its affected items.

The EC is assigned a "prerelease" status. Using a CAD drawing of the clock, the design engineer integrates the data from the drawing into the clock's BOM in ProductManager. In addition, affected items and **related ECs** are linked to the EC based on how they are going to be changed and what their statuses are. Deliverables are identified as well, including the design BOM with planned start and finish dates. Planned effectivities are included. As soon as the EC is created, the items that are going to be changed are protected and can only be worked on by the group assigned to the specified security level of the EC. Work continues on the BOM and items as the EC is finalized. For example, design engineers in Macon who belong to the security group have located a more heat resistant wiring scheme, defined product definition data for the new wires, added them as affected items in the EC, and created new BOM components. They have also learned that the paint on the clock face needs an additive to keep it from peeling when exposed to heat. Since the company mixes its own paints, the additive is included as a BOM component.

Next, the EC is sent for review in serial distribution. ProductManager will track the progression of the review based on due dates and each recipient or group of recipients. The review contains the approved REA, updated specifications for the clock, a CAD drawing of the clock, an indented BOM, a logical data reference object pointing to the new paint-mixing process, and comments concerning the heat tolerance levels of the clock's face plate. Included in the review are the manufacturing engineers in Macon, who disapprove the EC. They also have concerns about the face plate and want a replacement. This means the EC will have to be distributed again. This time, a purchased item, the clock face, is added to the attachments, and the EC is approved. Using ProductManager, the EC is tested for release readiness and then released to manufacturing. After the EC is released to manufacturing, design changes cannot be made to the affected items using the EC. Additional design changes will have to go through another EC.

The Pittsburgh and Macon manufacturing organizations can now make independent updates to their views of the data. At this point, affected items can be worked with independently of the design EC. The manufacturing sites are not changing the design, but are rather adding factors that affect how the clock is going to be built and installed. Pittsburgh has to alter the process for installing the clock. Instead of one clock assembly, it's decided that the clock will be stocked as two subassemblies in Pittsburgh. This changes how the clock is manufactured. The manufacturing BOM for Pittsburgh now shows that the two parts of the clock are assembled at a different step in the routing. Macon is a different story; their manufacturing engineers have to make changes to the clock itself. Their view shows how the clock will be built. Any additional planning or supplier data is added to the product definition data. When both manufacturing sites are satisfied with the design, the EC or affected items in the EC can be promoted to "effective" status, with an actual effectivity for each manufacturing site. The effectivity in the Pittsburgh manufacturing view is a product–unit effectivity based on the serial numbers on the stoves. Macon's effectivity is a date.

After an affected item or EC is in production, it can be closed. In the case of ABC Stove Company, the clock effectivity at the Macon facility took effect 25 days (the lead time required for the assembly and shipping) before the effectivity at the Pittsburgh site would take effect. Pittsburgh's effectivity was by serial number and was more flexible. When the new clock assembly arrived, it was installed in the stove after the old clock supply was depleted. With the new clock in the stove, a new configuration was established.

During the entire process, ProductManager managed and controlled the information. Sharing a database, design engineers were able to share and access current information, which helped keep the remote design organizations in touch. ProductManager was instrumental in introducing the items into production at the right time, assuring a well-planned, process-oriented release of work items. The use of ProductManager helped the company meet its goals for cost, time, and quality.

CHAPTER 3

Is ProductManager a Fit for Your Business?

Chapter 2 looked at the features of the ProductManager applications. This chapter will help you determine how well ProductManager fits your particular business needs. We will first cover some things you need to consider before choosing to implement any PDM system. Then we will guide you through a QuickFit analysis that measures your needs against the capabilities of ProductManager.

Do You Really Need a Product Data Management System?

Up to this point, we have discussed how a product data management (PDM) system can manage and control product data. If a business is involved in any level of design engineering or manufacturing, there's no doubt product data management plays some role. The question is, how effective and efficient are the current methods used to control product data? Many smaller manufacturing companies still use manual methods to control product data and must consider the inevitable step of converting to a computer-based PDM system as business volume and complexity grow. Larger companies may already have a computer-based PDM system installed. In either case, the management of a business must continually ask themselves if the current system is good enough.

You may already depend on computer systems to create product drawings, maintain inventory, and assemble your products. However, it may be that you need better control over your EC processes or you need to reduce the time it takes to put together a package for distribution. It may be time to consider using a PDM system to manage product release and change.

In a world of rapid technological change, businesses must constantly evaluate their operation in the light of revenue, cost, and quality goals, and make sure they employ all available means to remain competitive. Businesses increasingly have to decide whether to modify the current system or switch to another system that may be more efficient or provide more functions.

Among the questions you should be asking are "Will introducing a new system into my business pay off in the long run?" and "Can I integrate a new engineering management program into the PDM system I currently use to control my design and manufacturing process?" The discussions and tools provided in this chapter will help you answer these questions.

Many businesses use some form of concurrent engineering. A PDM system can be viewed as a tool that helps bring a business's development and manufacturing organizations into a single environment, working with the same data, drawings, schedules, and documentation. A PDM system removes organizational boundaries. If you work with product data, a computer program designed to manage that data will improve processes, reduce paperwork, and reduce cycle time.

ProductManager is one of the systems you should consider if you are ready to move into a new age of data management. As an open system, ProductManager can reside on several different UNIX-based platforms, which offers the user a choice of hardware vendors. These UNIX-based platforms can also support a wide range of applications in the design engineering and manufacturing environments, including CAD, CAM, communications, and process control.

ProductManager now runs on less expensive workstations while providing the same functions previously only available in the ProductManager mainframe environment. The functions of the mainframe version of ProductManager have been converted for use on workstations and offered as ProductManager/6000. The lower hardware cost makes workstations an attractive option for smaller businesses and, at the same time, provides a more flexible choice for medium and large businesses to control product data. For example, if your business is currently using a Sun, Hewlett Packard, or IBM system, you may be able to run ProductManager on the system along with your other applications, rather than having to purchase all new hardware. Furthermore, ProductManager uses the MOTIF user interface across all three environments. This reduces the time to train users on the new program.

The client/server architecture of ProductManager facilitates the distribution of information across multiple connected LANs. With its capability to exchange information between systems using an assortment of hardware and software, when ProductManager is coupled with drawing management programs it provides an integrated system for the creation, distribution, review, and approval of electronic work folders and their associated graphics, image, and document contents.

A PDM system may not be the answer for all businesses. If the current method of doing business works, with or without PDM, the expense and risk of change could outweigh the benefits of a new system. But at the same time, businesses are always looking for ways to streamline their operations, incorporate product changes on a more timely basis, and stay competitive. Implementing a PDM system is not risk free, and the right decision is not always obvious. However, you must also consider the risk associated with doing nothing while your competition may be aggressively streamlining its operation.

Examining Your Product Data Management Needs

After determining that a PDM system can address some of your business needs, the next step is to clearly define those needs. Whether your organization currently uses millions of dollars worth of computer systems or none at all, the way to begin determining your needs is to forget about computer hardware and software and look very closely at your business. All too often, businesses buy computer systems and then look for problems to solve.

Analyzing **critical success factors** for the business can be your starting point. These factors identify the areas of a business that are critical to its success: They must work without flaw if the business is to effectively carry out its strategy. For example, if a business incorporates a concurrent engineering strategy, critical success factors for the strategy may include a rapid method of communicating, an effective training program, a strong team organization, and shared information. The following steps are basic to determining your needs:

1. Establish a business strategy and set goals. What is the primary mission of the business? Start looking at information needs and flows to see if a computer system would improve the current flows.
2. Decide how to best reach the goals. Identify the critical success factors for each area that must function properly to meet overall business goals.
3. Communicate the goals to all employees.
4. Implement the strategy.

If you determine that a PDM system is right for your business, the next step is to work with the people who know your business needs and have ideas about what type of system will address those needs. Look for input from the design and manufacturing, systems and database administration, production planning, and quality areas of your business. Your customers are also valuable sources of information in determining your system needs and what it will take to meet those needs.

It's going to take some time, but don't take too long. If you spend months evaluating a PDM system, you may be losing ground to the competition. The amount of time you should take depends on whether you are implementing a new system or changing an existing one. It also depends on the size of the business. If a business has only six engineers who work with product data, it's not likely that it will take months or even weeks to evaluate your PDM needs. Larger businesses have more issues and people to deal with, and their evaluation may take longer. As we talk about evaluating PDM, keep in mind that the scope of all aspects we discuss can vary. In a small business, for example, a "steering committee" could consist of a single individual who understands the business's direction, rather than a group.

Here are a few suggestions for the kind of **evaluation teams** or individual expertise that you will need in order to decide on a PDM system and attain the goals a PDM system can help achieve:

Steering committee This group of people (or person in a smaller business) understands the vision and direction of the business. The steering committee can be a group of upper and middle managers or just the business owner. Based on recommendations from other evaluators, the steering committee will oversee and guide the integration of the business functions and processes to support the business's goals. It is vital to the success of changing the business that this group be in complete agreement on the new direction. They will weigh the technical risks of the system and establish the strategy for product data management in the business.

Design and manufacturing evaluation The design team will look at design needs and evaluate the different PDM systems under consideration in that light. They will work closely with the manufacturing team, which will evaluate the capabilities of the systems in release to manufacturing and control of part information. Both groups will determine whether a PDM system gives them the process control needed to meet data management objectives.

Systems evaluation This team is warranted by a business to evaluate the hardware and software that make up the PDM systems. They will look at performance, service, and maintenance factors; consider the best architecture for the business; and determine how the database will be set up. It is important for this team to recognize the future needs of the business and to help the steering committee in the development of a strategy.

Cost justification In smaller businesses, cost justification may rest on the shoulders of one person. In larger businesses, it may be assigned to a group of people with finance and statistical analysis skills. In either case, the cost of a PDM system and the hardware that supports it will be weighed against its benefits. Information from other individuals or teams will be evaluated by this group, taking cost factors into consideration.

The evaluation process will vary from business to business. Any organization that will be affected by a PDM system should be included in the evaluation process to help answer questions about the business strategy and data management needs. One of the first factors a company has to assess is the risk of altering the way it does business or introducing new processes into the business. There are indeed risks. If a business is profitable and produces a quality product on schedule, why would it want to change? The risks of introducing a new technology that doesn't help meet the business's goals could have a devastating effect on the bottom line. But taking the right risk can help a business become more efficient, more competitive, and more profitable.

The teams have to consider other factors in acquiring a PDM system. Instead of fully installing a companywide PDM system, a business can select a product or a single location to test the system, thereby lessening the risk and reducing the capital investment needed. Preparing the organization for change is another challenge. Complete management support is a must in managing change. Employees will be more supportive of the change if management shows support for it and demonstrates that it is in line with the business strategy. An education program will also help reduce resistance to change.

Help is available for evaluating business needs and PDM systems. Businesses can either use internal experts or work with consultants and hardware and software manufacturers to develop a business strategy and define the best approach to meet business goals. For a price, someone can always be found to help bring a computer system into your business. No matter which vendor you decide to work with, here are several questions you can ask about the vendor's capabilities and experience:

1. Does the vendor know your business, understand your goals, and feel comfortable with its ability to support the long- and short-term business strategy you have adopted?

   Miscommunication between you and the vendor can result in major problems in implementing the system. Make sure that everyone has the same goal for the long haul. Your vendor should understand your needs and the problems you face, along with how a data management system will help you meet your needs and solve your problems. The vendor should be willing to provide support and answer questions as long as you use the system. But remember that eventually you will have to stand on your own for day-to-day system operation. That means trained programmers, users, and administrators.

2. Is the vendor going to help you make objective technical decisions concerning hardware, software, and resources?

   The last thing you want is a PDM system that does not match your needs. An objective vendor will look across the various product lines and match them to your business needs, regardless of price (and their commissions). This means the vendor must know the systems and their capabilities and the various available options that are compatible with the product you purchase. Databases, bridges, and connectivity are concerns you both will share. An independent vendor can help you make system and component decisions.

3. How credible is the vendor and how much support will the vendor provide?

   Credibility is important in any business. Before you decide on a vendor, get some references and make some calls, but don't limit yourself to the references provided by the vendor. Credibility isn't only a question of ethics but includes experience, capability, and reputation. You also want to look for a vendor who will not only provide follow-up support such as training but will help you work through the problems associated with changing your business direction.

Resolve any concerns about the vendor you choose before you enter into an agreement. The previous questions should help you shorten your list of qualified vendors who can help you work through data management problems.

A final factor in examining your PDM needs is the extent of the changes you are going to make. If you are going from a total reliance on paper records to a completely automated system, you should take the time to look at all the processes in your business to see which ones can be eliminated or improved. After an automated system is in place, it will be more difficult to make these changes.

One of the buzz words in business today is "reengineering." This concept is advocated by Dr. Michael Hammer, the founder of the reengineering movement. He and James Champy authored *Reengineering the Corporation,* published by HarperCollins. The book describes the principles of reengineering a business. The authors point out that reengineering is the fundamental rethinking and radical redesign of business processes to achieve dramatic improvements in critical measures of performance, such as cost, quality, service, and speed. The ideas and suggestions in *Reengineering the Corporation* may help broaden your perspective on making process changes.

Let's take a look at some of the costs and benefits your evaluation teams will be looking at.

Costs Associated with a Product Data Management System

A business must not make a significant investment in a PDM system without understanding the costs associated with the hardware and software. Decisions have to be based on the long-term costs of implementing and maintaining the hardware and software over a period of years. An investment in a PDM system is expensive, and that's why you must be sure that it will fit your business strategy.

Three factors in determining how much a manufacturing company can afford to pay for a PDM system, or any computer-based system, are profit, maturity, and product. Profit accounts for what a business can afford to invest in equipment that can result in growth of the company. We're talking about net profit and available capital for investment in machining equipment or product data management hardware and software. If a business's profit margin is narrow, even more care should be taken in how capital investments are made.

The maturity of a business is also a factor in the risk and investment it can afford. A company that is new (5 to 10 years old) may not be able to take the risk of a major investment to improve operations, whereas a more mature company, one that needs a boost in productivity and innovation to go to the next stage of growth, may view the capital investment as an opportunity for rejuvenation. The mature company most likely has the financial stability or backing to take such a step. The last factor, and certainly not the least, is the kind of product the business produces and how it is produced. Some businesses make custom products one at a time, some mass-produce their products. The importance of this factor is how it affects the return on investment. How long will it take for a business to recover the capital investment in a tool that increases efficiency? If a product data management system improves productivity by 40 percent, how long will it take to recover the cost of the system and its ongoing maintenance costs?

Now let's look at the following costs that should be considered before making a PDM investment:

Hardware

Software

Technical support

Facilities

Education and training

Communications lines

Hardware

The computer hardware needed to run the PDM software costs money. If you already have a UNIX-based computer system, look at your current hardware and compare it with the hardware needed to run the PDM software. If they match, you don't have to purchase all new computer hardware. If you aren't that fortunate, however, hardware vendors are eager to construct a system installation package using their products. You will have to determine your performance requirements and make sure the hardware you purchase can provide that performance. Don't overlook the costs associated with the installation, set-up, and networking connections for your system.

Should you purchase a maintenance agreement for the hardware you purchase? No matter how you look at it, it's a gamble. The company you purchase the hardware from is betting that the system won't fail, and when you purchase the agreement, you are betting that it will fail. To keep the computer system performing at its peak, a maintenance agreement is a good idea. However, if your organization has people qualified to maintain the system, replace components, or upgrade the system, you can bypass this expense. The upside of a maintenance agreement is that you don't pay for service calls, replacement parts, or labor. Consult the sales or service representative of the company you choose to work with about any questions you might have regarding maintenance contracts.

Another option is to lease hardware. If you lease the equipment, you won't have to worry about a maintenance contract. Again, a sales representative of the company from which you lease the equipment can provide you with prices and terms.

Software

You must consider the PDM software you will purchase in conjunction with the hardware. The software has to be compatible with the hardware, and normally requires that you purchase other prerequisite software. Be sure to include these prerequisite software costs when comparing the costs of PDM systems.

When you purchase a ProductManager application, you are granted a 60-day unconditional money-back guarantee. This is a trial period during which you can use the software and determine whether or not it functionally meets your needs. If, during the test period, you find that ProductManager is not what you need, you can return it for a full refund.

Included with the ProductManager purchase price is technical support for as long as you use the program, or until IBM announces withdrawal of support for the program.

The ProductManager software is licensed on a **usage-level** basis. This means your purchase price is based on the maximum number of users who are going to use ProductManager at any given time. If you purchase a license for 20 users, only 20 people can be signed on at the same time. (You can have more than 20 users if they are not all signed on to ProductManager *at the same time*.) The ProductManager pricing structure uses a base price for each application and then adds a per-user charge for each application. In addition, there is an annual support fee for each application, which also includes a base price and a per-user charge.

Businesses that purchase ProductManager receive enhancements and future releases of the same version of the product at no additional charge. Keep in mind that significant new functions for the product may be offered as a product feature or in a new version of the software, in which case there would be an additional charge for the feature. You must purchase each ProductManager application based on the number of people using it. If additional users are added later, an upgrade fee is charged to reflect the new maximum number of simultaneous users. A point to consider about usage-level charges is how many users will be working on a PDM product at the same time. IBM user reviews indicate that as few as one of every seven potential users will be logged on at one time. According to these reviews, if a business has 200 employees that use a PDM system, it may only have to purchase software for 30 users.

A final factor--and this applies to the hardware as well--is the learning curve for the new system. Even after training, it is going to take a while for users to become efficient on the system, which will affect productivity.

Technical Support

Support for a software product spans a broad spectrum. It goes from basic technical support to full-range support services that may include **turnkey** solutions. Turnkey solutions are solutions that are set up specifically for a particular business, and may include implementation, modification, migration, education, and installation support. Naturally, this all comes at a price. Again, you have to decide what kinds of support you need. If your business already has the administrative and programming skills to support the software, you could save some support costs.

ProductManager software is backed by a service support center. The support center is staffed by people who not only are knowledgeable about the ProductManager system, but who also helped develop it. These representatives are available to assist you with any questions or problems you may have regarding the software. Technical support for ProductManager users is available by calling IBM-Assist. The IBM-Assist line connects you with ProductManager service representatives. Your call should be returned in less than an hour; the average response time is around 30 minutes. This free service covers product installation and use and is available from 8:30 A.M. to 6 P.M., Eastern Standard Time, Monday through Friday, for licensed ProductManager users. ProductManager Technical Services is another option for ProductManager users, but fees are charged for this 24-hours-a-day, seven-days-a-week service.

If you want to take technical support a step further, you can purchase access to IBM's **Remote Technical Assistance Information Network (RETAIN)**. This product support system provides online access to **ServiceLink** and **SupportLink**. ServiceLink lets you communicate with service representatives online to report problems to IBM, and SupportLink is a database that may contain the answer to a problem you are experiencing. By performing searches on keywords, you can get answers to technical questions about ProductManager. The online support also provides information about product updates.

Facilities

Along with deciding on locations for workstations and printers, you also have to determine the physical setup of the computer system. Some of your hardware may require **raised-floor environments**. In a raised-floor environment, the computing equipment sits on a floor installed 12 to 18 inches above the original floor. The raised floor permits air circulation beneath hardware such as mainframe computers to keep it cooler. Workstations can be operated at normal room temperature and thus don't need to be set on a raised floor. If you have a number of workstations in a small work area, though, you need to provide extra air flow to keep the area cool and comfortable for users.

Education and Training

Be sure not to overlook the costs of education and training. This is an area that warrants a larger investment than many businesses choose to make. Proper education can often make the difference between success and failure when installing any new system. Your users, administrators, and programmers need to become familiar with the hardware and software. If you don't have a maintenance contract on the hardware, you will probably also need to train someone to assist with the equipment and make minor repairs.

ProductManager comes with documentation to support system and database operations. In addition, the ProductManager Support Center will help get you started. Further educational opportunities are also available and important. Some alternatives are discussed later in this chapter.

Unless your business has object-oriented–knowledgeable programmers, you are going to have to provide education to help your programmers understand the class structures so that they can make any desired changes to the ProductManager source code. Simple tailoring is easily accomplished and does not require a great deal of programming skill. However, if programmers are going to modify the ProductManager programs by changing and recompiling source code, they need to know the basics of object-oriented technology.

IBM also holds **Teach the Teacher (T-3)** classes covering ProductManager. T-3 classes are primarily internal IBM classes, but ProductManager users and potential users are invited, free of charge, to these three-day sessions to learn first-hand about the product.

Communications Lines

Communications lines are what computers use to exchange information, whether it is across the room or overseas. Your expense here is going to be in cabling for LANs and cabling from the main computer to user terminals. Some businesses will already have the necessary cabling installed while others will be starting from scratch. The amount and type of cabling needed depends on the hardware setup you have. Also, depending on the hardware configuration, you may need a **bridge** to communicate between two LAN systems. A bridge is a device that allows the computers on two or more independent LANs to communicate with one another.

Another expense for businesses with operations in different locations is the telephone line cost of communicating. **Gateways** exist that allow the users on a LAN to share access to long-distance communications lines, which often helps reduce costs associated with communications. Communications line costs should be considered when sizing up the overall cost of implementing any computer-based system.

Benefits of a Product Data Management System

The only reason a business should install any new system is that it in some way will improve the profitability of the business. PDM systems are no exception. Now that we have explored some of the costs associated with implementing a PDM system, let's look at the potential benefits. In the past, design laboratories and manufacturing groups seemed to compete with each other instead of working together to design and produce a product. We now realize that there's no room for such internal competition when the external competition is so great. This is an area where concurrent engineering has proven its merit. Instead of designing a product and "throwing it over the wall," engineering groups are working closely with each other and with manufacturing to make sure a product is suited for production as designed.

Today there are approximately forty companies producing PDM systems--a number that is growing as more and more companies look for ways to efficiently handle information requirements. A PDM system helps eliminate organizational barriers by bringing design, test, process, production, manufacturing, facilities, and quality engineers into the first phase of product development. Online reviews and approvals that can reduce administrative and logistical nightmares between these groups make a PDM system a valuable investment.

We are going to discuss some of the benefits that should be considered before deciding whether or not a PDM system is right for your business. In addition, we will look at some dollar amounts for savings, based on user evaluations and actual savings. As we look at potential savings, we will use numbers that are realistically attainable, not numbers that stretch the limits of a PDM system. Keep in mind that different assumptions about the business environment being examined can produce a wide range of savings projections. Using basic savings figures from a variety of studies of ProductManager users and within IBM, we'll show you how ABC Stove was able to reduce its engineering cost by nearly 20 percent over a 5-year period with a PDM system.

Another important variable in the savings projection is the method a business currently uses to manage product data. If you're working in a manual paper-based PDM environment where ECs and REAs are created and approved in a hard-copy format, the savings with a PDM system will be greater than if your business already has a significant amount of automation in the release process.

The bottom line for our discussion is that if applied correctly, a PDM system will help reduce the cost of doing business. Now let's look at some potential benefits of implementing a PDM system: Reduced cycle time, increased productivity, and improved quality.

Reduced Cycle Time

The time it takes to design, release, and manufacture a new or modified product is called **cycle time**. Cycle times are important to businesses because the faster your business can react to changing customer requirements with new or modified products, the more competitive you will be and the more customers you will attract. When the product hits the market at the right time, there is a potential for greater sales. Reducing the time it takes to introduce and implement an engineering change from six weeks to a week or less is a challenging but realistic goal with a PDM system, especially if a business is currently using manual, paper-based methods of doing business. While not all PDM users see such a big change, it's not uncommon for a PDM business to drastically reduce the cycle time.

Let's again turn to the ABC Stove Company and apply data derived from industry studies of actual companies to illustrate how ProductManager can help reduce their cycle time. ABC Stove went from a manual, paper-based environment straight to a PDM system. Before purchasing ProductManager, the business had managed to get its average review cycle time from 45 days down to 36 days. But an average of 36 days seemed to be the bottom line. They were stalled there. Here are some of the roadblocks that prevented ABC Stove from further reducing the review cycle time:

Remote reviews Most of the time, review packages were mailed back and forth between Macon and Pittsburgh. Priority reviews were sometimes sent overnight, but did not always get to their destination the next day. Going both ways, the reproduction, mailing, and internal distribution of the packages took twelve days in the review process.

Rerouting of reviews when the primary reviewer is not available The primary reviewer was often not available. This meant someone had to identify an alternate reviewer and deliver the package, or wait until the reviewer returned. Averaging it out, two days were lost here.

Meetings for signing off on reviews Sign-offs required arrangements for meetings, calendar coordination, and a flight to Pittsburgh or a telephone conference followed by an overnight package to Pittsburgh. In either case, it added an average of five days to the cycle time of each review package.

Manual receipt and release of review numbers Assignment of numbers to REAs and ECs was handled by administrators. It took two days at each end of the cycle in Pittsburgh and Macon to receive the request, assign the number, and then release the review, resulting in six extra days in the cycle.

Disbursement of issue parts at remote manufacturing locations **Issue parts** are parts that must be removed from stock locations and disbursed to manufacturing. This activity occurred at the end of the review process and added another three days to the cycle time. By including the part on the EC, this step no longer adds cycle time but is performed before the rest of the cycle ends.

When ABC Stove purchased ProductManager, it lowered the average cycle time for review packages from 36 days to eight days. Depending on the level of automation, some businesses may not realize a 28-day reduction in cycle time using ProductManager, but others could realize an even greater reduction. A study conducted by an internal IBM group that switched to ProductManager after previously using a fair degree of automation in the release process indicated that seven days could be trimmed off a 12-day cycle time using a ProductManager system.

Figure 3.1 indicates the processes in which cycle time can typically be reduced by implementing ProductManager. These reduction figures are based on studies of multiple ProductManager users. The left column shows the savings

Reduced Cycle Time for Reviews				
Paper Process Savings	Total Cycle Time 36 days		Total Cycle Time 12 days	Automated Process Savings
5 days	↓	Receipt and release of numbers	↓	2 days
2 days		Rerouting of reviews		1 day
12 days		Remote reviews		2 days
6 days		Online sign-offs		1.5 days
3 days		Issue parts		0.5 day
Total Savings: 28 days	8 days		5 days	Total Savings: 7 days

Figure 3.1 ProductManager will reduce cycle times. The amount of time depends on the business environment. The figure shows the savings for a paper-based environment and for a more automated environment.

achieved when moving from manual, paper-based methods to ProductManager. The right column shows the more conservative savings that can be expected when moving to ProductManager from a partially automated release process.

Last year, ABC Stove spent $12 million, 4 percent of its $300 million revenue, on research and engineering. Before they installed ProductManager, the average cost of an EC was $10,800 and the cost of an REA was $6900. These figures are based on averaging the cost of engineering activities over the number of changes introduced, and will vary from business to business. Our automated ProductManager user's study determined that the reduced cycle time lowered the cost of keeping the review in the system by 3 percent for each day cut from the cycle time. If ABC Stove applied the same savings rate to just their 750 ECs, at 3 percent per day they would save nearly $4.6 million annually. Add in their REA reviews and they would save half of their annual budget. ABC Stove, converting from a paper-based system, is drastically reducing the days for review time. A 3 percent per day savings rate is optimistic. Let's look at the conservative side. If ABC Stove saved only 0.002 percent of the cost for each review for each day that was cut from the review cycle time, the company could save $453,600 for ECs and $216,000 for REAs. These savings are above and beyond normal productivity and administrative savings. The savings come from reducing **work in process**. With longer cycle times, the system is flooded with paperwork, and not everything in the system is being worked on. Controlling work in process adds efficiency to the review cycle. By reducing the cycle time, there is more potential for the same number of staff to create and resolve more ECs and REAs, or to reduce the number of staff and still maintain the current level of changes.

We have focused on the review process, but a PDM system also reduces the time it takes for the change to go through the manufacturing phase. In a concurrent engineering environment, manufacturing engineers are already looking at material requirements, sourcing parts, and working up purchase orders before the product is accepted into manufacturing. In addition, time is trimmed from the manufacturing cycle because item data is loaded during the review cycle. The same amount of work must be done, but groups can work concurrently to shorten the overall cycle time. ABC Stove removed 7 days from the manufacturing engineers' cycle time, thereby saving them another $167,400.

An automated system can turn what a major manufacturer spends on excessive work in process into savings that will cover the cost of the hardware and software that will perform these tasks for them. You might say it's like buying time. Companies are doing business in an age where reduced cycle times mean getting a product to the market when the consumer is ready to buy it. If they lose time in the logistics of getting a change incorporated, they're very likely to lose sales by not making the enhanced product available at the right time. Using PDM systems, cycle times are being reduced to meet these sales opportunities. Figure 3.2 shows how reduced cycle time can reduce scrap and rework costs and increase sales. As the cycle time is reduced, resulting

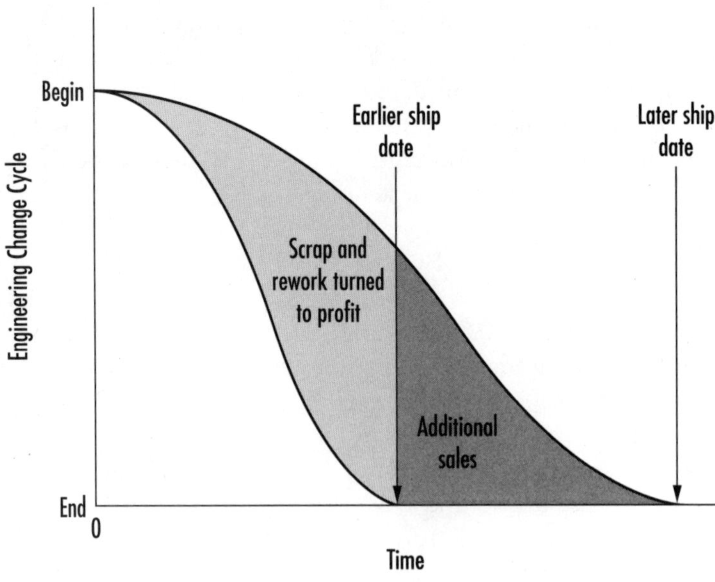

Figure 3.2 When time is cut from the development cycle, it also removes the scrap and rework associated with longer development times. This increases the profit margin for a product and the earlier ship date can result in additional sales.

in improved quality and reviews, the amount of rework and scrap is reduced. Less scrap and rework means that a business is going to realize a higher profit.

Besides saving on scrap and rework, the cycle time reduction also adds profit to the business through additional sales opportunities. Let's look at the potential loss to a business when the cycle time exceeds the time planned to introduce a new product. In many manufacturing environments, an old product is phased out as a new product is phased in. If a business plans to release a new product during the fourth quarter, the release process has to be fine-tuned to coordinate phasing out the old product and phasing in the new one. Suppose that in late September a problem pops up that will cause a three-week delay in getting the new product online. In the meantime, procurement has already stopped ordering parts for the old product, leaving the business with a product shortage during the changeover. With this shortage, the business loses significant revenue opportunity because it's not putting any product into the market. With a PDM system, there's less likelihood of a major breakdown in a development plan.

Figure 3.3 illustrates how sales may dip when a plan doesn't come together. The product sales line represents $50 million in annual sales. The dip in the product sales line shows the lost revenue caused by the lack of a product to sell due to the three-week lag in production. The box in the middle of the

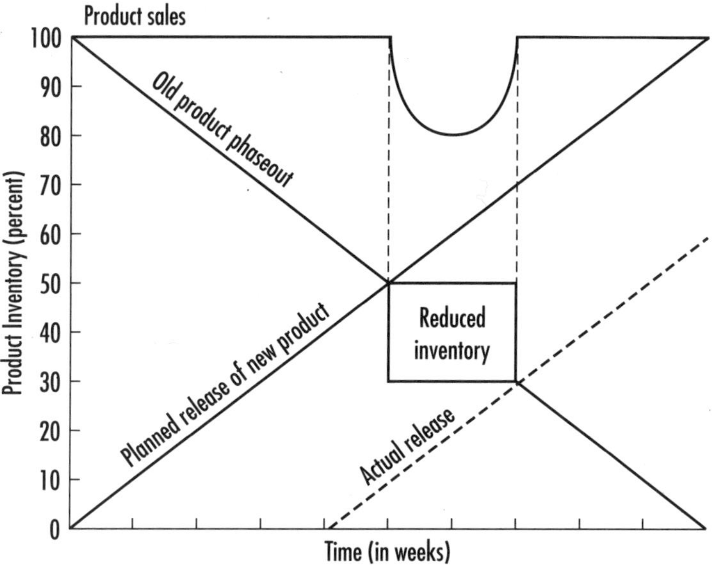

Figure 3.3 A PDM solution can reduce the likelihood of missing planned release dates. If a release date is missed, it can result in a reduction of inventory and lost sales.

figure shows an average of 20 percent reduction in inventory between the old product phaseout and the new product phase-in. This business lost $580,000 in revenue, which cannot be recovered, because of problems in the release process. By using a PDM system, such release problems can be avoided and releases can be planned for earlier dates, helping a company to meet windows of sales opportunities.

Increased Productivity

Getting more for your money is a goal for all businesses. We have seen how ABC Stove reduced its cycle time using ProductManager, which also offers potential productivity benefits. When companies are involved in a variety of changes across several lines of products, efficient use of resources is critical. So how did ABC Stove improve productivity with ProductManager? Let's see how by applying information about actual mailing, administrative, and record-keeping activities to ABC Stove. The information was gathered from potential and real ProductManager users and through IBM internal studies.

First, ABC was able to eliminate a number of record-keeping activities. Before ProductManager, ABC had 15 people at Pittsburgh and Macon who were dedicated solely to entering product item information into a database. This activity was performed for all product lines and included maintaining 100,000 items, creating 2400 new items and their associated numbers each year, and inputting miscellaneous information involved in manufacturing the products. Now, instead of passing their information on to administrators for inputting, engineers can work directly with the ProductManager system and let it manage and control the information. They can also interact with ProductManager through CAD integration. For example, they can place a specification on an EC review without having to exit their CAD tool and initiate a ProductManager session. Time is saved from shuffling the information on paper between the administrators and engineers. An engineer can now obtain a drawing or assign an EC number without going through an administrative staff person. The engineer also has more control over the entry of data into the system, and there's one less chance for transposition errors. Along with the factors described in reducing their cycle time, which also adds to productivity, ABC Stove has significantly improved records management productivity with ProductManager.

The second improvement in productivity hinged on the fact that 75 percent of the ECs resulted from REAs. REAs are not as labor intensive as ECs, but they still required people to track and coordinate. Letting ProductManager handle REAs has increased productivity at ABC in this area, too.

Third, productivity was improved when physical handling of reviews and item information by support personnel including secretaries, mail room personnel, and assistants was eliminated. Now their jobs are performed by the

PDM system, which electronically updates, delivers, and monitors approvals of review packages. The physical handling of information is time consuming, but administrative support personnel at ABC no longer have to track down EC package reviewers to give them a hard copy of the EC or retrieve one from them.

And last, the time for reproducing REA and EC packages was eliminated. ABC had two people at the Pittsburgh location whose only job was to copy, mail, and distribute review packages, and several administrators in Macon shared the reproduction and distribution responsibilities. When you consider their **burden rates**, the time they spent making copies and the cost of copiers and materials, the total cost of copying and distribution was significant. A burden rate is the cost of maintaining an employee, including salary, benefits, and overhead items such as office space. The average burden rate for each administrator was $60,000.

Based on these numbers, Figure 3.4 shows some of the productivity savings enjoyed by ABC Stove. While the figures are hypothetical, they are based on real user studies conducted by IBM between 1991 and 1993 for design and manufacturing areas.

Having a PDM system do the work of managing information and tracking changes enhances the efficiency of your staff and systems.

Improved Quality in Design and Processing

The term "off-spec" refers to a component that does not meet design specifications, and is therefore flawed. The more off-specs you have with a product,

Annual Productivity Savings for ABC Stove Company

Reduction in records entry and tracking in development and manufacturing	11 people ×$60,000	$660,000
Reduced item maintenance cost	4 people ×$60,000	$240,000
Reduced handling and reproduction	3 people ×$60,000 + $150,000 for mailing, copy equipment, and materials	$330,000
TOTAL		**$1,230,000**

Figure 3.4 Data entry, reproduction, and item maintenance expenses had a significant impact on ABC Stove's engineering budget. The figure summarizes annual savings the hypothetical business realized by using ProductManager.

the more problems there were with the original design. For example, when the metal into which a screw is designed to be inserted isn't strong enough to withstand the pressures produced by the screw, there is a problem. Using ProductManager and concurrent engineering practices, the stress engineer can flag such a problem before it goes to the next stage of development. Concurrent engineering gives the engineer the opportunity to flag the request at an early stage in development, and ProductManager provides the tool for the stress engineer to notify the other organizations of the problem in a timely fashion. In addition, the engineer's idea for fixing the problem can be submitted at the same time. Without a PDM system such as ProductManager, communication flows more slowly and can allow gaps of time where efforts are wasted on a design that's not going to work. ProductManager adds quality to the design by avoiding such problems. When you consider the cost of redesigning an item when it's in the final design stage or in manufacturing, you see that ProductManager can effect significant savings of time and money. ProductManager provides immediate access to initial or integrated designs and manages the exchange of information between engineering groups, greatly improving communication and eliminating the need for redesigns.

Design programs are becoming more sophisticated. Using these programs, after design engineers have designed a part, they can perform many of the necessary tests, such as stress tests, before the design even goes out for review. These tools are driving down the costs of design. Just as money can be saved through reducing scrap, money can be saved by completing designs that make a product more easily manufacturable. This reduces the need for future rework and ultimately increases the productivity of manufacturing. ProductManager provides a framework for managing drawings by helping an engineer locate, review, and change drawings. With controlled access, unauthorized use of drawings is prevented, saving rework time that would be necessary to fix unauthorized changes. Drawings can be retrieved from a remote database, changed, and inserted in a review package. Design rework may not be completely eliminated, but the number of times the design is kicked back and forth between manufacturing and development is reduced. In addition, designing for manufacturability increases productivity at the end of the cycle and reduces the need for redesign. By having complete control of design information and a management tool that provides for the efficient communication of design changes, manufacturing goals are more easily met. Less change, earlier visibility, and better tracking of changes contribute to higher and more consistent quality in the product.

ProductManager supports the exchange of information created from drawing tools such as CATIA for workstations, AutoCAD, Pro/ENGINEER, MICRO CADAM, and Professional CADAM. This facilitates efficient design review—an important quality function—from the initial design phase to the final design phase. A systematic approach to creating a product design like the approach ProductManager supports goes farther than just designing for manufacturability. It adds quality to the product by improving its reliability. Reliability of a product is the probability that the product will perform satisfactorily in its functions for a specified period of time. The quality of a design helps ensure that the standards are met. This reduces maintenance and service costs for the business and its customers.

Along with the quality that reviews add to a product, other quality issues exist that can be handled by ProductManager. Here are some of the quality issues the ABC Stove Company resolved by employing ProductManager:

Incorrect data This was created quite often when administrators transposed written instructions or item data from engineers while entering it in the database. The most frequent mistakes were in item statuses and numbers. Also, when processes were accidentally bypassed, errors were introduced that eventually caused problems in the development cycle. With ProductManager, engineers enter their own item statuses and their numbers are automatically assigned, reducing the opportunity to introduce errors. Under ABC's old system, assuming a data entry error rate of 2 percent for the 750 ECs and 560 REAs created annually, 15 ECs and 11 REAs resulted in extra work for engineers and administrators because of typographical errors or miscommunication. These types of mistakes resulted in 33 percent more effort in rework and expediting for the 15 ECs and 11 REAs, costing ABC Stove nearly $80,000 a year in problem-solving efforts. These savings potentials are pointed out in a 1992 IBM study of 32 design laboratories.

Different types of data Before installing ProductManager, ABC Stove used two systems for creating and tracking data. One was for mechanical item data on paper and another for electronic item data on computers. There was a lot of room for mistakes when these two sets of data were brought together in a complete product design. Occasionally, they didn't match. Fortunately for the stove company, the data problem only occurred in just over 1 percent of their ECs and REAs. But the damage was still significant because engineers had to rework data and sometimes redesign parts: The cost of their efforts was almost $60,000. Using ProductManager, the data is integrated on one system. Development and manufacturing personnel spend less time trying to resolve conflicts in data, again reducing the average cost for making changes to products.

Inaccuracies of release dates Either through oversight or lack of follow-up, ABC Stove had found that many date effectivities were inaccurate. This caused manufacturing problems as well as production control problems. Production control was not always aware of effectivities and there were often overstocks of old parts made obsolete by new ECs. ProductManager provided a sophisticated tracking system for effectivity that helped ABC Stove's production control organization improve floor space for its parts by nearly 15 percent. This saved ABC Stove $95,000 in handling and inventory costs. Again, the savings potential of PDM systems was pointed out in the 1992 IBM study of 32 design laboratories, and verified by the author in discussions with engineers about problems arising from capacity requirements.

Violation of EC release processes Controlling EC releases is another important step in meeting quality goals. Control ensures that the correct procedures are followed. ABC Stove documents correct release processes and distributes this documentation to all employees. Before ProductManager was installed, however, the manual distribution of an EC did not always get to the right people in a timely manner. Furthermore, manufacturing would sometimes receive incomplete EC folders missing a BOM or a drawing. ABC Stove now uses ProductManager to help identify the people who should receive each EC and then to distribute the EC electronically. ProductManager also makes sure everyone gets the same complete EC package, with all items at their most current revision level. Thus ProductManager adds quality to the design process by bringing control to EC distribution.

To put the importance of release processes into perspective for ABC Stove, let's apply actual process information gathered from ProductManager users to the 750 engineering changes ABC makes in a year. Before installing ProductManager, approximately 20 percent of those changes dealt with quality problems. Of these 150 quality-related ECs, more than 5 percent resulted from the failure of ABC engineers to follow correct release processes. One IBM study showed that as high as 7 percent of quality-related ECs are caused by failure to follow release processes. This figure will vary from business to business. Using ProductManager's release process, these kinds of errors are prevented. For ABC Stove, that's eight ECs and six REAs per year that would never have happened. By maintaining better control of its release process, ABC Stove now saves $10,800 for each EC and $6900 for each REA, or $127,800 a year.

Scrap and rework as a result of quality problems that could have been prevented by a PDM system had a significant impact on the cost of quality for our stove company. When Macon workers installed a defective purchased part in refrigerator motors, it was several weeks before it was discovered in testing. Three hundred of the motors had to be pulled out and reworked to replace the part. The problem was tracked to an incorrect motor configuration that had been provided to the part supplier. The ProductManager system could have prevented this problem with its product structure controls. The right BOM would have been identified for the refrigerator motor, including the correct part to be ordered. This particular quality problem cost ABC Stove $7000 to create and another $5000 to fix. ProductManager will not resolve all quality problems, but it will help reduce the chance of oversights and keep the business working with current design information. Using ProductManager, ABC Stove reduced errors in their design and manufacturing processes that would have caused scrap and rework expenses, and saved $160,000.

As ABC Stove discovered, controlling specifications and documentation associated with the product are important to the quality of a product. With the rapid changes typical in the development process, a document control program ensures that everyone is working with the same level or version of a document, whether it is a specification, test document, or manual. Document Control Manager provides an effective means of managing and working with product documentation, thereby improving the quality of a business's operations.

Savings Summary

From the previous sections, you can see that a major benefit of a PDM system is the reduced cost of doing business. While studies may vary, most find that businesses can pay for a new PDM system within a year. For ABC Stove, with an annual revenue of $300 million and a $12-million engineering budget, the investment can be recovered in less than four months. Since ABC met many of the hardware requirements by using and modifying cabling and computers already in place, the main cost was the purchase of software and hardware. ABC Stove spent $800,000 to implement ProductManager and saw a savings of $2.5 million in the system's first year of use. Implementation costs will vary, of course, based on individual business needs.

Figure 3.5 shows the estimated savings that ProductManager brought to ABC Stove. The figure shows savings after one, three, and five years. The Area of Savings column in the figure breaks down the areas in which ABC saved, as discussed in the previous sections. The greatest savings were realized in productivity. If you account for business growth and the potential gain in sales, the savings and economic impact of a PDM system could be even higher.

Each business has unique situations that need to be considered when calculating potential savings. This section has not covered all potential savings but has given you some areas to consider. Studies conducted by independent consulting groups and other PDM suppliers project PDM savings to be as high as 10 to 20 percent of a business's total annual revenues. A study by Coopers & Lybrand published in *Computer-Aided Manufacturing* (May 1991) discusses potential PDM savings. If their model is used--in which the potential revenue-producing opportunities are included, all savings are fully defined, and more aggressive savings statistics are used--ABC Stove would realize an even higher annual benefit with a PDM system than what we have projected here.

ABC Stove Savings Summary			
Area of Savings	**1st Year**	**3rd Year**	**5th Year**
Quality	$522,800	$1,568,400	$2,614,000
Reduced cycle time	837,000	2,511,000	4,185,000
Productivity	1,230,000	3,690,000	6,150,000
TOTALS	$2,589,800	$7,769,400	$12,949,000

Figure 3.5 The figure summarizes quality, reduced cycle time, and productivity savings ABC Stove realized after one, three, and five years using ProductManager.

Expanding the System with the Business

Most businesses must deal with constant change. When choosing a PDM system (or any system, for that matter), it makes sense to consider not only your current needs but also how the system and its vendor can meet your needs as they change. Think about the likelihood of whether each PDM vendor will be around to provide you with technical support and a stream of enhancements to keep their PDM system competitive in the future. Since no one knows what the future holds, this is a difficult question. The difficulty is compounded with PDM systems because they are relatively new to the industry, and thus largely without track records. PDM systems are also diverse. Some programs manage data at the PC level for small groups, while others are intended for larger businesses. Some are industry specific. With the diversity in the data management industry, some programs are not going to be right for your manufacturing business. You have to look at the merits of each program and its future if you have expectations of using the product for years.

The Multiple Virtual System (MVS) version of ProductManager is an established product. By the time the merits of the product were realized, however, businesses were looking at workstation systems for managing product data. With the functionality and features of an established mainframe product behind it, the workstation version of ProductManager was built on years of research and development that went into the mainframe version. Other PDM vendors may have extensive experience as well, and this should be considered before deciding on a PDM system.

Using ProductManager Outside of Engineering

Though this book discusses the engineering and manufacturing of products, product data management can be applied across a variety of industries that track and control information. Software development, process industries, and even the health care industry are examples of businesses that can benefit from a system that manages and controls information. The folder concept used by ProductManager is not limited to engineering applications. It can be used to review information associated with whatever kind of business you have. A business can use ProductManager to integrate other aspects of manufacturing into one system. This can include the tools, test equipment, and process plan data used by manufacturing.

In fact, IBM developed an application for hospitals using just the base application for ProductManager, Application Services Manager. It took only three people and one month to develop the new application, from requirements to delivery. The information management capabilities and folder processing of the application are applied to patient and treatment data and billing processes for hospitals in much the same way that they are used to create folders with distribution lists, contained objects, and review processes in the manufacturing environment.

IBM also plans to use ProductManager itself to manage the development of future versions of ProductManager software. The object-oriented nature of ProductManager allows it to meet a wide variety of needs, from equipment inventory to setting up and managing product demonstrations.

Assessing the Fit of ProductManager Using the QuickFit Analysis

After you have determined that a PDM system is needed and cost justified for your business and you understand the specific needs of your business, you are faced with a new question. Which PDM system will meet your needs? This is a very important question, but, unfortunately, not a simple one. There are many PDM systems on the market today. While clearly this book cannot tell you which one is right for your business, we will guide you through a quantitative process called **QuickFit Analysis** to help you assess how well ProductManager "fits" (meets the needs of) your business. QuickFit Analysis can also be used to assess the fit of any other PDM system, or any other type of application program for that matter. However, be aware that the QuickFit Analysis of ProductManager provided in this book should only be used for a preliminary look at the fit of ProductManager for your business. The ultimate method of analysis has to be defined by your business.

The QuickFit Analysis is a scoring system that matches the needs of a business, as defined by the user, against the functions of an application program. The user is first asked to score the importance of some common needs, and is then invited to add any other needs they have, based on their particular situation. The application program being analyzed is then given a separate score for each need, based on its ability to meet that need. The overall score of the application program is then compared to the maximum possible score to yield the QuickFit. The QuickFit Analysis also allows you to simultaneously assess the effect of other "add-on" programs designed to augment the functions of the application program. The score achieved by the application program together with its add-on programs is called the Extended QuickFit. To get a better understanding of the QuickFit Analysis, let's go through an example.

Sample QuickFit Analysis of a ProductManager Module

ProductManager consists of four applications. Each application is given a separate QuickFit Analysis. This allows potential users to assess the individual fit of each ProductManager application with their own needs. For our example QuickFit Analysis, we will again turn to our hypothetical ABC Stove Company to see how ProductManager's ASM application meets their business needs.

Figure 3.6 shows the example QuickFit worksheet that the ABC Stove evaluation team started with to determine whether the ASM function is right for their business. (Appendix A contains a complete set of QuickFit worksheets for all four ProductManager applications.) In the left column of the worksheet, there is a list of typical needs manufacturers have in the area of product data management. This list is provided simply as a starting point and a catalyst for thinking about needs. The first thing the ABC Stove team did was add any other PDM needs to this list, based on their particular situation. To keep our example simple, we will say that ABC Stove has only one additional need beyond those already provided on the QuickFit worksheet. The ABC Stove team added the need for electronic mail function to the analysis by writing it in at the bottom of the worksheet (*13. Provide electronic mail packages*). When performing your analysis, you may want to add many needs to the worksheet for your business. If you need more space than that provided at the bottom of the worksheet, simply make copies of the blank QuickFit continuation worksheet provided at the end of Appendix A. This allows your QuickFit Analysis to easily encompass many additional needs. The ability to add requirements is important because it allows the QuickFit Analysis to be tailored to the needs of any situation. Accurately reflecting all needs is critical to the accuracy of a QuickFit Analysis. However, be careful here not to add a need to the QuickFit

QuickFit worksheet

Name: ____________

Date: ____________

Application:
ProductManager/6000
Application Services Manager

Add-on programs:

Importance scale
0 = Not applicable
1 = Nice to have
2 = Of some importance
5 = Very important
20 = Critical

Application capability
0 = No support
1 = Some affinity
2 = Primitive support
3 = Significant support
4 = Complete support
5 = Extensive support

Add-on program capability
0 = No support
1 = Some affinity
2 = Primitive support
3 = Significant support
4 = Complete support
5 = Extensive support

Rate your business's CURRENT NEED to:	**Importance (0, 1, 2, 5, or 20)**	**Application Capability (0, 1, 2, 3, 4, or 5)**	**Application Score**	**Add-on Program (0, 1, 2, 3, 4, or 5)**	**Extended Score**
(Example)	**5**	**4**	(5 × 4 =)20	**1**	(5 × (4 + 1) =)25
1. Automatically generate item numbers.		× 5 =			
2. Convert a unit of measurement.		× 4 =			
3. Use drawing tools that are not a part of the product data management system.		× 3 =			
4. Provide user security across development and manufacturing areas.		× 5 =			
5. Identify drawings and their locations when they are not stored in a computerized file.		× 4 =			
6. Reduce the time to design and produce parts.		× 4 =			
7. Distribute CAD and CATIA drawings online.		× 4 =			
8. Run import and export jobs in batch.		× 4 =			
9. Tailor data management features to meet business needs and processes.		× 3 =			

Figure 3.6 The QuickFit worksheet ABC Stove will use to perform its QuickFit Analysis of Application Services Manager.

Rate your business's CURRENT NEED to:	Importance (0, 1, 2, 5, or 20)	Application Capability (0, 1, 2, 3, 4, or 5)	Application Score	Add-on Program (0, 1, 2, 3, 4, or 5)	Extended Score
(Example)	5	4	(5 × 4 =)20	1	(5 × (4 + 1) =)25
10. Control all information about users, companies, and distribution lists.		× 4 =			
11. Share development and manufacturing information across multiple locations.		× 4 =			
12. Track the progress of work reviews throughout the business.		× 4 =			
Add other requirements you want reflected in the Quickfit:					

(Use QuickFit continuation worksheets as necessary.)

Application score = (sum of this column)

Extended score = (sum of this column)

Perfect score = (sum of Importance × 5)

Perfect score = (sum of Importance × 5)

(Perform these calculations on the last worksheet page only.)

QuickFit = $\left(\frac{\text{Application score total} \times 100\%}{\text{Perfect score}}\right)$

Extended QuickFit = $\left(\frac{\text{Extended score} \times 100\%}{\text{Perfect score}}\right)$

Figure 3.6 (*Continued*)

worksheet for one ProductManager application that should be included on the worksheet for another application.

Next, the ABC Stove team filled out the worksheet. Figure 3.7 shows ABC Stove's completed QuickFit worksheet for ProductManager's ASM application. The first thing the ABC Stove team has to do is to weight all the needs listed on the worksheet by filling in the column labeled "Importance." The team rated the importance of these needs in their environment using the following scale:

0 = Not applicable: This capability is of no interest.

1 = Nice to have: This capability would be nice to have but its absence would be of little consequence.

2 = Of some importance: This capability is significant to us in the long-term future, but it is not critical now.

5 = Very important: This capability is very significant to us now or will become significant in the very near future, and its absence would be of considerable consequence.

20 = Critical: This capability is absolutely vital to our business.

The first business need listed is to automatically generate numbers for items. Since the stove company maintains thousands of items and is constantly creating new items, the team weighted this as a "very important" requirement and placed a 5 in the Importance column. They continued to rate each business need in the same manner. Notice that the stove company team did not weight converting a unit of measure as very important. Since ABC has no overseas development or manufacturing locations, they do not convert units of measure, but felt that it would be a nice feature to have. They gave it an importance of 1. Using this introspective method, the team completed the QuickFit worksheet.

After all the needs were scored, the ABC Stove team turned their attention to the ability of ProductManager's ASM application to meet each need. In this QuickFit worksheet and others in Appendix A, the application capability score for each need is provided for you in the column labeled "Application capability." The scores reflect the known capabilities of the application. This will save you much time and research effort when performing your QuickFit Analysis of ProductManager. However, the ABC Stove team must assign a score to the ProductManager application's capability to meet any additional needs they add to the QuickFit worksheet, using the following scale:

0 = No support: No capability to address this need.

1 = Some affinity: Provides foundation on which support for this need can be built.

2 = Primitive support: Provides minimal capabilities to meet this need.

3 = Significant support: Provides respectable but not complete capabilities to meet this need.

4 = Complete support: Provides complete capabilities to meet this need.

5 = Extensive support: Provides extensive capabilities to meet this need.

In determining the application capability score for the needs that they had added to the worksheet, the ABC Stove team turned to many sources, including the ProductManager support team, other users of ProductManager in both mainframe and workstation environments, and product demonstrations. Several consulting firms, such as CIMdata of Wellesly Hills, Massachusetts, or the Yankee Group of Boston, Massachusetts, also have detailed analyses of

QuickFit worksheet

Name: *ABC Stove Company*

Date: *12/5/99*

Application:
ProductManager/6000
Application Services Manager

Add-on programs:
Exchange
(A tailored program)

Importance scale
0 = Not applicable
1 = Nice to have
2 = Of some importance
5 = Very important
20 = Critical

Application capability
0 = No support
1 = Some affinity
2 = Primitive support
3 = Significant support
4 = Complete support
5 = Extensive support

Add-on program capability
0 = No support
1 = Some affinity
2 = Primitive support
3 = Significant support
4 = Complete support
5 = Extensive support

Rate your business's CURRENT NEED to:	**Importance (0, 1, 2, 5, or 20)**	**Application Capability (0, 1, 2, 3, 4, or 5)**	**Application Score**	**Add-on Program (0, 1, 2, 3, 4, or 5)**	**Extended Score**
(Example)	5	4	$(5 \times 4 =)20$	1	$(5 \times (4 + 1) =)25$
1. Automatically generate item numbers	5	× 5 =	25		25
2. Convert a unit of measurement	1	× 4 =	4		4
3. Use drawing tools that are not a part of the product data management system.	5	× 3 =	15	2 Exchange	25
4. Provide user security across development and manufacturing areas.	2	× 5 =	10		10
5. Identify drawings and their locations when they are not stored in a computerized file.	2	× 4 =	8		8
6. Reduce the time to design and produce parts.	20	× 4 =	80		80
7. Distribute CAD and CATIA drawings online.	20	× 4 =	80		80
8. Run import and export jobs in batch.	2	× 4 =	8		8
9. Tailor data management features to meet business needs and processes.	2	× 3 =	6		6

Figure 3.7 The completed QuickFit worksheet ABC Stove used for Application Services Manager.

Rate your business's CURRENT NEED to:	Importance (0, 1, 2, 5, or 20)	Application Capability (0, 1, 2, 3, 4, or 5)	Application Score	Add-on Program (0, 1, 2, 3, 4, or 5)	Extended Score
(Example)	5	4	(5 × 4 =)20	1	(5 × (4 + 1) =)25
10. Control all information about users, companies, and distribution lists.	2	× 4 =	8		8
11. Share development and manufacturing information across multiple locations.	20	× 4 =	80		80
12. Track the progress of work reviews throughout the business.	5	× 4 =	20		20
Add other requirements you want reflected in the Quickfit:					
13. *Provide electronic mail packages.*	20	× 5 =	100		100

(Use QuickFit continuation worksheets as necessary.)

Application score = (sum of this column)	444	**Extended score** = (sum of this column)	454
Perfect score = (sum of Importance × 5)	530	**Perfect score** = (sum of Importance × 5)	530
QuickFit = (Application score total × 100% / Perfect score)	84%	**Extended QuickFit** = (Extended score × 100% / Perfect score)	86%

(Perform these calculations on the last worksheet page only.)

Figure 3.7 (*Continued*)

ProductManager capabilities. It's critical that the capability of the application be accurately reflected in order to perform an accurate analysis.

Reviewing the first business need (Automatically generate item numbers), the stove company team found that ProductManager provides extensive support for this feature and agreed with the 5 in the Application Capability column. Next, they reviewed the capabilities of ProductManager to convert units of measure. While they have no short-term needs for this feature, they agreed that the application provides complete support. A 4 already appears in the column. The ABC Stove team continued down the list of needs, completing the Application Capability column.

After this step is complete, QuickFit Analysis now requires the team to perform some simple calculations. For each business need, the importance score is multiplied by the application capability score. The result is entered in the Application Score column. The score for the first business need was calculated like this: 5 × 5 = 25. The 25 was entered in the Application Score column. Similarly, the score for converting a unit of measure was calculated like this: $1 \times 4 = 4$.

Each business need is calculated until the Application Score column is complete. Next, the numbers in the Application Score column are summed, and the total is entered in the box at the bottom of the column. In this case, the ABC team totaled the column and entered 444 in the Application score box. The Perfect score box provides the measurement against which users can compare the results of the Application Score column. The perfect score is calculated by adding the numbers in the Importance column and multiplying that sum by 5 (the maximum application capability score). The stove company team found that the perfect score was 530 and entered the score in the Perfect score box.

To get the QuickFit for ProductManager's Application Services Manager application, the following calculations are performed:

$$\frac{\text{Application score total}}{\text{Perfect score}} \times 100 \text{ percent} = \text{QuickFit}$$

For the ABC Stove Company, this calculation was 444 divided by 530 and then multiplied by 100 percent, resulting in a rounded-off 84 percent. The company's QuickFit for the ASM application is 84 percent. Before interpreting this QuickFit result, let's complete the rest of the worksheet.

The two right-hand columns of the QuickFit worksheet allow for the calculation of an Extended QuickFit. This score allows the ABC Stove team to see how **add-on programs**--programs (besides the other ProductManager applications) designed to extend the functions of ProductManager's ASM application--might help improve the fit for their particular situation. There are several add-on programs available to extend the functionality of ProductManager. In addition, a company can develop its own add-on programs to provide needed functions.

In our example, ABC Stove is developing their own add-on program for exchanging information between their legacy systems and ProductManager. Called "Exchange," the add-on program allows drawings to be imported into the ProductManager system. This helps meet business need #3, "Using drawing tools that are not a part of the product data management system." The Exchange program will add capability to Application Services Manager by acting as an interface between the other drawing systems and ProductManager. The ABC Stove team decided that ASM and Exchange together provide a combined capability score of 5 (extensive support) for need #3. Since ASM itself rates a 3, we then rate Exchange a 2 to get a combined capability score of 5.

The Extended QuickFit can now be calculated. After adding the score in the Application Capability column to the number in the Add-on Program column, we multiply the sum by the number entered in the Importance column:

$$(\text{Application capability} + \text{Add-on program}) \times \text{Importance} = \text{Extended score}$$

The resulting number is then entered in the Extended Score column for each of the needs. For the add-on program Exchange, which addresses business need #3, the application capability score of 3 was added to the add-on program score of 2, and this sum was multiplied by the importance score of 5 to get an extended score of $(3 + 2) \times 5 = 25$. The 25 was then entered in the Extended Score column. This calculation is done for all needs for which add-on programs will be used. For those needs without add-on programs, the application score is carried over to the Extended Score column.

After calculating the extended score for their add-on program, the ABC team was ready to calculate the overall ASM Extended QuickFit just as they did the QuickFit. They first summed the numbers in the Extended Score column and entered that figure, 454, in the Extended score box at the bottom of the column. The perfect score, 530, remains the same and is carried over. To get the Extended QuickFit for ProductManager's Application Services Manager plus the add-on program Exchange, the stove company's team performed the following calculation:

$$\frac{\text{Extended score total}}{\text{Perfect score}} \times 100 \text{ percent} = \text{Extended QuickFit}$$

For the stove company, this calculation is 454 divided by 530 and then multiplied by 100 percent, resulting in a rounded-off 86 percent. The Extended QuickFit for ProductManager's Application Services Manager and the add-on program Exchange is thus 86 percent.

Interpreting the QuickFit Analysis Results

By completing the QuickFit Analysis, the ABC Stove team is trying to determine whether or not ProductManager warrants further investigation. While there is not a cutoff score, a general rule of thumb for QuickFit Analysis is that anything over 60 percent warrants further investigation. The QuickFit Analysis score for the ABC Stove Company was 84 percent. The comparison of the needs of the company with the capabilities and functions of ASM indicated that the company should consider the application. When the add-on program Exchange was factored into the assessment, the Extended QuickFit score climbed to 86 percent.

Even though ABC's QuickFit Analysis provided a high QuickFit score, the stove company should look closely at any needs rated as either very important or critical that have a combined application capability and add-on program score of less than 4 (that is, application capability + add-on program < 4). This will point the company to the most critical areas to investigate further; it must find a way to meet these needs. If you can't find a way to meet the needs rated as either very important or critical, the system will have a higher risk of failure, even though it has an acceptable overall QuickFit.

To get the Average QuickFit for all of the ProductManager applications in which the ABC Stove Company is interested, it averages the individual QuickFits for all four applications. Let's suppose that average is 83 percent. When combined with the add-on programs, the Average Extended QuickFit rises to 90 percent. By calculating the Average QuickFit and Average Extended QuickFit scores for the applications, the ABC Stove team can gain a better overall understanding of ProductManager and, based on their needs, a better understanding of how much the program will help them. The increase from 83 to 90 percent points out that the company should be looking at add-on program opportunities to enhance the performance of ProductManager. It also means that the costs of the add-on programs must be included in the justification for purchasing ProductManager.

Since ABC Stove is considering other product data management programs, its team can perform a QuickFit Analysis on those programs as well. By using the same set of needs (they are the same on the worksheet for each application) and importance scores, the users can use the QuickFit results to compare the respective fit of each program. Along with QuickFit Analysis, other factors such as technical support, costs, and education must be taken into consideration. The QuickFit numbers are effective when comparing programs, but should be only one factor in the final decision to purchase a PDM system.

After completing all QuickFit Analysis and identifying the areas that warrant further investigation, it is time to take the next step in the decision-making process. This can include attending product seminars, attending demonstrations of the products, or visiting manufacturing companies who use the products. Don't worry too much if the businesses you visit aren't identical to yours; no business is. What you are looking for are the factors that have caused their implementation to succeed or fail. Chapter 4 will deal with some critical implementation issues.

Performing Your Own QuickFit Analysis

When you are ready to perform a QuickFit Analysis of ProductManager for your business, all of the necessary QuickFit worksheets can be found in

Appendix A. However, some do's and don'ts must be considered before performing the analysis.

Do carefully consider and define your needs. Start with the set provided on the QuickFit worksheets and add more needs to the list, based on input from all areas of the business that will be affected if the proposed system is implemented. You will probably learn of new needs as a natural consequence of your evaluations. This is fine, but make sure you remain consistent in your importance ratings as you discover new needs. Without well-understood and accurately rated needs, you will end up wasting time and resources.

Do use the QuickFit Analysis technique to compare the fit of all the application program alternatives you are considering. Make sure you use the same set of needs and importance ratings for every application program you analyze. Be thorough when researching the application programs' capacities to meet each need. Software companies may not be forthcoming about the limitations of their programs. Demonstrations of the functions in question are one good way to better evaluate an application's capability against a given need. Assign the application capability score only after you can make an accurate judgment.

Do consider the individual QuickFits for each application as well as the average QuickFit for all modules that are part of the system. This will help you see more clearly the overall fit of the proposed system.

Don't use QuickFit as your only criterion for selecting an application program. A carefully done QuickFit Analysis gives you a good picture of a proposed system's fit with your particular requirements, and this fit is of critical importance. However, assuming that there is more than one system with an acceptable fit, there are many other things to consider. These include vendor stability, overall manufacturing strategy (such as CIM), technical support from the vendor, vendor references and reputation, product cost and terms, conversion from your current environment, compatibility with your current computing networks, and the skills of your business's personnel. Use QuickFit as just one input to the decision-making process.

Don't ignore any needs that you rate as very important or critical that have a combined application capability and add-on program score of less than 4 (Complete support). These needs must be met in some way. You must figure out how you will meet them if the proposed system is implemented. Your alternatives include selecting an available add-on program that better meets your needs, working with ProductManager Services to find a solution, developing your own custom add-on program, or changing a business process. You should also ask yourself if you have overrated the importance of the need and whether the support provided by the proposed system is actually sufficient.

ProductManager Add-on Programs

As mentioned before, one data management system will not meet all the needs of all businesses. With the tailoring features of ProductManager, users can create their own interface programs or purchase add-on programs that enable ProductManager to perform the way that best meets the business's needs.

These programs are not part of ProductManager, but can be purchased to extend product functions such as redlining drawings or placing ProductManager documentation online for easy access. The optional programs we will list here are not the only programs available to provide extended support. Before deciding to tailor ProductManager or to create your own program, consider whether one of the existing add-on programs can meet your business needs. Here are several questions to ask while you are evaluating add-on products:

Does the program present a seamless user interface? A seamless interface makes navigation between programs less complicated.

Does the optional program work with the ProductManager database or does it build its own? Having two or more independent databases with redundant information provides an opportunity for error introduction every time one database is updated and the other is not.

Is the program supported? Can you count on technical support and a stream of product enhancements?

Now let's take a look at some add-on programs that can be used with ProductManager:

Common Data Facility/MVS

This facility links ProductManager users on LANs to information stored in mainframe environments. Common Data Facility/MVS provides centralized control of information for users working in either a mainframe or workstation environment. The facility also provides ProductManager users an interface with other mainframe resource managers that it has access to, such as databases on legacy systems.

Transmission Control Protocol/Internet Protocol (TCP/IP)

The communications protocol most widely used in the engineering field is Transmission Control Protocol/Internet Protocol (TCP/IP). Developed by the U.S. Defense Advanced Research Projects Agency, this protocol is popular in networks that are comprised of products from multiple vendors. TCP/IP is used by ProductManager to communicate with other systems in a LAN environment. It is also a key element in ProductManager's client/server implementation. When ProductManager needs to communicate with other programs, TCP/IP provides the link that enables communication.

Distributed Application Environment's Entry Communications System/6000

Distributed Application Environment (DAE) can be used to exchange information with systems that don't use the TCP/IP protocol. Distributed Application Environment's Entry Communications System/6000 is a client/server-based extension to the computer's operating system. When used with Common Data Facility/MVS, DAE Entry Communications System/6000 can access drawings and data objects stored in mainframe repositories. Other protocols can also be used in the AIX or UNIX environments, but only Entry Communications System/6000 supports applications in the DOS, OS/2, UNIX, AIX, VM, and MVS environments. It also provides the capability to access and move drawings, images, and other data objects within and between LANs.

DataBridge and DataBuilder

What about different systems that contain information required by ProductManager? The data may be different in structure, nomenclature, and values format. One of the recommended tools for exchanging information between systems is the combination of DataBridge and DataBuilder, developed by International TechneGroup Incorporated in partnership with IBM. These tools support relational database systems that use SQL, whether they are legacy systems or other product data management programs. The bridge and builder are used to define and work with data models so that a neutral schema of data can be developed that different systems can work with. A schema is a set of statements in a data definition language that describes the structure of a database. For example, if there are different systems for managing engineering changes, materials control, and shop/floor control, the bridge and builder provide the means to bring together the data and map it so that the data in each system matches that in the others. Data from non-ProductManager systems can then be imported into a ProductManager system file. DataBridge and DataBuilder are also PDES/STEP compliant.

Don't be misled into thinking that it's simple to build such a bridge between systems. Although PDIF files handle information between ProductManager systems, handling information between noncompatible systems is not as easy. Programmers for your business know the data formats your business is currently using. They will have to determine the best system for your business for exchanging information and then implement formats that facilitate this data exchange.

Preview

Preview 4.3 is a product used to access engineering and manufacturing data in CIM environments. Produced by Rosetta Technology, the program brings workstation graphics to users on their Xstations in an AIX or UNIX environment and meets IGES standards. Using Preview, engineers can view and work with drawings. In addition to the IBM systems, Preview can be used with Sun Microsystems and Hewlett Packard servers connected to the RISC System/6000 on local area networks.

Preview provides **redlining** capabilities. Redlining is marking up a drawing by overlaying it with another file. When you redline a drawing, you do not change it but rather create a layer in the drawing that can be shared with other engineers for review. Preview's redlining feature comes with a palette that includes drawing functions, editing capabilities, optimal viewing, and measurement facilities. Users can use the palette or pull-down menus to work with drawings. Using layers for redlining graphics, engineers can work with designs while leaving the original drawing protected.

AIX BookManager READ/6000

BookManager READ/6000 brings ProductManager documentation online. With this optional program, users can search the complete ProductManager library from their workstations. Postscript files are also available from the library, which enables the printing of hard copies of the documentation.

Tailoring ProductManager

How do you go about modifying ProductManager to make it work the way you want? Depending on the nature of the change, it can be performed by one of several groups of users. If it's a simple change, the end user or administrator may be able to do it. If it is more complex, it will require either an administrator or an experienced programmer to perform. We'll look at how ProductManager can be modified, from the simplest to more complex changes. The following sections describe each user group and their responsibilities for tailoring the system. Let's start our discussion with what end users can do to change how the system works for them.

End Users

Normally, end users can personalize only a few functional aspects of the system, such as distribution lists, nickname files, processing options, and national language preferences. They can also change the keyboard requirements, choosing a setup for either a 12- or 24-function key keyboard.

Administrators

The next level of modifying ProductManager is the administrator level. Administrators can change panel terminology, data elements and lengths, function key text and actions, default values, and business processes.

Administrators can work with product libraries to change the panels. The panels can be displayed by the user interface's panel viewer function before they are introduced into the system. Using **dialog tags**, a tagging language that defines panel appearance and behavior, administrators can define what panels look like, how information is displayed on them, and what action bar and function key options are available for the panel. Administrators also use dialog tags to maintain data-entry fields. They can delete a field or select not to display it. A number of data-entry fields have **prompts**, in which case a user can select to see a list of acceptable entry values for the field. The list that appears is called a **varclass (variable class)**. The variable class is also used to define translations and perform validity checking. The tagging language is used to define or remove attributes for varclasses. Varclass information includes numerical ranges, character streams, and alphanumeric values.

Administrators can also define online help information and messages, menu selections, and field names and lengths. ABC Stove uses the term "business change" instead of "engineering change" to make product changes. An ABC administrator can use dialog tags in the product library to change the reference on the panels so that ABC engineers see the term they are familiar with. In addition to changing terms, panel layouts can be modified. For example, list panels have columns, and administrators can delete, add, or change columns. If a new column is added, however, a programmer will have to add the logic for the attribute. Data-entry fields can also be changed, added, or deleted. After changes have been made, administrators can use the panel viewer function to preview changes before they are put into use.

Administrators can change system **default values**. Default values are values that are predefined so that the user doesn't have to define them every time a new file or record is created. ProductManager comes with some defaults already defined, for example, the number of days it takes for a folder to become delinquent is eight. These values can be changed, however, if they don't fit the way your business operates. Administrators can change defaults by changing class data attributes.

Business factor tables are used in a number of ways to control the behavior of ProductManager. They reside in the ProductManager database and control the logic flow of the programs. Administrators can set the row and column values in the business factor tables to meet the system behavior the business prefers. The columns in these tables contain behavior logics, while the fields contain the values for each logic. For example, in Figure 3.8, Behavior 1

Business Factor Table before Modification

Key Values	Behavior 1	Behavior 2	Behavior 3	Behavior 4
Development	Y	N	N	Y
Prerelease	N	Y	N	N
Release	N	N	Y	Y

Business Factor Table after Modification

Key Values	Behavior 1	Behavior 2	Behavior 3	Behavior 4
Development	Y	N	N	Y
Prerelease	N	Y	N	N
Release	N	N	Y	Y
Production	Y	N	N	Y

Figure 3.8 Business factor tables are used to add or change ProductManager logic. When a business wants to add "production" as another status in the release process, the business factor table can be modified.

could indicate whether a certain level of authority is required to work with an EC, while the rows indicate progressive statuses of an EC. Business factor tables exist for many types of ProductManager objects. Columns in business factor tables can be changed, or new rows and columns can be added to the table to meet a business's needs. As with list panel columns, if new columns are added to a business factor table, a programmer should add the logic.

Figure 3.8 shows the business conditions for ECs that ABC Stove uses with ProductManager. The upper table shows the conditions before the table was modified. The company engineers wanted to add "production" as a new status for an engineering change. The lower table is the same table, after it was modified to include "production" as a status. Administrators can perform this task because the logic already exists for the behavior.

Programmers

Any time new attributes are added to the database that have to be read or written, programming skills are required to alter the program. Examples of tailoring that should be performed by programmers include building new classes, adding attributes to object classes, adding new business processes, and changing user exits.

The tailoring of classes and their attributes and methods is performed online with the user interface. This means that programmers can sign on to ProductManager and make the changes from within the system. They work with the application program interface (API), which is a set of application-specific commands that can be issued directly by the application program. It simplifies the job of application programmers, who do not need to be involved with the details of hardware interaction. The interface contains ProductManager classes and features that support information exchange within the ProductManager system. Programmers can change classes by overriding the initial values of a class attribute. When a class is changed, its functions within the system may be affected. Programmers can also create new parent classes and create or change attributes and methods for classes.

The ProductManager interface displays a list of classes that can be altered. They are called **exposed classes**. Because of **data integrity**, some objects are not exposed for tailoring and cannot be changed. Data integrity protects objects that may be parts of another object. If a part number is a part of a BOM, the relationship between the item and BOM would be destroyed if the part number were deleted along with the object, so the object and its class are not exposed for tailoring.

Even if an object is not exposed, programmers can add programming logic to its class through **user exits**. User exits are predefined points in ProductManager that enable businesses to insert their own programs, such as additional verifications for ECs before they are added to the database, or changes to the flow of reviews. This feature helps programmers redefine business processes without jeopardizing critical business information. While the tailoring of ProductManager to specific business needs requires skilled and knowledgeable programmers and administrators, the overall benefit is a data management product that supports the way *you* want to use the system.

ProductManager Reference Library

Whether you are assessing the fit of ProductManager or considering making modifications to your ProductManager program, the ProductManager reference library is a useful resource. Books in the ProductManager library explain the functions, concepts, and panel flows of the program. The library is organized so that each type of user can easily locate publications containing information appropriate for their needs. There are publications for the following types of ProductManager users:

End user Uses the system application programs to create, maintain, and manage a product's engineering and manufacturing definition data.

ProductManager administrator Maintains the system functions for the end user. The administrator requires some programming knowledge.

Security administrator Sets up and maintains the security of the system applications. This administrator configures the security system, establishes security procedures, and implements security checks created by the business.

Database administrator Maintains the design and integrity of the business's system databases. This administrator needs to be an expert in database theory and practice.

System administrator Sets up and maintains links between ProductManager systems and non-ProductManager systems. This administrator also maintains links between system users on different nodes and networks and between the system and the batch environment, where a group of jobs run on a computer at one time on the same program. The system administrator requires a high level of programming knowledge.

Programmer Installs, integrates, tailors, maintains, and upgrades the ProductManager system and application software. The programmer also writes add-on application programs for the system.

Depending on how a business supports ProductManager, jobs may vary between user groups. It's likely that one person will perform several of the administrative or programming jobs, or that a small group will share all the responsibilities of maintaining the system. Regardless of how a business sets up ProductManager support, the library is task oriented and provides the degree of information required by each position.

The most common use of ProductManager is by the end users. A set of books for end users includes *Using Application Service Manager,* which covers the base application. There are also books for the individual applications. *Using Product Change Manager and Product Structure Manager* contains information about working with product data, and *Using Document Control Manager* guides users through working with documents.

These books start with the basics. The first chapter in each book discusses signing on to the ProductManager system, working with the action bar, and using the product's panels. The remaining chapters discuss the business processes for each ProductManager feature and provide step-by-step instructions for completing tasks. For example, the book for the base application discusses the folder concept and takes you through the folder tasks, while the books for the applications discuss the engineering change process and take you through the steps.

Administering ProductManager provides assistance to system and security administrators. Details concerning administrative tasks such as network communications configuration, national language support options, and security system configuration are included in the book. *Diagnosing Problems* is a guide that provides instructions for completing basic diagnostic procedures, and contains information about system exception codes.

When working with more complex information, database and system administrators can look at *Customizing ProductManager.* This book provides an overview of tailoring ProductManager to your business. Included in the book are discussions on modifying dialog tags and business factor tables, and working with Intermediate C language and DB2 packages. Intermediate C language is an IBM variation of C language.

Database Reference provides details about the general design and contents of the ProductManager databases. This reference illustrates the structure of each physical database along with the data elements that make up the databases. Included in the reference are logical data models and model database tables.

In addition, the system administrator may have a need for *Programming Concepts,* which describes ProductManager's object-oriented design principles and presents a technical overview of the applications and the key base components. The book also explains how to use the application programming interface, and can be used as a reference for developing applications integrated with the ProductManager base component.

The programmer who works with the ProductManager system should be familiar with all aspects of using and controlling the system. Each of the books listed up to this point was written for a particular user group, but the programmer must be familiar with all the concepts discussed in all the books. Another book available to users, but especially useful for the programmer, is *DB2 Physical Design Diagram.* Since ProductManager works in conjunction with this popular database management program, the book is an important tool for managing information.

A number of other books and packages are available that help users understand the concepts and tasks used to work with ProductManager. The *Guide to Engineering Management* is a good starting point for learning about an engineering information management system. It highlights general steps for installation planning. The introductory package *ProductManager: Engineering Management Edition* explains the CIM approach to managing product data. The package includes information about the benefits of AIX, UNIX, and TSO platforms.

Another book that deals with ProductManager's MVS environment contains information and procedures for upgrading from one ProductManager MVS release to another. *Migrating ProductManager* includes instructions on how to migrate, or upgrade, your current database environment and application model to a later release. User books are available in softcopy format via the BookManager Read/6000 add-on program, and introductory material is available in a CD-ROM format.

Figure 3.9 lists the books (some on CD) that make up the ProductManager library, along with their document numbers.

Book Title	IBM Form Number
Introducing ProductManager	
Guide to Engineering Management	GC38-8000
Roadmap to Information	SB35-4217
ProductManager General Information	GB35-4306
ProductManager Application Services Manager	GB35-4307
ProductManager Product Change Manager	GB35-4308
ProductManager Product Structure Manager	GB35-4309
ProductManager/6000 Platform Brief	GB35-4310
ProductManager Introducing Folder	GB35-4315

Figure 3.9 The ProductManager reference library provides documentation for each product user group. The publications and their IBM form numbers are shown.

Book Title	IBM Form Number
Material on installation, planning, and tailoring for use with Application Services Manager	
ProductManager/6000 Licensed Program Specifications	GB35-4314
Application Services Manager/6000 Program Directory	PRGDIR570W
Database Reference	SB35-4300
Customizing ProductManager	SB35-4299
Migrating ProductManager	SB35-4305
Programming Concepts	SB35-4302
Diagnosing Problems	SB35-4301
Administering ProductManager	SB35-4298
Using Application Services Manager	SB35-4303
Product Change Manager/6000 **Product Structure Manager/6000**	
Using Product Change Manager and Product Structure Manager	SB35-4304
Document Control Manager/6000	
Using Document Control Manager	SB35-4339

Displayable softcopy publications for
ProductManager/6000: Engineering Management Edition

Book Title	CD-ROM Number
Roadmap to Information	SK2T-5839
General Information Flyer	SK2T-5839
ProductManager Application Services Manager Flyer	SK2T-5839
ProductManager Product Change Manager Flyer	SK2T-5839
ProductManager Product Structure Manager Flyer	SK2T-5839
ProductManager/6000 Platform Brief	SK2T-5839

Figure 3.9 (*Continued*)

CHAPTER 4

Implementing ProductManager

Depending on how well you plan, implementing any computer solution in your business can be like throwing water or gasoline on a fire. This chapter will first go over the implementation experience of some hypothetical manufacturers of varying sizes. The latter part of the chapter gives you some pointers on planning for a data management system and discusses services and education you might want to consider if you install ProductManager.

Implementation Examples

To help you see what it is like to implement a PDM system in a manufacturing company, we will look at the implementation experiences of three hypothetical manufacturers: one small, one medium-sized, and one large. We will first examine the problems they faced that are typical in the manufacturing arena. Then we will describe how they applied ProductManager to meet their specific needs. These scenarios will help you better understand the capabilities of ProductManager and the advantages of properly managing product information.

Small Business Implementation

Our first company is Ben's Bearing Assemblies. It is a small company in Cincinnati, Ohio, that produces bearings, shims, and bearing housings. Ben's was founded 21 years ago and, as such, is a well-established business. Last year the company revenues amounted to $4 million. Ben Jones, the owner and lead marketer, is pleased that the company is respected and conducts much of its business with repeat customers and their referrals. He's worked hard to earn the company's reputation as a reliable and quality-oriented supplier. Ben's business is a combined pull and make-to-order manufacturing operation. The business does not mass-produce bearings, so they subcontract out any large orders to another manufacturer.

Ben's Bearing Assemblies has three design engineers, and an intern on a revolving basis. One engineer works with metallurgy and sizing factors, another with stress and materials, and the intern does minor updates to drawings. The third engineer is an expert on bearings. He doesn't have an engineering degree, but he helped Ben get into the bearing business and has a thorough knowledge of that business. He is the lead designer and also runs the company while Ben is away. The rest of the business is made up of stock, manufacturing, and procurement employees--45 altogether, including two production managers who roll up their sleeves and fill in for employees when there's a need.

While he is pleased that his business is surviving and even growing at a slow pace, Ben would like to see his company grow faster. Ben also has another concern: He lost several valuable contracts last year because he could not meet time and cost factors specified by one of his long-term customers. Ben knows that other bearing manufacturers have shortened their production cycles. He asked himself how they managed to do it and still maintain the quality that customer specifications call for.

Ben and his engineers started looking at their processes and discussed the lost business. Bearing specifications either arrived by mail or are hand carried to the bearing shop by Ben or a customer. The specifications were then used to create electronic drawings. His engineers used a computer drawing tool for design work, but for any drawings other than the current files on each engineer's personal computer, they used a hardcopy and diskette library to serve as a central repository. The engineers work as a team on each design. When a design was ready, a verbal agreement around the room sent it out to the manufacturing area. Ben feels he has the best engineers in the business, but he began to realize that they needed more control of the designs and better tools in order to meet his long-term goals.

Ben and his group identified their problems, one of which lay in retrieving drawings. The hardcopy files of drawings were not always in order, and they tended to get separated from their corresponding diskette files. Also, the files that were stored in their drawing software program could only be accessed from one personal computer and thus could not be easily shared with the other engineers. They found themselves looking over each other's shoulders because they couldn't view a drawing at their own personal computers. Generally, the team did not have a consistent method of accessing the most current level of a bearing assembly. In some cases, they had to start a design from scratch because a similar design could not be found.

The engineers, though working in the same room, had problems sharing information. Design changes were considered complete when the lead engineer announced he was sending a complete design out to the manufacturing area. This system worked as long as the metal and stress engineers were sitting next to him at the time. If one of the engineers was not present, however, her hand-written comments may not have been available for consideration. Even with a small work group, a missed review can have a negative impact on a design.

The time had come for Ben to make a decision. His lead engineer and long-time friend encouraged him to continue as usual, based on the business's success. He resisted the idea of capital investment, and felt that a more structured approach would take away from the creativity and efficiency of the designers. They are a close-knit team. Why would added structure bring efficiency to the group? He felt that the computers they already had would take the company where it needs to go. Ben didn't agree; he felt that the potential benefits of a PDM system were worth the risks and investment. He thought a product data management system would help accomplish three goals:

1. Establish product document control
2. Reduce time spent in locating documents
3. Share information online and improve productivity

After viewing product demonstrations, using QuickFit comparisons, and visiting other manufacturers, Ben decided to use ProductManager to get a handle on the out-of-control documentation retrieval problem.

Ben's Bearing Assemblies opted for the minimum solution because it would do all that was needed to keep costs down while meeting their business needs. Ben purchased the Application Services Manager and Document Control Manager applications, along with the add-on Preview. Ben's business already had good control over the materials and manufacturing processes for making bearings, so he didn't need the PCM and PSM applications. Ben needs ASM for the folder capabilities and to enable the system, but he's most interested in the DCM application. Instead of drawings being scattered in locations from the production floor to the drawing library, they would reside in online files so his engineers can work with them on their PCs. There is no ProductManager customization required to meet Ben's needs. He doesn't have a programmer and does not plan to alter the functionality of the system.

Based on the requirements of the software and price and performance evaluations, Ben decided to go with an IBM RISC System/6000 Model 250.

This included a desktop workstation, which he assigned to the lead engineer. Ben already had three 486-class PCs with windows capability. These PCs and the Model 250 would all be attached to an Ethernet LAN set up in a single large work area. The Model 250 he purchased is capable of supporting up to seven users, so Ben has some room for growth. Figure 4.1 shows the work area for Ben's group after ProductManager was installed, and the hardware, software, and peripherals needed to implement ProductManager. Ben had to configure his PCs to communicate through the LAN using X-emulator software. Each PC and the RISC terminal would be equipped with 16-MB/second Token-Ring adapters to allow them to communicate over the LAN.

After the hardware and software had been installed, Ben's engineers received tutoring on the system through the ProductManager Implementation service, a fee-based program in which IBM implements the system and provides help with skills transfer. On-site support was available through the program until the bearing engineers felt comfortable with the system. The ProductManager representative helped make the initial load of Ben's existing drawing data into the ProductManager system. During this initial setup of ProductManager, DCM took information from Ben's existing PC files and placed it into the ProductManager repository. As time permits, the group will scan the hardcopy drawings and move them into their ProductManager repository as well.

With ProductManager, Ben's engineers can now go to one place to find the most current drawings. Then the engineers can work with the drawings using Preview. This capability improves productivity and reduces the duplication of work. A design that may have taken 30 minutes just to locate can now be pulled up in seconds and revised in less than an hour.

Ben's design team is now more productive and has the time to work as a team on those rush orders. When he receives an overnight request for a bearing, he feels more confident that the order can be fulfilled.

The concern raised by the lead engineer about too much structure was proved to be unfounded when they learned that folder distribution could be tailored by each user. If the stress engineer feels that the metals engineer needs to review the design, he can quickly add the engineer to his distribution list. If not, he can send it straight to the lead engineer for review and approval. This also means each engineer can review drawings and make his suggestions for changes by redlining the drawing using Preview--all from his own PC.

Implementing ProductManager has taken a good deal of effort at Ben's Bearing Assemblies. However, they are now geared to more efficiently manage product data. This will allow the engineers to reduce cycle time and make Ben's business more efficient and more profitable.

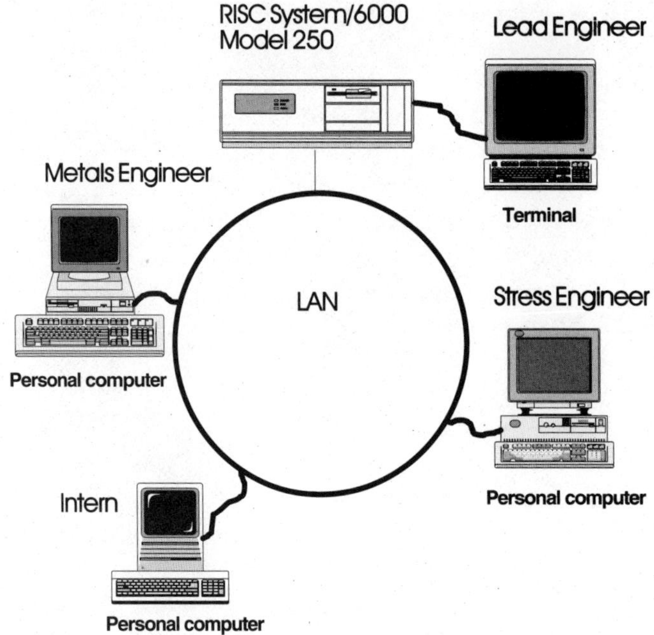

Ben's Bearing Assemblies Setup Requirements

Hardware

RISC System/6000 Model 250

- 128 megabytes of RAM
- 2 gigabytes of DASD
- 8-mm tape drive
- Color monitor
- 6019-19 graphics display adapter
- Token-Ring adapter 16 M-bit

Software

ProductManager/6000 applications

- Application Services Manager
- Document Control Manager

DB2/6000 database
Preview drawing display
AIX operating system

Peripherals

Existing 486-class PCs with windows
Token-Ring adapter 16 M-bit
X-emulator software
Token-Ring wiring and cabling

Figure 4.1 Ben's Bearing Assemblies system layout with a Model 250. Also shown are the setup requirements for Ben to begin running ProductManager.

Medium-Sized Business Implementation

Our medium-sized business, Engines Inc., produces complete engines and engine parts including crankshafts, pistons, and motor blocks used by major manufacturers. Located in Akron, Ohio, Engines Inc. has been building motors for 50 years. The overall responsibility of design and manufacturing belongs to the operations manager, Jack Hays. He has been working on a special project directed by the company's advisory group. They want Engines Inc. to become a more aggressive competitor and a low-cost producer as it goes into its sixth decade of operation. Last year, Engines Inc. revenues amounted to $250 million. Jack has been working with a consultant and his management team to find ways to better use business resources and reduce the cost of doing business. Engines Inc. has 1700 employees. This figure includes design and manufacturing engineering groups, which are located in separate buildings. The design group is in the main headquarters, and the manufacturing group is located in the manufacturing complex.

Engines Inc.'s problem was that its engineers were bogged down in a daily paper chase, which created longer cycle times and excessive scrap and rework for the business. In addition, some engineering areas were left out of the EC review cycle. By the time they had input into the design, the initial design phase was complete. If they found a problem, it meant more redesign and wasted time and effort. Using a manual distribution process, nearly 400 engineering changes were processed last year. On average, that meant that the Engines Inc. staff made 20 copies of a four-inch thick stack of paper each day. This stack typically included specifications, test procedures, and drawings with redline mark-ups. It took 12 full-time coordinators to control documentation and coordinate ECs.

On a typical day, the coordinators received REAs from all areas of the business. They assigned numbers to ECs and tracked their progress through the system. This meant making copies of and distributing proposed changes, setting up review and approval meetings, and writing and distributing final approvals. After an EC was approved, the team updated any databases affected by it, stored the EC in their library, made microfiches of the drawings, and filed the original drawings. Along with coordinating activities, they also staffed and maintained a library where engineers could request copies of drawings to work from. Though it wasn't efficient, the system worked. Normally there was no problem in obtaining a drawing, except for the time it took to walk to the library, make the request, and get the drawing.

Jack's engineers wanted better control of change processes. Earlier this year, a project was delayed two days while a misplaced change package was tracked to a manufacturing engineer who was out of the office for an emergency. The process was stalled because the engineer, a reviewer, carried his review comments with him. According to the consultant, an online review package could have been recovered immediately or delegated to another reviewer.

Some areas of the business used computer systems to manage information. The company used a mainframe computer for finance, material requirements planning, and purchasing. Design engineering also kept some of its current drawings on the mainframe, but most drawings and part information were scattered about in a variety of formats, from hardcopy references to isolated online files. Engines Inc. did not have an overall PDM system in place. If a drawing were recent, a manufacturing engineer might have called a design engineer for a copy rather than using the time-consuming process of getting it through the library. The manufacturing engineers worked with another drawing system, so each of the two groups had to create its own definition of a product structure.

Jack knew that the capital for new design and business management tools was in this year's budget, and the consultant had recommended a PDM system that could bring development and manufacturing information into a single framework. Past problems of working with manual drawings and business change packages have had a significant impact on cycle time. Manual processes meant that not all engineers had the most current designs. Here is what Engines Inc. wanted from a PDM system:

1. A more efficient review process
2. Less time and fewer people to make a change
3. Less scrap and rework due to inadequate design reviews

Jack and his team decided on a ProductManager solution. Engines Inc. went with all four ProductManager applications. ASM and PCM would improve the review process, while PSM would save time in making changes to part definitions. Whether or not they should also get DCM was a toss-up for Jack and his team at first. Some team members wanted to wait until the change process was in place before tackling documentation. However, looking at document demands, strained library resources, and the need for immediate access to information, they concluded that DCM would directly support what they wanted from a PDM system, and included it in their ProductManager package. For hardware, they chose the RISC System/6000 platform and AIX operating system. At the time, the engineers were using a variety of hardware and software, including Hewlett Packard, Sun Microsystems, and RISC System/6000 workstations. Many of the engineers had 486-class machines with windows capabilities, while some did not even have terminals. Those without terminals still did drawing board work.

After defining its business needs, the Engines Inc. team, working with ProductManager technical support, decided that a Model 590 machine would provide the computing power required to manage the company's product data. The 590 was set up on a 30-person LAN connected to two Model 370s on two more LANs, all in the design engineering area. This combination provides the system performance level required by Engines Inc.'s design engineers. Instead of using a single large LAN, the smaller LANs were selected to reduce cabling costs and network traffic. The Model 590 acts as the system server, and contains the ProductManager database, code, and tables; the Model 370s run the ProductManager applications; and the 70 users in this building use PCs to work with the applications. This networking structure links marketing with the design engineering groups and provides good performance and flexibility.

Two more Model 370 LANs were required to bring the same support level for higher performance to the manufacturing area. The manufacturing engineers spend much of their time in the manufacturing area and will therefore spend less time on the ProductManager system than the design engineers will. Two more 370 LANs in the manufacturing building (connected to the 590 LAN in design) will provide the performance level required for 40 users in the building. These users include manufacturing engineers and the materials and purchasing groups. There are 250 people altogether, but they are not full-time system users, so Engines Inc. only has to pay for 40 users (in addition to the 70 users in design and marketing) under the usage-level charge. With some cabling and ports already in place and the PCs available for configuring and connecting to the LANs, Jack just needed to run LAN cabling and a fiber-optic cable between the two buildings to complete the network. Figure 4.2 shows the system layout between Engines Inc.'s two buildings and the hardware, software, and peripheral requirements the business needed to get started with ProductManager.

Engines Inc. already had a variety of workstations, which could be used with ProductManager by upgrading them to X Version 11, Release 4 (X11R4). Jack also wanted all his engineers on the system, so he added Xstation Model 150s for those engineers that didn't already have their own workstations.

After the decision was made to purchase a PDM system, Jack's team knew that the implementation of the system would require a lot of attention in the beginning. Engines Inc. does not have the skills, expertise, or resources to devote to educating users and tailoring the new ProductManager system. They signed up for fee-based education on the system for their users and an administrator. They also wanted to tailor ProductManager to their specific needs. Working with ProductManager's dialog tags was simple enough for their administrator, but adding new logic to support specific business requirements would require programming assistance. Although it entailed additional cost,

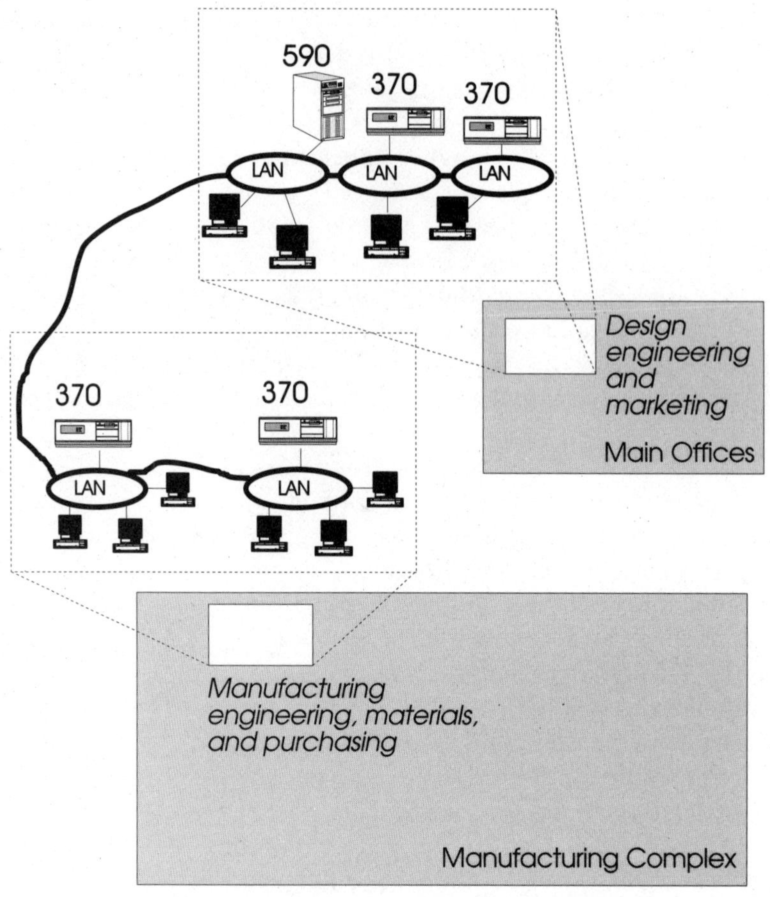

Figure 4.2 Engines Inc. system layout using a Model 590 to run ProductManager for design and manufacturing engineering, marketing, materials, and purchasing. Also shown on the next page are the setup requirements for Engines Inc. to begin running ProductManager.

the group decided to purchase the ProductManager Customization service for the more difficult programming.

Implementing a PDM system at any company isn't an overnight endeavor. At Engines Inc. it meant overtime. While they were learning ProductManager, design and production had to continue using manual methods for a while, because Jack couldn't risk using only ProductManager to manage the information until the database was complete. Engineers and coordinators received hands-on experience with the system as they loaded part information that wasn't included in the initial data load. It took nearly a month, but Jack felt assured that when the switch was made to ProductManager, all the critical information would be there.

Engines Inc. Setup Requirements

Hardware

(1) RISC System/6000 Model 590
- 384 megabytes of RAM
- 6 gigabytes of DASD
- 8-mm tape drive
- Color monitor
- 6019-19 graphics display adapter
- Token-Ring adapter 16 M-bit

(4) RISC System/6000 Model 370
- 128 megabytes of RAM
- 2 gigabytes of DASD
- 8-mm tape drive
- Color monitor
- Token-Ring adapter 16 M-bit

(6) Xstation Model 150
- 2 megabytes of video RAM
- 10 megabytes of RAM
- Token-Ring adapter 16 M-bit

Software

ProductManager/6000 applications
- Application Services Manager
- Product Change Manager
- Product Structure Manager
- Document Control Manager

DB2/6000 database
AIX operating system

Peripherals

Existing 486-class PCs with windows
Bring workstations to X11R4 compliance
X-emulator software for PCs
Token-Ring wiring and cabling
Windowing system
Token-Ring adapter 16 M-bit
Fiber-optic cable between buildings

Figure 4.2 (*Continued*)

After several weeks of operation, engineers have started seeing the benefits of a computer solution. They have more control over their work, spend much less time handling paper, and take no more walks to the library. The coordinators are being phased into other operations as ProductManager assigns numbers, manages reviews, and provides packages for distribution throughout Engines Inc. The physical library still remains, but is used as an archive. A coordinator will spend the next nine months cataloging the archived files using ProductManager's DCM application.

As users are becoming more familiar with the system, Jack has noticed that the business is moving faster. Before, it took more than three weeks, and sometimes longer, to work an engineering change through their manual process. Checking around, Jack found that some reviews are now going through in four days. There are still occasional meetings, but the packaging of information is quite efficient and has eliminated most of the needs for face-to-face meetings. Counting the time it took to get ProductManager up and loaded with their data, Jack feels he'll see a return on the investment within six months. He is using less paper and fewer copiers and staff. The cycle time to make a change has been cut by 66 percent, meaning he's producing more products for the money.

Along with improved productivity has come better quality. While it wasn't as noticeable as the increase in productivity at first, it didn't take much longer for the full benefit of a more efficient design process to hit home. Manufacturing engineers were the first to notice that design review packages were more complete. They were spending less time on the phone with design engineering trying to track down missing part definitions and specifications. Using ProductManager and its REA process, manufacturing engineers were identifying potential problems before they got too far along in the system. They were beginning to reduce rework efforts that had plagued them under the old system. The bottom line is that Engines Inc. can now build more engines in the same amount of time, and with better quality.

Large Business

ACME Autos opened its doors in the early 1960s, when several executives from the automobile industry combined their money and talents to introduce a new line of economical transportation. Backed by investors, the business grew, and thanks to the efforts and financial wizardry of its founders, has obtained a respectable market share in the auto industry. Last year was the best ever, with over $1 billion in sales. With suppliers across North America, ACME Autos has manufacturing locations in Galveston, Texas, and Monterrey, Mexico. The final assembly of the cars is performed at ACME's Cleveland, Ohio, facility, where the company is headquartered.

ACME's locations were selected based on availability of suppliers, materials, labor force, and expertise. For example, Monterrey provided both a cheaper workforce and the capability of obtaining electronics at a lower cost than they could be obtained in the United States. So the electrical systems such as the ignition system, lights, dashboard, and small motor assemblies are produced in Monterrey. Galveston, on the other hand, offered the industrial technology, petroleum products, and shipping facilities to produce the transmissions, tire-and-wheel assemblies, seats, and glass products for the cars. Cleveland builds the chassis and car bodies and assembles the final product.

Most design work was handled with the CATIA computer-aided design programs, which provide some modeling and rapid prototyping capabilities. Cleveland maintained a mainframe database for the drawings and specifications. ACME's remote southern locations could access the mainframe for most of Cleveland's current designs. The remote locations maintained their design data on their own local systems until a design was complete, at which point it was stored in Cleveland's mainframe database. The system worked because engineers from the remote locations spent half the year in Cleveland integrating designs and reviewing changes to ensure they were all working from the same design. Close attention to the review process was a part of ACME's concurrent engineering program.

While the business continued to grow, it was not without problems. The CEO, Dwayne Wilson, was worried. He saw the trends and knew that eventually his company would have to expand its product line and reduce the time it took to produce a new design and get it to the market. In the past, the company was successful because it found a market niche for its high-quality, economical cars. Dwayne knew that the business was maturing, and while consumer response to their line of cars had been good, the business had saturated its market niche. To expand the company from that point, ACME would have to develop new models and find new market niches.

While expanding production was a concern, ACME also had supplier problems cropping up. The business relies heavily on suppliers to meet its production and financial goals. Reliable suppliers had helped bring ACME to their current stage of maturity. However, although Dwayne felt that his company could meet the new production challenges, he was no longer sure about the suppliers. They had always met ACME's schedules and supplied good quality parts in the past, but the future dictated that cycle times be reduced, quality improved, and a tighter relationship formed between his company and the suppliers. Dwayne took a look at the suppliers ACME uses to see where the problems lay.

First, there are off-the-shelf suppliers. Roll-sheet steel is used to manufacture car bodies, and can be obtained from several suppliers. No problems existed with these suppliers because after a phone call from ACME, the needed part would be shipped immediately. Next is the build-to-order supplier. This is where Dwayne started seeing problems. ACME provides engineering specifications to its build-to-order suppliers. When purchasing locates and contracts with a supplier that can provide a part, specifications are sent to the supplier, who begins to build the part from the specs. The Galveston location sends specifications to Texas Brakes, a build-to-order manufacturer, to build the brake assembly. When there was a flaw in the design, work was stopped while the necessary changes were implemented. Valuable time and resources were spent to fix such designs.

ACME Autos also deals with specification-buys. An example of a specification-buy supplier is our medium-sized hypothetical business, Engines Inc. Its engineers have been asked to develop engines for ACME cars. Spec-buy suppliers were another problem area for ACME. For example, although Engines Inc. is a reliable and high-quality supplier, they had to interact daily with ACME engineering groups to work through design and production issues. This slowed the design process due to travel, frequent meetings, and mailing time.

Finally, Dwayne looked at assembly contractors. These suppliers assemble parts according to ACME's specifications and BOMs. There were problems here as well. For example, due to a constant state of design improvement, one of these suppliers assembled 300 radiator units with the overflow valve on the wrong side because the design change was slow in getting to the supplier.

Several months ago Dwayne, along with his senior business managers, formed a steering committee to start looking at a new strategy for the company. They agreed the basic strategy should be to become more competitive in other market niches, increase the market share in their current niche, and create a framework for managing all product information, particularly to develop a concurrent engineering environment throughout the supplier system. With this consensus on the direction they should take, the committee decided to focus on the data management work item. They called in people with more expertise and formed evaluation teams that included representatives from marketing, engineering, information systems, and finance to start looking at the business and how its new goals could be implemented. ACME expected a PDM system to help them do three things:

1. Implement international electronic folder communications
2. Enhance concurrent engineering capabilities
3. Bring suppliers into the development loop

After intensive examination of PDM systems and their vendors, and much discussion, the ACME evaluation teams and steering committee elected to go with ProductManager to provide the information management framework. ACME purchased all four ProductManager applications and three ProductManager installations, one for each location. This would improve performance at each location and keep traffic on dedicated lines between the locations at a manageable level. Each location would run all four ProductManager applications. Using network IDs and ProductManager remote functions, each location would thus be able to conduct its own operations efficiently and, when needed, communicate with the remote locations.

The folder capabilities of ASM and PCM met ACME's electronic communications needs, while PSM and PCM offered a wide variety of functions for concurrent review processes, including a tailorable review process. DCM would also enhance the concurrent engineering process by providing immediate, up-to-date product information.

The Cleveland location required support for 140 design and manufacturing engineers, while Galveston has needed support for 50 users, and Monterrey for 30. It was decided that a RISC System/6000 Model 990 at Cleveland would serve as the central repository for all three locations and would run one

ProductManager installation. There are four engineering groups in Cleveland: two in design and two in engineering. Three Model 590s were installed to act as large-application servers for three LANs. The 590s also act as clients of the Model 990 by receiving information from the ProductManager repository and database. Model 370s were attached to each LAN to improve system performance. Each user can access the RISC System/6000 ProductManager servers through personal computers or Xstations connected to the RISC System/6000s by a 16-M-Bit Token-Ring LAN.

Galveston installed a Model 590 to handle its installation of ProductManager. This additional installation of ProductManager at Galveston increases the businesswide performance of the ProductManager system. Galveston engineers handle a large number of ECs that do not have to be sent to Cleveland or Monterrey for approval. Galveston can also access the Model 990 database for current product information, so engineers can download that information to their own database at Galveston, work with it until a change is implemented, and then send the new version back to the Model 990 at Cleveland. By adding a Model 370 and a second LAN, Galveston obtained ample performance to meet the needs of their 50 design and manufacturing engineers, and network traffic was reduced. Again, the Galveston engineers can access ProductManager through their UNIX workstations, PCs, or newly purchased Xstations, all attached to a new LAN.

Monterrey also installed a Model 590 to run ACME Auto's third installation of ProductManager. Since many of their parts are assemblies, they do less actual design work. The Model 590 gives Monterrey's 30 engineers the same system efficiency as Galveston's combination of Models 590 and 370. As in the other ACME locations, the engineers at Monterrey will access ProductManager from their existing UNIX workstations, existing PCs, or through new Xstations attached to the LAN. Figure 4.3 shows a broad view of how ACME Autos' system looks and the hardware, software, and peripherals required by ACME Autos.

ACME needed to upgrade its PCs so they could be attached to the LAN and participate in X Windows communications. Since ACME was going to communicate between locations, a tool for running distributed client/server applications was also required. ACME selected the Distributed Application Environment add-on program to facilitate the exchange of information between Cleveland, Galveston, and Monterrey. Along with bridge modems, dedicated to handling data flow between LANs and different locations, and cabling, the final need was a phone line for transmitting reviews and folders between locations and accessing the Cleveland repository.

With a solid programming skills base, ACME didn't need to spend a lot of time educating administrators and programmers on the new system. With a small amount of education, the ACME programming group was able to do their own customization of ProductManager. For answers to their questions,

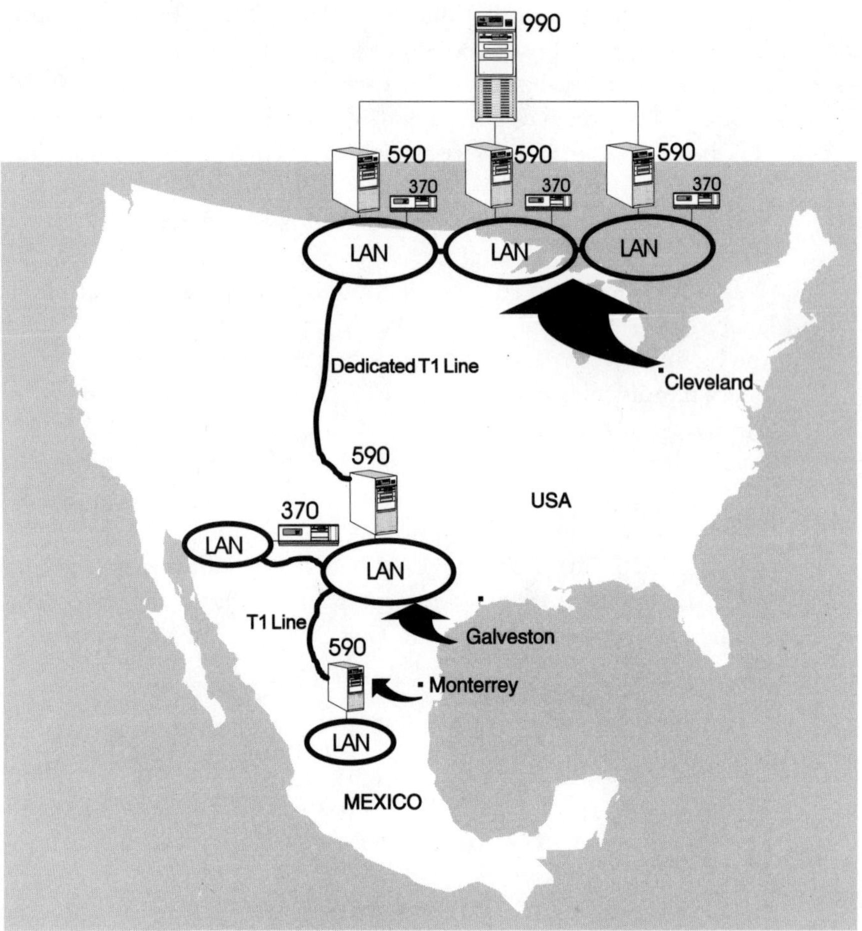

Figure 4.3 ACME Autos system layout using a Model 990 that serves as a central repository for all three ProductManager installations and runs Cleveland's ProductManager program. The Model 590s in Galveston and Monterrey also run an installation of ProductManager. Also shown on the next page are the setup requirements for ACME Autos to begin running ProductManager.

they purchased ProductManager Technical Services, a premier service that offers 24-hours-a-day, seven-days-a-week support for customers. ACME's biggest investment in education was in the area of end-user education for its engineers. ACME Autos enrolled its end users and administrators in the ProductManager application courses on using ASM, PSM, and PCM. These courses helped them understand the basic concepts of the system and how to use the application.

As with Engines Inc., it took ACME time to phase in all the ProductManager functions. ACME did have an advantage, however. Part definition data and most drawings and specifications were already stored in their computer

ACME Autos Setup Requirements

Hardware

(1) RISC System/6000 Model 990
- 512 megabytes of RAM
- 16 gigabytes of DASD
- 8-mm tape drive
- Color monitor
- 6019-19 graphics display adapter
- Token-Ring adapter 16 M-bit

(5) RISC System/6000 Model 590
- 384 megabytes of RAM
- 6 gigabytes of DASD
- Token-Ring adapter 16 M-bit

(4) RISC System/6000 Model 370
- 128 megabytes of RAM
- 2 gigabytes of DASD
- Token-Ring adapter 16 M-bit

(20) Xstation Model 150
- 2 megabytes of video RAM
- 10 megabytes of RAM
- Token-Ring adapter 16 M-bit

Software

ProductManager/6000 applications
- Application Services Manager
- Product Change Manager
- Product Structure Manager
- Document Control Manager

DB2/6000 database
AIX operating system
DAE program

Peripherals

Existing 486- and 386-class PCs with windows
Bring workstations to X11R4 compliance
X-emulator software for PCs
Token-Ring wiring and cabling
Windowing system
Token-Ring adapter 16 M-bit
Dedicated T1 lines

Figure 4.3 (*Continued*)

systems in different formats. Some definition data also had to be loaded manually, but this was accomplished in only three weeks. At the same time, other product information was being loaded into the Model 590s in Galveston and Monterrey. This was the first time since the company started that all product definition data was available in the same format. There were still drawing files that had been created in different programs, but they could all be packaged in a single folder for review.

The management team had helped prepare the business for change. Its engineers were already supporters of concurrent engineering and were anxious to apply ProductManager features to take concurrent engineering a step further. Within several weeks of starting to use ProductManager for real work, they found that the electronic folders and reviews were helping them exchange information more efficiently. While the engineering groups had had some online distribution before, it didn't compare to the functions that came with the new system. Now they are able to have ProductManager monitor when reviews are due back, control the distribution of the review, and merge review comments. When a design engineer is changing an axle design, the design review is sent online to the engineers in Galveston for their input. Formerly, a review would have been sent online a part at a time, sometimes resulting in an incomplete review. Now, the ProductManager package not only keeps the information together, it also maintains a history of the review, a process that used to be performed manually by engineers.

ACME was on its way to a successful application of ProductManager. But the story doesn't end there. The next section describes how they included some of their major suppliers in the development loop.

The Extended Enterprise

We have discussed three business scenarios to help you visualize how you might use ProductManager in your business. To complete the ProductManager picture, we will now build on these examples to illustrate how ProductManager can be used to help manage information between different companies. Let's assume that our three hypothetical companies--Ben's Bearing Assemblies, Engines Inc., and ACME Autos--do business with each other. Wanting to enhance its concurrent engineering program, ACME now has the opportunity to extend concurrent engineering past its business boundaries and into its suppliers' design areas.

We briefly discussed agile manufacturing at the end of Chapter 1. Let's look at what might be possible if ACME and its suppliers decide to pull it all together. Because of its dependence on suppliers, ACME is looking at the concept of an extended enterprise, in which a cooperative is formed between a parent business (customer) and its suppliers to share product information and reduce the time it takes to design and build a product. Using a product data management program, the extended enterprise can bring the major supplier groups associated with a product to the same level of design and review efficiency as the parent company.

Ben's Bearings is a supplier for Engines Inc., which is a supplier for ACME Autos. An agreement between the three businesses to work with similar systems would make an already successful relationship an even better one. Ben's usually received specifications for bearings from its customer, Engines Inc., but what if ACME Auto sent specifications to Ben's and the engine company simultaneously? Before Engines Inc. can determine their overall requirements, Ben's engineers have a design that works for the bearings. Not only have internal organizational boundaries been removed, but business boundaries have been removed as well.

To more fully illustrate this concept, let's focus on a specific supplier to see how a ProductManager solution can make a difference in cycle time and supplier involvement. ACME's Galveston facility builds wheel assemblies, but the brake shoes are subcontracted out to Texas Brakes. When ACME Auto dealers expressed concern about brake shoes not engaging properly, ACME wanted to react quickly. ACME design engineers at Galveston studied all aspects of the braking system. When they thought they had the solution, a request for engineering action, including the problem analysis and solution, was submitted electronically. It went to Cleveland and to Texas Brakes, which is a remote user on the ACME's Galveston ProductManager system. Giving Texas Brakes access to ACME's ProductManager system had made Texas Brakes more responsive to ACME without requiring Texas Brakes to install their own ProductManager system. The relatively small costs associated with connecting to ACME's system can be shared by the businesses.

It didn't take the Texas Brakes engineers long to see that ACME's solution to the problem with the brake shoes was not the best approach. The ACME design engineer had suggested that ACME modify its wheel hub. Instead, the brake shoe engineer suggested that the dimensions of the brake shoe be modified. It was a less expensive alternative and could be implemented more quickly. The REA was changed, turned into an EC, and approved, all in one day. Texas Brakes implemented the setup for the new shoes the next day and they were in production the day after that. Without close cooperation, Texas Brakes engineers would not have reviewed the request until it was approved, or maybe even until after it was an approved EC. It would have resulted in days or maybe weeks of working through to the final solution.

Using the product data management technology of ProductManager, ACME Autos continues to make progress toward their corporate strategy of involving suppliers at the design integration stage of development. Their system works with Texas Brakes as a remote user. It works even better with Engines Inc. and Ben's Bearing Assemblies, who have complete ProductManager systems. The layout for this extended enterprise across the state of Ohio is illustrated in Figure 4.4. It's 50 miles from Cleveland, where ACME Autos is located, to Akron, where Engines Inc. is headquartered. It's another 320 miles from Akron to Cincinnati, where Ben's Bearing Assemblies provides vendor support for both companies. Engines Inc. keeps several engineers traveling between Akron and Cleveland to work through specification details. They also occasionally send an engineer to discuss engine bearings with Ben Jones in Cincinnati.

ProductManager reduces the need for travel. In the extended enterprise, each business has access to an application of ProductManager. By tying the systems together, a network can be formed allowing for communications and exchange of information, such as review packages or specifications, between the groups. Notice that ACME Autos and Engines Inc. will mostly exchange REAs and EC reviews, while Engines Inc. and Ben's Bearing Assemblies will mainly exchange specifications and drawings. But if ACME needs a bearing, it can send the specification to Ben's, who can produce the design and send it back to ACME Autos for review. No more long hours on the road carrying review packages. Although Ben didn't purchase the PCM and PSM applications, he can still work with specifications that arrive in an electronic folder.

There were no additional hardware requirements for any of these three businesses to establish this Ohio connection. All that was needed were dedicated and secure phone lines between the three applications, and a common communications protocol.

Managing change and responding to a changing market are going to be the key to ACME Autos' success during the next 10 years, as they try to break into new market niches. A PDM system will give them control and help them manage change. If ACME is successful, its suppliers are going to contribute to that success and share in it. The benefits of a PDM system across enterprises will help all the businesses involved meet their quality and costs goals and reduce cycle times.

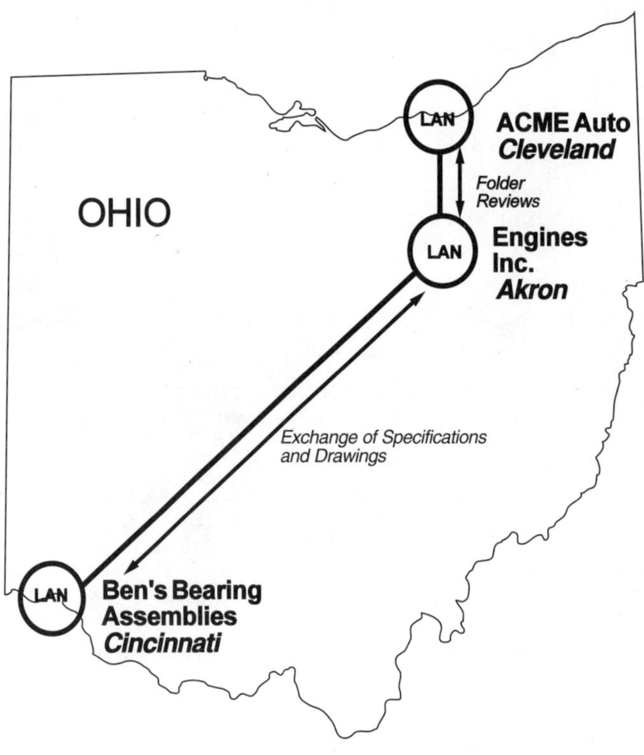

Figure 4.4 The extended enterprise network used between ACME Autos and its supplier companies in Akron and Cincinnati.

Implementation Tips and Techniques

The implementation of any PDM system, including ProductManager, is critical to a smooth transition to information management. A thorough implementation plan can minimize problems associated with converting from one system to another. An implementation plan is an outline of the tasks required to introduce a new program into a business. Appendix B provides implementation planning forms for ProductManager to help you create your own implementation plan. The plan must be written down and communicated to everyone in the business. Everyone from the top management to the person who coordinates engineering changes to end users who will work with the system must have a thorough understanding of how business processes may change and how they will be expected to perform their jobs in the future. Basic understanding of the implementation plan should be considered a critical success factor, just as the business strategy is a critical success factor that all employees must understand in order for the business to succeed.

An implementation plan needs visible support from top management in the business. This support can be demonstrated by executives who attend meetings relating to the implementation of the new program, and who take a personal interest in the project. Emphasizing the success of the project can help motivate those responsible for implementing it. If the boss is on the scene and supportive of the plan, it also helps reduce resistance to making the change.

The implementation plan needs to have well-defined activities assigned to people by name, with expected completion dates. It's important to have the plan include regular "checkpoint" meetings to review the plan, determine the progress that has been made toward meeting it, and work through time and resource problems. Senior management should attend or conduct these meetings, which can result in the plans being altered, depending on progress made or lack thereof.

An implementation plan should also have subplans to support it. These plans can include more detailed activities such as education, security, and upgrading and customizing applications. The education plan, for example, should include information about training programmers in object-oriented technology, teaching skills that end users will need to complete tasks, and training a database administrator. Providing quality education to everyone involved will ensure that a business gets the most out of the new data management system through knowledgeable users.

Another key element of the implementation plan is moving information from your current system into your new system. This is called conversion. You can determine conversion requirements by looking at two models of your business. One is the "as-is" model, and the other is the "to-be" model. To get to the "to-be" model, you must first understand where you are. If you are starting from a manual operation with few or no computers, the choices are simpler. The data will have to be typed into the new computer. If you are converting data from an established business database, you want to preserve the existing database at least until you have the new system up and running. You have several problems to work through here. First, you have to see how the old and new databases interrelate. You will want to load your current business data into the new database. You will most likely need a communications protocol to exchange information between computer programs. A protocol enables information to be communicated between databases. It means you will have to work through the media that run the databases to see how data can be mapped from one system to another. **Mapping data** means reformatting a set of values so that they can be used by another program or system. It's a kind of translation. Product data interface format files are used with the ProductManager program to help with this data transfer.

Second, you have to determine what information in the existing database should be mapped to fields in your new database. This determination has to be made during preinstallation sessions with technical representatives who know the new database and the old database. It has to be a part of the implementation plan. Planning for information exchange is critical to the smooth implementation of ProductManager. Along with databases, other elements such as the platform, operating system, and each application have to be considered in the implementation plan. You need to determine the prerequisites for installing each element and plan for postinstallation testing.

Complete a general implementation plan, and then add subplans that provide the minute details for installing ProductManager. As each plan is developed, assign the people responsible for completing each phase of the plan, along with start and finish dates.

ProductManager Services and Education

An important element in choosing a data management product is not only the strength of the company that stands behind the product, but also the reputation and credibility of the service the company provides. You cannot buy a product and be left to work through your specific business needs, training, and implementation on your own. Along with the no-charge technical support and education provided by the ProductManager team, there are a wide variety of fee-based services that can assist your business in evaluating and implementing ProductManager.

Several of these services give you an opportunity to judge the capabilities of ProductManager before you commit to a particular program or direction for your data management needs. Others help with the nuts and bolts of implementing ProductManager. Let's take a quick look at some of the services available to help with the transition to a PDM system:

ProductManager Try-It gives you an opportunity to install ProductManager on your hardware for a limited period of time to assess its capabilities before you decide on a product data management program. It shows your business what skills are needed for working with ProductManager and what the product can do for your business. By understanding the product and the skills required to work with it, you can better determine whether ProductManager is right for your business.

Engineering Release and Change Control Assessment identifies the strengths and weaknesses of your current engineering environment. IBM representatives can then make recommendations and assist you in determining the benefits of ProductManager.

Engineering Release and Change Control Reengineering takes a closer look at your product data management processes and information flows. The focus of this service is to look at the processes, procedures, and software support for your current system application in the context of the product data management field.

ProductManager QuickStart helps establish an initial installation of ProductManager. QuickStart begins the training process for database administrators and end users.

ProductManager Implementation supports planning for and implementing ProductManager. The implementation is completed in phases that include requirements, system architecture, code and test, customization, and skills transfer. Implementation services can be obtained based on your needs. For example, if your employees have the skills to implement the product, the skills transfer option can be excluded from the agreement.

ProductManager Customization assists you in tailoring your installation of ProductManager. It includes custom code to help your business meet its expectations of the product. Tailoring can help you extend the functions of the application model, create user exits, and change the ProductManager panels.

ProductManager Migration provides services that can range from converting from an MVS ProductManager installation to a UNIX environment to upgrading from one release of ProductManager to the next release.

Joint Development is an option for businesses that have unique requirements. IBM provides your business with experienced developers and program architects to work with you to develop a ProductManager application specifically designed for your business. The joint development effort can also be related to future releases of ProductManager.

ProductManager Skills Transfer is a series of education sessions conducted by IBM representatives in a classroom or hands-on environment to assist your business. These sessions help you incorporate your business's terminology into the ProductManager environment. Several courses are offered, from introductory sessions to application-specific courses. The ProductManager team is also available to provide sessions on the specific skills your business may need to acquire.

ProductManager Technical Services is the premier service offered for ProductManager. It provides 24-hours-a-day, seven-days-a-week support to customers. Included in the service is an assigned account specialist to work with you through installation and customization. Direct support from the ProductManager support and development team through conference calls and visits are part of the package.

Education is an important part of implementing the ProductManager solution. The services offered by IBM can be tailored to each user group for the system. Figure 4.5 shows the education categories used for ProductManager. The figure shows different levels of users across the top. These levels include the executive management, managers and project team leaders, end users, administrators, and programmers. Each user group receives education based on their needs and responsibilities in the company and how they will work with the ProductManager system. The rows in Figure 4.5 show the types of education and training each level of user group is involved with. The asterisks indicate fee-based services.

Executive management normally receives some high-level education on the features and concepts, but are not trained on using the system. Their support and involvement can set the tone for the project implementation by reinforcing commitment to the project. Executive management education for ProductManager ranges from documentation and demonstration diskettes about the product to video and PC Storyboard presentations. Department managers and project team leaders can receive education similar to that of executive management, but their education also includes topics related to implementing the product. This group is very involved in making assessments about the current engineering system and evaluating how ProductManager can improve the system. They are also involved in reviewing data management processes and data flows in the business and in deciding how ProductManager is applied to processes and flows.

	Executive management	Managers and team leaders	Users	Database and system administrators	Programmers
ProductManager features and concepts	• Stand-up presentations • Video • ProductManager introduction folder	• Application courses* • ProductManager introduction folder	• Application courses* • ProductManager QuickStart*	• Application courses* • ProductManager QuickStart*	• Object-oriented overview*
Tailoring	NA	• Engineering release and change control re-engineering* and assessment*	NA	• ProductManager implementation and customization* • Skills transfer*	
Product use	NA	• Using documents • ASM • PCM and PSM • DCM	• Using documents • ASM • PCM and PSM • DCM	• Using documentation • Administrative documentation • Problem diagnosis • Database reference • Support line	• Programming documentation • Problem diagnosis • Customization documentation • Support line

Figure 4.5 ProductManager services and education and how they relate to each user group. The asterisks indicate fee-based services and education.

The user group will actually use ProductManager to perform their jobs. They need education about what the system can do and how they can make it do it. ProductManager Services offers classes to get this group up and running on the system. The administrators need some familiarization with how to use the product, along with extensive education on working with the system and its database. The implementation and customization service and the skills transfer service can provide further education if needed.

Programmers require knowledge and experience in the object-oriented programming field. If a business already has these skills, then maybe all that is needed is education in implementation and customization, and skills transfer.

If you want a first-hand view of ProductManager, you can see the product demonstrated at a variety of trade shows and seminars around the world. Call an IBM representative to find out where ProductManager is going to be demonstrated. For customers who are nearing a decision on a PDM system, plant tours are available to give you a chance to see the product as it is used.

QuickFit Worksheets for ProductManager Applications

Use these worksheets to perform your own QuickFit Analysis on any or all ProductManager application programs. Feel free to make copies of these worksheets only as you need for your own personal use in performing QuickFit Analyses for your business.

QuickFit worksheet

Name:

Date:

Application:
ProductManager/6000
Application Services Manager

Add-on programs:
Preview
BookManager/6000
DataBridge and Builder

Importance scale
0 = Not applicable
1 = Nice to have
2 = Of some importance
5 = Very important
20 = Critical

Application capability
0 = No support
1 = Some affinity
2 = Primitive support
3 = Significant support
4 = Complete support
5 = Extensive support

Add-on program capability
0 = No support
1 = Some affinity
2 = Primitive support
3 = Significant support
4 = Complete support
5 = Extensive support

Rate your business's CURRENT NEED to:	**Importance (0, 1, 2, 5, or 20)**	**Application Capability (0, 1, 2, 3, 4, or 5)**	**Application Score**	**Add-on Program (0, 1, 2, 3, 4, or 5)**	**Extended Score**
(Example)	**5**	**4**	(5 × 4 =)20	**1**	(5 × (4 + 1) =)25
1. Automatically generate REA, EC, and item numbers.		× 5 =			
2. Convert a unit of measurement.		× 4 =			
3. Use drawing tools that are not a part of the product data management system.		× 1 =		4 Preview	
4. Provide user, function, and data security across development and manufacturing areas.		× 5 =			
5. Identify drawings and their locations when they are not stored in a computerized file.		× 4 =			
6. Reduce the time to design and produce parts.		× 4 =			
7. Distribute CADAM and CATIA drawings online.		× 4 =			
8. Run import and export jobs in batch.		× 4 =			
9. Tailor data management features to meet business needs and processes.		× 3 =			
10. Control all information about users, companies, and distribution lists.		× 4 =			

QuickFit worksheet

Name: ____________

Date: ____________

Application:
ProductManager/6000
Application Services Manager

Add-on programs:
Preview
BookManager/6000
DataBridge and Builder

Importance scale
0 = Not applicable
1 = Nice to have
2 = Of some importance
5 = Very important
20 = Critical

Application capability
0 = No support
1 = Some affinity
2 = Primitive support
3 = Significant support
4 = Complete support
5 = Extensive support

Add-on program capability
0 = No support
1 = Some affinity
2 = Primitive support
3 = Significant support
4 = Complete support
5 = Extensive support

Rate your business's CURRENT NEED to:	**Importance (0, 1, 2, 5, or 20)**	**Application Capability (0, 1, 2, 3, 4, or 5)**	**Application Score**	**Add-on Program (0, 1, 2, 3, 4, or 5)**	**Extended Score**
(Example)	5	4	(5 × 4 =)20	1	(5 × (4 + 1) =)25
11. Share development and manufacturing information across multiple locations.		× 4 =			
12. Track the progress of work reviews throughout the business.		× 4 =			
13. Create and distribute electronic review packages.		× 4 =			
14. Save time locating remote drawings.		× 3 =			
15. Access application program interface (API) programs using product panels.		× 4 =			
16. Integrate processes and tracking programs into one consolidated system.		× 3 =			
17. Reduce the use of hardcopy specifications, drawings, documents, and parts lists.		× 4 =			
18. Automatically change the security placed on an item when its status changes.		× 4 =			
19. Establish network with remote installations of product data management system.		× 4 =			
20. Resend reviews and merge the comments with the original review.		× 4 =			

QuickFit worksheet

Name:

Date:

Application:
ProductManager/6000
Application Services Manager

Add-on programs:
Preview
BookManager/6000
DataBridge and Builder

Importance scale
0 = Not applicable
1 = Nice to have
2 = Of some importance
5 = Very important
20 = Critical

Application capability
0 = No support
1 = Some affinity
2 = Primitive support
3 = Significant support
4 = Complete support
5 = Extensive support

Add-on program capability
0 = No support
1 = Some affinity
2 = Primitive support
3 = Significant support
4 = Complete support
5 = Extensive support

Rate your business's CURRENT NEED to:	**Importance (0, 1, 2, 5, or 20)**	**Application Capability (0, 1, 2, 3, 4, or 5)**	**Application Score**	**Add-on Program (0, 1, 2, 3, 4, or 5)**	**Extended Score**
(Example)	5	4	(5 × 4 =)20	1	(5 × (4 + 1) =)25
21. Monitor delinquent folders and create delinquency reports.		× 4 =			
22. Electronically delegate reviews to alternates.		× 4 =			
23. Recall and redistribute reviews after they have been sent.		× 4 =			
24. Adhere to PDES/STEP standards.		× 3 =			
25. Work in a heterogeneous environment using multiple clients.		× 4 =			
26. Complete online support with help text, messages, and help for messages.		× 5 =			
27. Access to books using online facility.		× 0 =		3 BookManager/6000	
28. Customize the appearance and functions of program panels:					
a. Change values for promptable information.		× 4 =			
b. Enable or disable functions on a product panel.		× 3 =			
c. Change panel terminology, help text, and messages.		× 4 =			
29. Include organization identifiers and text in automatically generated numbers.		× 4 =			

QuickFit worksheet

Name:

Date:

Application:
ProductManager/6000
Application Services Manager

Add-on programs:
Preview
BookManager/6000
DataBridge and Builder

Importance scale
0 = Not applicable
1 = Nice to have
2 = Of some importance
5 = Very important
20 = Critical

Application capability
0 = No support
1 = Some affinity
2 = Primitive support
3 = Significant support
4 = Complete support
5 = Extensive support

Add-on program capability
0 = No support
1 = Some affinity
2 = Primitive support
3 = Significant support
4 = Complete support
5 = Extensive support

Rate your business's CURRENT NEED to:	**Importance (0, 1, 2, 5, or 20)**	**Application Capability (0, 1, 2, 3, 4, or 5)**	**Application Score**	**Add-on Program (0, 1, 2, 3, 4, or 5)**	**Extended Score**
(Example)	**5**	**4**	(5 × 4 =)20	**1**	(5 × (4 + 1) =)25
30. Translate information entered in English to other languages.		× 4 =			
31. Distribute reviews in parallel, serial, or mixed order.		× 4 =			
32. Capability of working with several programs using the same screen.		× 4 =			
33. Notifications and messages regarding the progress of reviews.		× 4 =			
34. Archive system actions through event logging.		× 2 =			
35. Integrate with MVS systems.		× 0 =		4 DataBridge & Builder	
36.		× =			
37.		× =			
38.		× =			
39.		× =			
40.		× =			
41.		× =			

(Use QuickFit continuation worksheets as necessary.)

Application score = (sum of this column)

Extended score = (sum of this column)

Perfect score = (sum of Importance × 5)

Perfect score = (sum of Importance × 5)

QuickFit = $\left(\frac{\text{Application score total} \times 100\%}{\text{Perfect score}}\right)$

Extended QuickFit = $\left(\frac{\text{Extended score} \times 100\%}{\text{Perfect score}}\right)$

(Skip these calculations if you use any QuickFit continuation worksheets.)

QuickFit worksheet

Name: ____________________

Date: ____________________

Application:
ProductManager/6000
Product Change Manager

Add-on programs:

Importance scale
0 = Not applicable
1 = Nice to have
2 = Of some importance
5 = Very important
20 = Critical

Application capability
0 = No support
1 = Some affinity
2 = Primitive support
3 = Significant support
4 = Complete support
5 = Extensive support

Add-on program capability
0 = No support
1 = Some affinity
2 = Primitive support
3 = Significant support
4 = Complete support
5 = Extensive support

Rate your business's CURRENT NEED to:	**Importance (0, 1, 2, 5, or 20)**	**Application Capability (0, 1, 2, 3, 4, or 5)**	**Application Score**	**Add-on Program (0, 1, 2, 3, 4, or 5)**	**Extended Score**
(Example)	**5**	**4**	$(5 \times 4 =)20$	**1**	$(5 \times (4 + 1) =)25$
1. Provide a consistent means for incorporating product changes and releases to manufacturing.		$\times$ 5 =			
2. Reduce REA and EC review time.		$\times$ 4 =			
3. Produce complete and accurate REA and EC electronic distribution.		$\times$ 4 =			
4. Control numbers assigned to REAs and ECs.		$\times$ 5 =			
5. Involve other organizations in initial design phase.		$\times$ 4 =			
6. Track progress of REAs and ECs through the approval process:					
a. Monitor delinquencies.		$\times$ 4 =			
b. Provide history.		$\times$ 4 =			
c. Control release of changes to manufacturing.		$\times$ 4 =			
d. Control reviewers and information flow.		$\times$ 5 =			
e. Tailor review processes.		$\times$ 3 =			
7. Place items under EC control.		$\times$ 4 =			
8. Control effectivity coordination between development and manufacturing.		$\times$ 4 =			

QuickFit worksheet

Name: ____________

Date: ____________

Application:
ProductManager/6000
Product Change Manager

Add-on programs:

Importance scale
0 = Not applicable
1 = Nice to have
2 = Of some importance
5 = Very important
20 = Critical

Application capability
0 = No support
1 = Some affinity
2 = Primitive support
3 = Significant support
4 = Complete support
5 = Extensive support

Add-on program capability
0 = No support
1 = Some affinity
2 = Primitive support
3 = Significant support
4 = Complete support
5 = Extensive support

Rate your business's CURRENT NEED to:	**Importance (0, 1, 2, 5, or 20)**	**Application Capability (0, 1, 2, 3, 4, or 5)**	**Application Score**	**Add-on Program (0, 1, 2, 3, 4, or 5)**	**Extended Score**
(Example)	5	4	(5 × 4 =)20	1	(5 × (4 + 1) =)25
9. Relate corequisite and prerequisite EC dependencies.		× 4 =			
10. Automatically associate a distribution list with an REA or EC.		× 2 =			
11. Attach specifications, BOMs, and related material to an EC.		× 5 =			
12. Track versions of items and their BOMs.		× 4 =			
13. Track configurations of products by date or unit effectivity.		× 4 =			
14. Track configurations of products by batch or lot number.		× 2 =			
15. Improve EC and MEC coordination between locations.		× 3 =			
16. Access history and previous BOM structures from within an EC.		× 4 =			
17. Control the release of print specifications prior to approval of EC.		× 4 =			
18. Provide feedback from manufacturing for engineering changes.		× 4 =			
19. Reduce unauthorized changes to items in prerelease status.		× 4 =			

QuickFit worksheet

Name:

Date:

Application:
ProductManager/6000
Product Change Manager

Add-on programs:

Importance scale
0 = Not applicable
1 = Nice to have
2 = Of some importance
5 = Very important
20 = Critical

Application capability
0 = No support
1 = Some affinity
2 = Primitive support
3 = Significant support
4 = Complete support
5 = Extensive support

Add-on program capability
0 = No support
1 = Some affinity
2 = Primitive support
3 = Significant support
4 = Complete support
5 = Extensive support

Rate your business's CURRENT NEED to:	**Importance (0, 1, 2, 5, or 20)**	**Application Capability (0, 1, 2, 3, 4, or 5)**	**Application Score**	**Add-on Program (0, 1, 2, 3, 4, or 5)**	**Extended Score**
(Example)	**5**	**4**	(5 × 4 =)20	**1**	(5 × (4 + 1) =)25
20. Release a portion of an EC early to increase lead time.		× 3 =			
21. Include drawings, such as CAD or CATIA, in REA and EC reviews.		× 3 =			
22. Establish a less formal EC process without using affected items.		× 4 =			
23. Control multiple release levels with one EC.		× 5 =			
24. Predefined approval process:					
a. Formal sign-off procedure.		× 4 =			
b. Capability to modify process.		× 2 =			
c. Make programming changes to process.		× 3 =			
25. Flexibility to change REA and EC processes to meet specific business needs.		× 2 =			
26. Assign REA and EC reviewers based on their responsibilities and status levels.		× 4 =			
27. Provide easy-to-use product change system for users:					
a. Bypass REA and EC details to work with higher-level summaries.		× 2 =			

QuickFit worksheet

Name: ____________________

Date: ____________________

Application:
ProductManager/6000
Product Change Manager

Add-on programs:

Importance scale
0 = Not applicable
1 = Nice to have
2 = Of some importance
5 = Very important
20 = Critical

Application capability
0 = No support
1 = Some affinity
2 = Primitive support
3 = Significant support
4 = Complete support
5 = Extensive support

Add-on program capability
0 = No support
1 = Some affinity
2 = Primitive support
3 = Significant support
4 = Complete support
5 = Extensive support

Rate your business's CURRENT NEED to:	**Importance (0, 1, 2, 5, or 20)**	**Application Capability (0, 1, 2, 3, 4, or 5)**	**Application Score**	**Add-on Program (0, 1, 2, 3, 4, or 5)**	**Extended Score**
(Example)	5	4	(5 × 4 =)20	1	(5 × (4 + 1) =)25
b. Easy-to-use interface.		× 4 =			
c. Little complexity to screen flow.		× 3 =			
28.		× =			
29.		× =			
30.		× =			
31.		× =			
32.		× =			
33.		× =			
34.		× =			
35.		× =			

(Use QuickFit continuation worksheets as necessary.)

Application score = ____ (sum of this column)

Extended score = ____ (sum of this column)

Perfect score = ____ (sum of Importance × 5)

Perfect score = ____ (sum of Importance × 5)

(Skip these calculations if you use any QuickFit continuation worksheets.)

QuickFit = ____ $\left(\frac{\text{Application score total} \times 100\%}{\text{Perfect score}}\right)$

Extended QuickFit = ____ $\left(\frac{\text{Extended score} \times 100\%}{\text{Perfect score}}\right)$

QuickFit worksheet

Name:

Date:

Application:
ProductManager/6000
Product Structure Manager

Add-on programs:

Importance scale
0 = Not applicable
1 = Nice to have
2 = Of some importance
5 = Very important
20 = Critical

Application capability
0 = No support
1 = Some affinity
2 = Primitive support
3 = Significant support
4 = Complete support
5 = Extensive support

Add-on program capability
0 = No support
1 = Some affinity
2 = Primitive support
3 = Significant support
4 = Complete support
5 = Extensive support

Rate your business's CURRENT NEED to:	**Importance (0, 1, 2, 5, or 20)**	**Application Capability (0, 1, 2, 3, 4, or 5)**	**Application Score**	**Add-on Program (0, 1, 2, 3, 4, or 5)**	**Extended Score**
(Example)	**5**	**4**	(5 × 4 =)20	**1**	(5 × (4 + 1) =)25
1. Maintain up-to-date product definition data on all items:					
a. Complete descriptions of items.		× 5 =			
b. Design attributes.		× 5 =			
c. Manufacturing and engineering data.		× 5 =			
d. "Where used" information.		× 5 =			
e. Reference documents for an item.		× 5 =			
f. Planning codes and item status.		× 4 =			
2. Maintain supplier lists and preferences for each item.		× 5 =			
3. Define internal and external suppliers for all items.		× 4 =			
4. Determine cross-references between vendor and company part numbers.		× 5 =			
5. Maintain ownership of parts and subassemblies.		× 4 =			
6. Retrieve and work with item BOMs:					
a. Include substitute components in BOM.		× 5 =			
b. Include optional components in BOM.		× 5 =			

QuickFit worksheet

Name: ________

Date: ________

Application:
ProductManager/6000
Product Structure Manager

Add-on programs:

Importance scale
0 = Not applicable
1 = Nice to have
2 = Of some importance
5 = Very important
20 = Critical

Application capability
0 = No support
1 = Some affinity
2 = Primitive support
3 = Significant support
4 = Complete support
5 = Extensive support

Add-on program capability
0 = No support
1 = Some affinity
2 = Primitive support
3 = Significant support
4 = Complete support
5 = Extensive support

Rate your business's CURRENT NEED to:	**Importance (0, 1, 2, 5, or 20)**	**Application Capability (0, 1, 2, 3, 4, or 5)**	**Application Score**	**Add-on Program (0, 1, 2, 3, 4, or 5)**	**Extended Score**
(Example)	**5**	**4**	(5 × 4 =)20	**1**	(5 × (4 + 1) =)25
c. Include operation data in BOM.		× 5 =			
7. Automatic BOM creation from drawings.		× 4 =			
8. Maintain master and individual routings.		× 3 =			
9. Reduce likelihood of out-of-date product information.		× 4 =			
10. Automatically assign item numbers by department or organization.		× 5 =			
11. Establish group classification for items.		× 2 =			
12. Maintain hundreds of thousands of items.		× 5 =			
13. Maintain design and manufacturing BOM views of the same item.		× 4 =			
14. Identify obsolete items.		× 5 =			
15. Maintain a current parts list on ECs and MECs.		× 4 =			
16. Create reports related to items and BOMs:					
a. Explosion, indented, and summarized.		× 4 =			
b. Implosion, indented, and summarized.		× 4 =			

QuickFit worksheet

Name:

Date:

Application:
ProductManager/6000
Product Structure Manager

Add-on programs:

Importance scale
0 = Not applicable
1 = Nice to have
2 = Of some importance
5 = Very important
20 = Critical

Application capability
0 = No support
1 = Some affinity
2 = Primitive support
3 = Significant support
4 = Complete support
5 = Extensive support

Add-on program capability
0 = No support
1 = Some affinity
2 = Primitive support
3 = Significant support
4 = Complete support
5 = Extensive support

Rate your business's CURRENT NEED to:	**Importance (0, 1, 2, 5, or 20)**	**Application Capability (0, 1, 2, 3, 4, or 5)**	**Application Score**	**Add-on Program (0, 1, 2, 3, 4, or 5)**	**Extended Score**
(Example)	5	4	(5 × 4 =)20	1	(5 × (4 + 1) =)25
c. Net difference between items and BOMs.		× 4 =			
d. View both item information and its BOM.		× 4 =			
17. Consolidate the systems used to create BOMs.		× 4 =			
18. Update and work with non–EC-controlled data.		× 4 =			
19. Identify part numbers that are not used.		× 4 =			
20. Have predefined item status levels and controls for managing product releases.		× 4 =			
21. Maintain item yields and lead times.		× 4 =			
22. Track and control information dealing with items and products.		× 4 =			
23. Work with manufacturing and engineering information for items and assemblies.		× 4 =			
24. Access drawing tools while working within a PDM system.		× 3 =			
25. Provide multiple views of product structures so each manufacturing unit has its own view.		× 4 =			

QuickFit worksheet

Name:

Date:

Application:
ProductManager/6000
Product Structure Manager

Add-on programs:

Importance scale
0 = Not applicable
1 = Nice to have
2 = Of some importance
5 = Very important
20 = Critical

Application capability
0 = No support
1 = Some affinity
2 = Primitive support
3 = Significant support
4 = Complete support
5 = Extensive support

Add-on program capability
0 = No support
1 = Some affinity
2 = Primitive support
3 = Significant support
4 = Complete support
5 = Extensive support

Rate your business's CURRENT NEED to:	Importance (0, 1, 2, 5, or 20)	Application Capability (0, 1, 2, 3, 4, or 5)	Application Score	Add-on Program (0, 1, 2, 3, 4, or 5)	Extended Score
(Example)	5	4	(5 × 4 =)20	1	(5 × (4 + 1) =)25
26. Ease of use to rename item attributes.		× 3 =			
27. Establish and maintain multiple BOM views.		× 3 =			
28. Standardize parts use across product lines.		× 4 =			
29. Ensure remote locations have same level of drawings to work from.		× 4 =			
30.		× =			
31.		× =			
32.		× =			
33.		× =			
34.		× =			
35.		× =			

(Use QuickFit continuation worksheets as necessary.)

Application score = (sum of this column)

Extended score = (sum of this column)

Perfect score = (sum of Importance × 5)

Perfect score = (sum of Importance × 5)

QuickFit = $\left(\frac{\text{Application score total} \times 100\%}{\text{Perfect score}}\right)$

Extended QuickFit = $\left(\frac{\text{Extended score} \times 100\%}{\text{Perfect score}}\right)$

(Skip these calculations if you use any QuickFit continuation worksheets.)

QuickFit worksheet

Name:

Date:

Application:
ProductManager/6000
Document Control Manager

Add-on programs:

Importance scale
0 = Not applicable
1 = Nice to have
2 = Of some importance
5 = Very important
20 = Critical

Application capability
0 = No support
1 = Some affinity
2 = Primitive support
3 = Significant support
4 = Complete support
5 = Extensive support

Add-on program capability
0 = No support
1 = Some affinity
2 = Primitive support
3 = Significant support
4 = Complete support
5 = Extensive support

Rate your business's CURRENT NEED to:	**Importance (0, 1, 2, 5, or 20)**	**Application Capability (0, 1, 2, 3, 4, or 5)**	**Application Score**	**Add-on Program (0, 1, 2, 3, 4, or 5)**	**Extended Score**
(Example)	**5**	**4**	(5 × 4 =)20	**1**	(5 × (4 + 1) =)25
1. Include the most current specifications with an REA or EC.		× 5 =			
2. Comply with ISO/9000 documentation standards.		× 3 =			
3. Track and control the approval of documents associated with product changes.		× 4 =			
4. Maintain versions of documents that relate to the corresponding product version.		× 5 =			
5. Provide all users the same up-to-date version of specifications and documents.		× 4 =			
6. Control access to business documents during development.		× 4 =			
7. Work with documents using workstation editors:					
a. Update specifications and spreadsheets.		× 4 =			
b. Create product descriptions.		× 3 =			
c. Work with drawings.		× 4 =			
8. Reduce need for hardcopy documentation by providing online review capabilities.		× 4 =			

QuickFit worksheet

Name:

Date:

Application: ProductManager/6000 Document Control Manager

Add-on programs:

Importance scale
0 = Not applicable
1 = Nice to have
2 = Of some importance
5 = Very important
20 = Critical

Application capability
0 = No support
1 = Some affinity
2 = Primitive support
3 = Significant support
4 = Complete support
5 = Extensive support

Add-on program capability
0 = No support
1 = Some affinity
2 = Primitive support
3 = Significant support
4 = Complete support
5 = Extensive support

Rate your business's CURRENT NEED to:	**Importance (0, 1, 2, 5, or 20)**	**Application Capability (0, 1, 2, 3, 4, or 5)**	**Application Score**	**Add-on Program (0, 1, 2, 3, 4, or 5)**	**Extended Score**
(Example)	5	4	(5 × 4 =)20	1	(5 × (4 + 1) =)25
9. Retrieve information related to a particular EC, item, or affected item.		× 4 =			
10. Purge out-of-date documentation from storage.		× 4 =			
11. Reduce manual handling and copying of documents.		× 4 =			
12. Ensure on-time delivery of prints and specifications.		× 4 =			
13. Perform online reviews of documents that support product changes or business processes and respond to the reviews electronically.		× 5 =			
14. Search and sort documentation within a "vault."		× 4 =			
15. Maintain document archives.		× 4 =			
16. Control the release of documents associated with parts and assemblies.		× 4 =			
17. Track changes to stored documents.		× 4 =			
18. Work with multiple formats for documents.		× 3 =			
19. Add new documents and drawing tools.		× 4 =			

QuickFit worksheet

Name:

Date:

Application:
ProductManager/6000
Document Control Manager

Add-on programs:

Importance scale
0 = Not applicable
1 = Nice to have
2 = Of some importance
5 = Very important
20 = Critical

Application capability
0 = No support
1 = Some affinity
2 = Primitive support
3 = Significant support
4 = Complete support
5 = Extensive support

Add-on program capability
0 = No support
1 = Some affinity
2 = Primitive support
3 = Significant support
4 = Complete support
5 = Extensive support

Rate your business's CURRENT NEED to:	**Importance (0, 1, 2, 5, or 20)**	**Application Capability (0, 1, 2, 3, 4, or 5)**	**Application Score**	**Add-on Program (0, 1, 2, 3, 4, or 5)**	**Extended Score**
(Example)	**5**	**4**	(5 × 4 =)20	**1**	(5 × (4 + 1) =)25
20. Use multiple tools to work with a document.		× 3 =			
21. Associate documents with items and ECs.		× 4 =			
22. Launch ProductManager from within a drawing tool.		× 3 =			
23. Maintain history of product documentation.		× 4 =			
24.		× =			
25.		× =			
26.		× =			
27.		× =			
28.		× =			
29.		× =			
30.		× =			

(Use QuickFit continuation worksheets as necessary.)

Application score = (sum of this column)

Extended score = (sum of this column)

Perfect score = (sum of Importance × 5)

Perfect score = (sum of Importance × 5)

QuickFit = $\left(\frac{\text{Application score total} \times 100\%}{\text{Perfect score}}\right)$

Extended QuickFit = $\left(\frac{\text{Extended score} \times 100\%}{\text{Perfect score}}\right)$

(Skip these calculations if you use any QuickFit continuation worksheets.)

QuickFit continuation worksheet

Name:

Date:

Application:

Add-on programs:

Importance scale
0 = Not applicable
1 = Nice to have
2 = Of some importance
5 = Very important
20 = Critical

Application capability
0 = No support
1 = Some affinity
2 = Primitive support
3 = Significant support
4 = Complete support
5 = Extensive support

Add-on program capability
0 = No support
1 = Some affinity
2 = Primitive support
3 = Significant support
4 = Complete support
5 = Extensive support

Rate your business's CURRENT NEED to:	**Importance (0, 1, 2, 5, or 20)**	**Application Capability (0, 1, 2, 3, 4, or 5)**	**Application Score**	**Add-on Program (0, 1, 2, 3, 4, or 5)**	**Extended Score**
(Example)	**5**	**4**	(5 × 4 =)20	**1**	(5 × (4 + 1) =)25
	×	=			
	×	=			
	×	=			
	×	=			
	×	=			
	×	=			
	×	=			
	×	=			
	×	=			
	×	=			

(Use QuickFit continuation worksheets as necessary.)

Application score = (sum of this column)

Extended score = (sum of this column)

Perfect score = (sum of Importance × 5)

Perfect score = (sum of Importance × 5)

QuickFit = $\left(\frac{\text{Application score total} \times 100\%}{\text{Perfect score}}\right)$

Extended QuickFit = $\left(\frac{\text{Extended score} \times 100\%}{\text{Perfect score}}\right)$

(Perform these calculations only on the last QuickFit continuation worksheet for this application.)

APPENDIX B

ProductManager Implementation Plans

This appendix presents a general implementation plan that will help you plan for and install the hardware and operating system, the ProductManager program, and its applications. The series of tables guides you through activities you should consider before and after acquiring ProductManager. Activities are listed in the recommended sequence, but many of them can be performed concurrently. A point to remember is that some of the services associated with tailoring and training are fee-based services offered by ProductManager.

General Implementation Plan

Activity or Task	Responsible Person	Start Date	Finish Date
Getting started 1. Assign project leader. 2. Determine technical resources and skill levels: a. Programming. b. System management. c. System administration. d. Database administration. 3. Identify business and IBM technical contacts. 4. Prepare schedule for implementation: a. Identify events. b. Create a time line. c. Establish checkpoints in the schedule. **Physical installation requirements** 1. Plan computer system layout: a. Planning guide for hardware products. b. Space needs for computers. c. Power sources. d. Uninterruptible power supply. e. Physical security. 2. Plan local workstation and printer layout. 3. Plan equipment needs for furniture, racks, and cabling. 4. Order equipment. 5. Implement plans for system layout: a. Designate user locations. b. Remodel.			

Activity or Task	Responsible Person	Start Date	Finish Date
c. Telephone and power outlets. d. Power supply. e. Security. 6. Prepare installation areas: a. Run cables. b. Install hardware and equipment. c. Provide adequate ventilation with clusters of systems. **Operational requirements** 1. Plan for system security: a. Review ProductManager security information. b. Assign security administrator. c. Plan for user IDs and passwords. 2. Assign key administrative personnel: a. Operating system administrator. b. ProductManager administrator. c. Database administrator. d. Programming support. e. Hardware maintenance and operators. 3. Conduct preinstallation survey with IBM technical-support personnel: a. Define customizations. b. Define users and local and remote locations. c. Decide on optional software. d. Determine content of initial data load. e. Define business processes. 4. Plan for system backups: a. Backup schedules. b. Disaster recovery. c. Off-site backup and storage.			

Activity or Task	Responsible Person	Start Date	Finish Date
5. Plan for supplies: a. Special forms. b. Stock forms and paper. c. Printer supplies. d. Tapes and diskettes.			
6. Organize product documentation: a. Assign librarian. b. Consolidate materials. c. Plan for tailored technical information. d. Determine Document Control Manager objects.			
Education requirements			
1. Plan for education needs: a. Management team. b. Operators and administrators. c. End users. d. Object-oriented technology.			
2. Arrange for training sessions: a. Coordinate with IBM support. b. Plan for QuickStart sessions. c. Plan for skills transfer and support sessions.			
3. Arrange for classrooms and lab.			
4. Conduct classes for setup personnel: a. Operating system and platform administrators. b. Database and ProductManager system administrators. c. Programmers.			

Activity or Task	Responsible Person	Start Date	Finish Date
System installation			
1. Verify readiness of physical location.			
2. Ensure receipt of manuals and their availability during installation.			
3. Install equipment and operating system and verify that it is operational.			
4. Back up system.			
5. Install prerequisite software (Note: for the AIX system, obtain software license passwords for NETLS and DB2/6000).			
6. Perform system testing.			
7. Install optional software and perform backup.			
8. Assign initial users and passwords for operating system and platform.			
9. Begin end-user education.			
ProductManager/6000 installation			
1. Review program directories for each application to be installed.			

Activity or Task	Responsible Person	Start Date	Finish Date
2. Install ProductManager/6000 software: a. Obtain 8-mm tape for installation. b. Create a file system. c. Install and tailor applications. 3. Obtain license passwords for each ProductManager/6000 application purchased. 4. Install and tailor printers. 5. Install and tailor Xstations. 6. Configure protocols. 7. Install and tailor add-on programs that may include: a. Preview. b. Entry Communications System/6000. c. BookManager READ/6000. 8. Verify and test ASM by creating and deleting a folder. 9. Verify and test PCM and PSM: a. Create and delete an EC. b. Create and delete an item. 10. Tailor ProductManager with IBM technical support based on preinstallation survey results: a. Define part number schema. b. Apply company nomenclature. c. Identify local and remote locations if there is more than one ProductManager installation.			

Activity or Task	Responsible Person	Start Date	Finish Date
d. Establish interfaces to legacy systems. e. Establish system security. f. Establish print capability. g. Define logical data reference objects.			
11. Perform initial data load of existing business data: a. Extract data from legacy systems. b. Convert data to PDI-formatted files. c. Import PDI files to ProductManager.			
12. Initialize tables, including locations, number generation, person data, and company data.			
13. Verify and test data.			
14. Begin operations.			
Post-installation procedures			
1. Establish disaster recovery procedures.			
2. Back up systems.			
3. Apply updates to ProductManager and applicable prerequisite software.			
4. Tailor documentation as required.			
5. Continue education as required.			

Index

READER FEEDBACK SHEET

Your comments and suggestions are very important in shaping future publications. Please jot down your thoughts here, photocopy this page, and fax to (904) 934-9981 or mail it to:

Maximum Press
Attn: Jim Hoskins
605 Silverthorn Road
Gulf Breeze, FL 32561
Fax (904) 934-9981

COMMENTS: